WITHDRAWN

THE WORKS OF SHAKESPEARE

EDITED FOR THE SYNDICS OF THE
CAMBRIDGE UNIVERSITY PRESS

BY

SIR ARTHUR QUILLER-COUCH
AND   JOHN DOVER WILSON

TWELFTH NIGHT

OR

WHAT YOU WILL

AN ATATIS SVÆ 27
1 5 8 9

John Bull

TWELFTH NIGHT
OR
WHAT YOU WILL

Shakespeare

CAMBRIDGE
AT THE UNIVERSITY PRESS
1949

PUBLISHED BY
THE SYNDICS OF THE CAMBRIDGE UNIVERSITY PRESS

London Office: Bentley House, N.W. 1
American Branch: New York

Agents for Canada, India, and Pakistan: Macmillan

First edition 1930
*Second edition 1949

* *Places where slight editorial changes or additions introduce variants from the first edition are marked by a date* [1949] *in square brackets.*

Printed in Great Britain at the University Press, Cambridge
(Brooke Crutchley, University Printer)

CONTENTS

THE FRONTISPIECE, WHICH IS REPRODUCED FROM A
PAINTING BY AN UNKNOWN ARTIST NOW IN THE EXAMI-
NATION SCHOOLS, OXFORD, SHOWS DR JOHN BULL, GRESHAM
PROFESSOR OF MUSIC 1597–1607, AND ORGANIST TO KING
JAMES I, ONE OF THE MOST DISTINGUISHED MUSICIANS
IN A GREAT MUSICAL AGE

TWELFTH NIGHT

I

Questions concerning the text of this play and the date of its first production will be treated in their proper place. It is enough to say here of the text that none is discoverable earlier than the 1623 Folio, and indeed this was probably its first appearance in print, if we may guess so much from the fact that the licence granted to the printer specifies 'soe manie of the said copyes as are not formerly entred to other men,' and *Twelfth Night* is one of these. For the date: It is not mentioned in Meres' list, of 1598: but it *is* mentioned in a diary discovered either by Collier or by Hunter among the Harleian MSS in the British Museum. Collier first published it in 1831, but it was Hunter who identified the diarist as one John Manningham, barrister of the Middle Temple. The entries extend, with gaps, from Christmas 1601 to April 14, 1603, and under 'Febr. 1601' occurs the following:

Feb. 2.—At our feast wee had a play called Twelue night or what you will. much like the commedy of errores or Menechmi in Plautus, but most like and neere to that in Italian called Inganni a good practise in it to make the steward beleeue his Lady widdowe was in Loue with him by counterfayting a lettre, as from his Lady, in generall termes, telling him what shee liked best in him, and pre-scribing his gesture in smiling his apparraile etc. And then when he came to practise making him beleeue they tooke him to be mad.

Manningham's 'our feast' was Candlemas (Purifica-tion of the Blessed Virgin), Feb. 2, 1601–2. He does not say or hint that he was witnessing a first performance: but he gives the impression that the play was a new one: and if we take *Twelfth Night* to be something more

definite than a mere fancy-title, it seems a reasonable guess
that Shakespeare had written it for presentation on the
preceding Twelfth Night (Epiphany), 1602. For what
stage he intended it, whether public or private—or, if for
a private entertainment, at what patron's command—we
know not. But it carries throughout the atmosphere
of a happy Twelfth Night revel, written for a polite
audience, and with just so much of irresponsible extravagant fooling—of What You Will—as would amuse
such an audience without scandalising. Be it remembered too, that such an audience would include a
number of children, to whose delight tradition consecrated this innocent *Saturnalia*, this *Fête des Rois*. For
the legend came out of St Matthew's Gospel: and it ran
that the Fairy Befana (or Epifania) found herself too
busy with household affairs to look after the Three
Kings as she ought when they set forth for Bethlehem
following the Star, but promised to await their return.
And so she did: but they, after presenting their gifts,
'being warned of God in a dream that they should not
return to Herod, departed into their own country
another way.' Wherefore (the tale is) every Twelfth
Night Befana watches for them; and when they do not
return, in penance and in sorrow for the Innocents slain
in Rama, she walks the night-nurseries before morning
and fills the children's stockings with toys. No doubt in
course of time the *Fête des Rois* would become sophisti-
cated, as has happened to Pantomime in these later years.
Yet it remained, down almost to our own day, a children's
Saturnalia, a frolic of 'dressing up' and mimicking the
absurdities of their elders, under presidency of a 'Lord of
Misrule'; and obscenities such as we pardon, however un-
willingly, in the ordinary 'musical' farces of to-day, and a
Shakespearian audience accepted as a kind of fun proper
to Comedy, would offend us yet in Pantomime even as they
would have offended in a Twelfth Night show: *Maxima
debetur pueris reverentia*. We shall have more to say on

this point, but for the moment content ourselves with noting that the play, with all its laughing tolerance of ginger and cakes and ale (ancient concomitants of Twelfth Night), never strays into lewdness: that, in particular, the Clown Feste (i.q. *Festus*, master of the feast and its Lord of Misrule) is remarkable among Shakespeare's Fools not only by eminence of wit and satiric philosophy, but by keeping them both clean of bawdry.

Allusions in the text of the play tend to confirm rather than to cast doubt upon the date generally assigned to it: and on the whole, for our critical purpose here, we may assume that date to be 1601–2 or near-about.

And this just accords with the date which any sensitive critic (without, perhaps, being able to cite better evidence than an inner certainty slowly acquired by study, not producible in Court) must feel to be the right date for *Twelfth Night*; a play which is a summary on the edge of a pause:

a box where sweets compacted lie:

—a summary of all the old happy comedies, an immediate successor to *As You Like It*. Years later, under the placard of 'A Comedy' Shakespeare was to attempt dramas of reconciliation—*The Winter's Tale* and *The Tempest*—to end happily but on a deeper note. It is always dangerous to generalise upon Shakespeare's notion of a comedy and its quiddity. But we may agree that after *As You Like It* and *Twelfth Night* a gulf opens, to be crossed on the terrible footholds of the great Tragedies; and that, beyond them, a different Shakespeare emerges into so much of the sunny side of life as experience allows him to accept as real and to enjoy; which, when one comes to examine it, mainly consists in hope and a sort of faith that, if *he* had the remaking of this world, the sins of the fathers should *not* be visited on the children but rather redeemed by them, and the promise of this world renewed by force of youth and innocent love. An ageing man's fond illusion, perhaps! But what better trust has any one of us?

II

But we are (say) at 1601, and are dealing with a Shakespeare thirty-seven years old; with a playwright who has mastered the dramatic trick and can play with it at will; with an artist on the verge of using his skill to conquer the new kingdom of Tragedy: with a man who (however we speculate on the cause of it) had somehow acquired, or was in process of acquiring, a distrust of men's loyalty and a suspicion alive to smell the fitch in woman's purity; a man who could have said with Ruskin:

The fashion of the time renders whatever is forward, coarse, or senseless in feminine nature too palpable to all men . . . and the chance of later life gave me opportunities of watching women in states of degradation and vindictiveness which opened to me the gloomiest secrets of Greek and Syrian tragedy. I have seen them betray their household charities to lust, their pledged love to devotion. I have seen mothers dutiful to their children as Medea; and children dutiful to their parents as the daughter of Herodias . . .

'but my trust is still unmoved,' he continues, 'in the precious—of the natures that are so fatal in their error.' And so it remained with Shakespeare who, knowing all about Goneril, could invent an Imogen, deal charitably with Doll Tearsheet, interpret Cleopatra.

III

In 1601, then, we see Shakespeare, a man of thirty-seven, with a record of Comedy prosperously attempted, standing on the brink of that dark kingdom of Tragedy which he has yet to explore and to conquer if he can—

Pondering his voyage; for no narrow frith
He has to cross.

Nor (as we hope to show) is it fanciful to see him, so poised for flight, in *Twelfth Night* casting a backward comprehensive glance upon his old playmates and leaving them in this play (with its under-burden of melancholy) his Farewell to Comedy.

But, to make this clearer, we must first devote a page or so to its alleged 'Sources'—a task we usually undertake against our will, with the proviso that three times in four Shakespeare's 'sources' are as likely as not any man's or everyman's sources. Now and again, to be sure—as with *Romeo* or *As You Like It* or the Roman plays—we can point to some definite piece of another man's writing and demonstrate that Shakespeare used it as his material: and, where this can be done, we find our understanding of him and his ways of work enlarged and our criticism correspondingly the surer. But this source-hunting becomes futile and even dangerous if the pursuit of it encourage the notion that Shakespeare was the kind of man to borrow his minutest or his most ordinary effects from this or that suggestion discoverable in this or that obscure pamphlet or Italian *novella*: that his habit was, so to speak, to walk around a library telling himself 'I want a new plot' and picking out books with a 'Will this do?' 'Will this other give me a hint?' To take one of his devices for an illustration —that of the girl who dons boy's apparel and follows her lover in guise of a page. It was a favourite with him, as with a score of playwrights in an age when women's parts were enacted by boys: but it is as old as the hills, and it were a confusion of industry with idleness to hunt the suggestion back through medieval to ancient literature, to chase Julia or Rosalind or Viola panting back through time and space and into Noah's Ark.

The truth is, as Stephen Gosson reports in *Plays Confuted* (1581), that Shakespeare's contemporaries were ransacking Latin, French and Italian comedies to

fetch home grist to their mills; and if we say that Shakespeare, that powerful inventor, was also a great economist of invention (as he undoubtedly was, having learnt
that thrift as an apprentice in furbishing up old dramas),
why then we must follow it up by admitting that he was
sufficiently master of his trade to sit and watch more
menial men doing his work for him.

For useful critical purposes, then, we hold that
hunting after any distant wildfowl of 'originals' can
only justify itself as harmless recreation—no farther
—until it fetch home some bird from whose wing
Shakespeare demonstrably feathered one of his
arrows.

The subject of Shakespeare's possible sources for
Twelfth Night has already been pretty exhaustively
treated by Furness in his edition of the play and by
Mr Morton Luce in his admirable volume in *The Arden
Shakespeare*—a book which can hardly be overrated
for its intelligent painstaking. To them the reader must
be referred; but for our present purpose we may be
content with the following summary.

John Manningham, as we have seen, found *Twelfth
Night* 'much like the commedy of errores or Menechmi
in Plautus, but most like and neere to that in Italian
called Inganni.' Now there were two Comedies of
that name: (1) *Gl'Inganni*, by Nicolo Secchi, or Secco,
first acted in 1547 and printed at Florence, 1562:
(2) *Gl'Inganni*, by Curzio Gonzaga, Venice, 1592: with
a third (3) by Domenica Cornaccini, Venice, 1604,
which we may leave out of account. But none of these
Inganni's bears much resemblance to *Twelfth Night*:
and it is generally supposed that Manningham's memory
confused *Gl'Inganni* with *Gl'Ingannati*, a comedy presented at Siena in 1531. *Gl'Ingannati* was published
at Venice in 1537 in a volume entitled *Il Sagrificio*—
the 'sacrifice' being a preliminary and ceremonious
offering-up of sonnets, madrigals, etc. sung to the lyre

as each member of the Intronati[1] casts on the altar some
love-token of a lost mistress: the Comedy following this
'induction,' Gl'Ingannati, may have been brought into
England by a troupe of Italian players who performed
before Elizabeth in 1577-8. But this is unnecessary
guess-work: for the play had a European vogue. It was
translated into French by Charles Estienne, physician
(Lyons, 1543), and adapted for the French stage under
the title of Les Abusés in 1549: for the Spanish, by Lope
de Rueda in 1556. The French version fathered a Latin
one, Laelia, given at Queens' College, Cambridge, in
1595[2]. But apart from translations and adaptations of
the play, the story occurs in Bandello's Novelle, ii. 36
(Lucca, 1554), Cinthio's Hecatommithi (Monte Regale,
1565) and Belleforest's Histoires Tragiques, vol. iv (Paris,
1570). The list may finish with an English version of
the story, The Historie of Apolonius and Silla, found
in Barnabe Rich's Farewell to Militarie Profession
(London, Robert Walley, 1581), a version long accepted as the vera origo of Twelfth Night and printed—
a poorly told tale—on that supposition in Hazlitt's
Shakespeare's Library.

From all this it is obvious—if the quest be worth
pursuing—that Shakespeare, writing in 1601 or there-
abouts, had plenty of sources to irrigate his invention, if
he chose to draw upon them. A more useful conclusion
would seem to be that the primal source dates back beyond Boccaccio, beyond Plautus (out of whom Shakespeare had dipped a pailful for The Comedy of Errors),
and is in fact as old as the hills.

---

[1] One of these offerings, un Cupido scolpito, dono della sua
Donna, is cast into the flames by Messer Agnol Malevolti, a
name which may have suggested 'Malvolio.' But the term
mala voglia ('evil concupiscence') is frequent in Bandello,
v. infra.

[2] Edited by Dr Moore Smith from a MS in Lambeth
Palace.

For it cannot be too often or too strongly pointed out that the exploration of Shakespeare's 'sources' varies greatly in the amount of profit it yields to us, but still more in the *kind* of profit. Where, for example, we know that he had Holinshed's *Chronicles* before him, we can learn (with wonder) something of the dramatic genius which pounced on a passage of it for *Macbeth*, to expand and work tragedy upon it. Still more usefully we can read North's *Plutarch* alongside *Antony and Cleopatra* and follow the magical process as it converts by a few touches good prose into great poetry. Quite usefully again, where we know the dramatist is working in *As You Like It* upon Lodge's novel of *Rosalynde*, we can watch him and what his skill makes of it. But when, as with *Twelfth Night*, the story is a primal one, and we have a dozen sixteenth-century versions capable of providing a hint here or a phrase there, the quest may easily turn to a folly of delusion. And after all, for our relief, no one has yet found Shakespeare a debtor to anyone for Malvolio.

IV

Whomsoever Shakespeare plundered, or may have plundered, at one time or another, it is certain he never used so constant a victim as himself. No one can piece together the scraps of information and gossip left to us and construct out of them any biography to satisfy a mind reasonably scrupulous in separating good evidence from bad—no one, after every baffling attempt to build, out of fragments that again and again break in his hand, a figure of Shakespeare as he lived *totus teres atque rotundus*, can survey the result—without admitting that he has made shift to force his own conception of what consummate genius ought to be into the mould of a plain man of business. (And this we suppose to lie at the root of the Baconian and other heresies.) But a like difficulty in scene after scene must tease anyone who examines the plays themselves. Here is a man so prodigal of invention that every situation teems with thought and metaphor, throws out tendrils, foliage, fruit, as a volcanic soil obeys the heat beneath. And yet this poet who apparently cannot help himself is found, on examination, to be a strict economist, almost a niggard, of all his superabundance.

The solution may, after all, be simple enough. As the younger Dumas once boasted, 'Give me two trestles, four boards, three actors, one passion, and I will make you a drama,' so this paradox of Shakespeare may perhaps be explained by a mighty indolence, such as may easily beset a great artist who has mastered his trade. 'I have toiled hard enough at the theatre to know its tricks: I have toiled even harder, from *Venus and Adonis* on, at the more difficult business of putting beauty into speech: I have acquired the mastery of that, too—*une jolie façon de dire les choses*; moreover I have lived in the country, in London, at its Court, and have suffered. You demand a new play of me? Well, fetch me an old one—any old story with stuff in it, and I will make it new enough.'

In dealing with several of the Comedies we have had to face this paradox; but *Twelfth Night* forces it upon us everywhere. From beginning to end we find it a tissue of incidents, of characters, of situations, which have been proved effective by previous stage-experiments. Confusion of identity (out-Plautusing Plautus) has been worked in *The Comedy of Errors*, with the shipwreck that leads to recognition, and the friendly ship-captain who goes to explore the strange town. This friendship of an elderly man for a youth reappears in *The Merchant of Venice*, and Antonio, the friend's name in that play, is Antonio again in this. Viola again—the boy-actor exchanging skirts for trunk-hose, revives Julia, and like Julia attends her chosen lover as a page—revives also

Portia, Nerissa, Jessica, Rosalind—all by different ways of playfulness working up towards Imogen, paragon of women in boy's attire. We all recognise Sir Toby and Aguecheek as sibs to Falstaff and Slender: the trick played on Malvolio is cross-cradle with that played on Beatrice and Benedick—and so on. Even Viola's

> Make me a willow cabin at your gate

echoes *As You Like It*; as her famous lines on her supposed sister,

> My father had a daughter loved a man...

echo, with a deeper note, Katharine's story in *Love's Labour's Lost* of the man who killed her sister—

> He made her melancholy, sad, and heavy—
> And so she died: had she been light, like you,
> Of such a merry, nimble, stirring spirit,
> She might ha' been a grandam ere she died....
> And so may you...for a light heart lives long.

Out of this account we leave for a while the echoes of mere music in our play. But we summarise for the moment, with Barrett Wendell, its many self-derivative origins—

Twelfth Night, far from being essentially different from his former plays, is perhaps the most completely characteristic we have yet considered. For what reason we cannot say—indolence we might guess in one mood, prudence in another—he was exceptionally economical of invention, except in mere language. Scenes, characters, situations, devices which had once proved themselves effective he would constantly prefer to any bold experiment. This very economy of invention, perhaps, contained an element of strength; it left his full energy free for the masterly phrasing and the spontaneous creation of character which has made his work lasting. Strong or weak, however, the trait is clearly becoming almost as characteristic as the constant concreteness of his style: and nowhere does it appear more distinctly or to more advantage than when we recognise in

would suppress it. His downfall, again, is just of the sort
to tickle a child's humour—the sort of risibility that does
not reach beyond the sheer fun, for instance, of seeing a
solemn personage slip up heels-aloft on a slide of butter.

Let us remind ourselves, too, that *Twelfth Night* contains no bawdry: that Feste, while one of the most
philosophical of Shakespeare's clowns, is also the cleanest
mouthed; that the jolly back-chat of Sir Toby, Sir
Andrew, Maria, Fabian runs innocent throughout as
battledore and shuttlecock: that the plentiful disorder of
Olivia's household, in short, is never that of a disorderly
house. Even the love-making never passes beyond such
simple romantic play as children have learnt from their
fairy-books and take as much for granted as the glass
slipper fitted by the Prince on Cinderella. No hearts
break; passion never obtrudes upon sentiment, save by
a hint. Orsino sighs; Viola sighs with a difference;
Olivia, presented as love-proof, suddenly capitulates to
love for a disguised maid and then as impetuously tosses
her cap over the mill, to marry the twin-brother. Everything ends happily and, as it began, to the pretty illusion
of music.

VII

But it is high time to reverse the shield and attempt to
show how by Shakespeare's magic he turns this Christmas romp into pure and delicate Comedy appealing to
the knowledge, the refined intelligence, even to the
wistful memories, of cultivated men and women. As
John Earle said of 'A Child'—

We laugh at his foolish sports, but his game is our
earnest; and his drums, rattles and hobby-horses but the
Emblems and mockings of man's business. His father hath
writ him as his own little story, wherein he reads those days
of his life that he cannot remember, and sighs to see what
innocence he has out-lived.

Something of that melancholy—of that wistfulness at least, resides in many, if not in most of old childish songs: for example in—

> Nous n'irons plus au bois,
> Les lauriers sont coupés,

or

> Au clair de la lune,
> Mon ami Pierrot,
> Prêtez-moi ta plume
> Pour écrire un mot.
> Ma chandelle est morte.

One knows—and has liked to know—men of middle age, who at Christmas-time make a ritual of spending an hour or so over a volume of Hans Christian Andersen, or Perrault's tales, or *Alice in Wonderland*, or even Jules Verne—Sentiment, if we choose to frown—

> What a little thing
> To remember for years,
> And remember with tears!

But sentiment is a fact.

VIII

But sentiment is also, and doubtless, a danger. Its true place resides in the Aristotelian mean. Lacking that tenderness of heart which it predicates, a man tends to vulgarity of soul, hard commercialism: with excess of it he tends to flaccidity of fibre, easy practice with likes and dislikes—to become, like Charles Kean's cook, 'of that happy disposition I can love any man.'

Now this, the worst trap of sentiment, may be summarised as Self-deception: and (as George Meredith pointed out in his famous Essay) the Spirit of Comedy being in the end identical with common-sense, Self-deceit must always be Comedy's favourite target.

If you believe that our civilisation is founded on common-sense (and it is the first condition of sanity to believe it),

you will when contemplating men, discern a Spirit overhead. . . .

Its common aspect is one of unsolicitous observation, as
if surveying a full field and having leisure to dart on its
chosen morsels without any fluttering eagerness. Men's
future upon earth does not attract it: their honesty and
shapeliness in the present does; and whenever they wax
out of proportion, overblown, affected, pretentious, bom-
bastical, hypocritical, pedantic, fantastically delicate:
whenever it sees them self-deceived or hoodwinked, given
to run riot in idolatries, drifting into vanities, congregating
in absurdities, planning short-sightedly, plotting de-
mentedly; whenever they are at variance with their pro-
fessions, and violate the unwritten but perceptible law
binding them one to another: whenever they offend sound
reason, fear justice; are false in humility or mined with
conceit, individually or in the bulk—the Spirit overhead
will look humanely malign and cast an oblique light on
them, followed by volleys of silvery laughter. That is the
Comic Spirit.

Now in *Twelfth Night*, as in *Gl' Ingannati* ('The
Duped')—as in *A Midsummer-Night's Dream*, for that
matter—everyone deceives or is deceived, while several
deceive to be deceived in turn. 'We are cheated,' says
Dowden, 'by our fellow-mortals, by fortune, by accident; but always the chief deceiver is ourself—our senti-
mentality, our vanity, our fears, our egoism.'

That is shrewd criticism: and accepting it we may
note of *Twelfth Night* that, of the three main self-
deceivers, two get off lightly and happily, set free to
laugh at themselves because they have hurt none but
themselves, and that but gently: while the Comic Spirit
whips Malvolio far more severely because *his* egoism
has set him up to be a judge of others, to condemn.

IX

Orsino, but for the grace of God and the clemency of
circumstance, might have come to as evil an end as
King Richard II. He has the same gift of saying things

beautifully when they do not help the immediate situation. He is discovered as being in love, but his 'fancy' is bred less of the heart than of the head, and in fact he is in love with being in love. He toys with it as with a lap-dog, stroking its ears: he feeds it on music—'Give me excess of it'—

> that, surfeiting,
> The appetite may sicken, and so die....
> That strain again! it had a dying fall:
> O, it came o'er my ear like the sweet sound
> That breathes upon a bank of violets;
> Stealing and giving odour....Enough, no more!
> 'Tis not so sweet now as it was before.

Quite so: he does not even make his own music; he commands it to be brought in excess, and then complains of surfeit thus—

> O spirit of love, how quick and fresh art thou,
> That, notwithstanding thy capacity
> Receiveth as the sea, nought enters there,
> Of what validity and pitch soe'er,
> But falls into abatement and low price,
> Even in a minute...So full of shapes is fancy,
> That it alone is high fantastical.

There we have him; a virtuoso who cannot mount or ride, but plays at punning and woos his Inamorata by messenger. As for the music, Shakespeare knew a great deal about it[1]: knew about it from the music of the spheres down to triple time, plain-song, tonic intervals and the proper handling of lute and viol. But he also knew how music can illude men of cheap character. He puts his most-quoted praise of it into the mouth of the worthless Lorenzo (*Merchant of Venice*, Act 5)—

> Sit, Jessica. Look how the floor of heaven
> Is thick inlaid with patens of bright gold,

[1] See, for example, *Shakespeare and Music* and *The Poets and Music*, by Edward W. Naylor, Mus.D. (Dent and Sons).

> There's not the smallest orb which thou behold'st
> But in his motion like an angel sings,
> Still quiring to the young-eyed cherubins...

and so on, through an amorous lecture. But as in the last
Act of *The Merchant*, as in the 'moated grange song' in
Measure for Measure, so in this play, it is Shakespeare
who brings in the music exactly to the mood *he* commands: and here he commands better than Orsino—the
wayward, wistful singing of Feste. Orsino, commanding
much music and a page with the impressive name of
Cesario, finds himself in the end fortunately possessed
of a—Viola.

Olivia is plainly a self-deceiver after another fashion.
She plays with *mourning*; but is easily cured. (Manningham mistook her for a widow.) It has somewhere
been suggested that the stage-tradition which habits and
presents her as a staid *châtelaine*—a *femme de trente ans*
or so—is a mistake; that her swift barter of mourning
for love and of one love at a moment's notice, for another, better befits an irresponsible girl, as her letting her
household shift under a Steward's superintendence ill
consorts with years of presumable prudence. It may be
so; but acquaintance with matronly ladies and the
strength of their impulses may incline us to reflect that
the stage-tradition is not so wrong after all.

As to Malvolio, we are not so sure that stage-tradition
is correct, making him the character assigned to the
'star' actor of a Company. One bears the tradition in
mind, with all that Charles Lamb says about him. We
remember, too, that King Charles I wrote 'Malvolio'
upon his copy of the Second Folio preserved in Windsor
Castle (as he wrote 'Parolles' against *All's Well*), these
impersonations having apparently left on his mind the
most vivid portrait in each. And no doubt it happened:
an eminent actor took charge of Malvolio, as eminent
actors have always taken charge of Shylock. But even
allowing that Shakespeare had a way of making his un-

pleasant characters somehow sympathetic, we would maintain that the stage-tradition of making Shylock and Malvolio too 'sympathetic' (and to that extent too important) puts these characters out of the picture, to the defacement of the total scheme. Malvolio, of course, is not a 'Puritan' in any historical sense, but a Puritan only as an incarnation of the abstract Puritan's besetting foible—that of self-righteousness, of making himself a judge of others. Through this, and through the complacent arrogance bred by that habit of mind, he comes to grief. As the Comic Spirit might put it, he tries to lift himself up by his own cross-garters: and he is incorrigible as a nagging woman—as all such kill-joys are. 'You have done me wrong, notorious wrong—I'll be revenged on the whole pack of you.'—And so he goes out, impenitent, his hypocrisy still wrapped about him for a cloak of maliciousness. We all know that type of man and have a sort of pitying respect for him because he will never learn. But we should not allow his figure to dominate this play any more than we should allow his kind to dominate our daily life.

X

Viola, too, deceives and is deceived; prettily entrapped towards the end by womanish fear in the business of the duel; hers being the blame of this through playing the boy. But Viola is Viola. Shakespeare just makes her lovable: and if we ask how or why—as how or why he makes sweet Anne Page lovable—we critics are as sapient as any lover who asks Jove (who knows all about it but will not tell) why men and gods fall in love. One small point in her courtship may be noted, because it touches a point in the sister-play of *As You Like It*. There is just a touch of the minx in Rosalind and Viola both, as they would each have her suitor 'build him a willow cabin by her gate.' But Viola keeps up her boy-game to the end; while if Orlando does not detect Rosalind's from the start, he is more of a fool than the play gives us excuse for supposing him. At any rate, by contrast with Rosalind Viola appears less a creature of flesh and blood; diaphanous somewhat; a princess out of fairy-tale; yet indubitably a princess, born to arrive after pretty adversities at her heart's desire and live happy ever after. To put it in one way, she is just the sort of maiden that a sound middle-aged man, with a heart not unresponsive to youth and romance, would choose for a ward: to put it in another, she is one of those Shakespearian women—such as Perdita and Miranda—concerning whom one feels that on a perfect stage they could only be impersonated by one gifted by the gods to combine fresh transient beauty with inherited breeding.

As for Sir Toby, Sir Andrew, Maria, the players-up in the intrigue, who can fail to recognise their originals? Of Sir Toby one might say—were it permissible to be said with delicacy—that he is Falstaff flattened out; a Falstaff in two dimensions; a figure in which (as Burke said of another social phenomenon) vice has lost half its evil by losing all its grossness; or rather, has lost all its evil by losing half its grossness. For Belch, like Falstaff, is a social phenomenon, a derelict of the decaying feudal times, a gentleman who, by course of time and change reduced to the employ of a hanger-on, has lost neither the ways of a past age, nor its joviality, nor its manner. Like Dogberry, he has 'had losses': but these relics of better times he preserves with his out-at-heel boots and the pardonable infirmity of going to bed in them. As for Aguecheek, he is Slender *redivivus*, with his vanity, conned aphorisms, thin canary beard and trick of pulling it while he glances down his legs; the sort of fool we all know and welcome in company, and follow to his grave regretfully, wishing more food for pastime were left to us. While, as for Maria, if we derive her down from Mistress Quickly, through the Quickly of *The Merry*

Wives—albeit as unregenerate men we sigh over her gradual refinement—we must admit her true to the old breed.

XI

Still, and with all respect to Malvolio, to his hold upon 'star' actors, to all his claim, not disputed, upon Shakespeare's sole begetting, we must hold and insist on holding Feste, Master of the Revels, to be the master-mind and controller of *Twelfth Night*, its comic spirit and president, even as Puck is comic spirit and president of *A Midsummer-Night's Dream*. Unscathed by the slaps and side-blows of the plot, in the end he gets dismissed out into the cold: and that is Shakespeare's last word of irony—as it is with his last word on the poor loyal Fool in *Lear*. But while the play lasts, and his business, Feste has it in charge. Does the Duke demand music? Feste provides it; but it is something other than the Duke demands. As, when he sings 'O mistress mine' he is rewarded by Aguecheek with 'A mellifluous voice, as I am true knight,' so, when he sings that incomparable ditty 'Come away, come away death,' the Duke rewards him with coin and is answered by the artist with a recommendation to get a tailor to make him a doublet of changeable taffeta to fit an opal-shifting mind—

I would have men of such constancy put to sea, that their business might be every thing and their intent every where, for that's it that always makes a good voyage of nothing.... Farewell.

His philosophy too, as Swinburne has noted, is pure Rabelais—pure Pantagruel purged of Panurge. It would have saved many commentators much time had they perceived this; and that when Feste is airily fooling Aguecheek with quotations from an alleged Hermit of Prague who opined that 'whatever is, is,' or the history of Pigrogromitus and the Vapians passing the equinoctial of Queubus, they search libraries. The Vapians managed it naturally because

> They went to sea in a sieve, they did;
> In a sieve they went to sea....

XII

Twelfth Night, then, coming just after *As You Like It*, just before the great tragedies, and written for the traditional mad-cap close of Christmas feasting and revels, has been called Shakespeare's farewell to mirth: and for this leave-taking (although theatrical leave-takings and 'positively last appearances' not infrequently tend to repetition) Shakespeare summons up a troop of characters recognisable by us as our old favourites—with a difference. Delightful to read—and so delightful to witness that no one who has missed seeing it staged can guess the full of its charm or the thrill of that truly Aristotelian ἀναγνώρισις upon which it concludes—a play of one piece compact, compelling and holding you to its mood —this *Twelfth Night*, analysed in the study, becomes a texture or tissue of shadows, of afterthoughts, the ghostlier the more poetical. Arden, with its greenwood sunshine, has faded into Illyria, perilously near fading into Elysium. The mirth abides; but it reaches us from a distance, its *dramatis personae* move in the beams of a lunar rainbow. They move to music, but to music with 'a dying fall' as a fountain in a garden at night, and it has changed from the robust note of 'Love is crownéd with the prime' to 'Youth's a stuff will not endure'—a very slight change, but subtle, delicate, if we listen. The reader, aware of this change, becomes aware also that the play, for all its gaiety, is agonising a spell upon him: as might a woman eager for love, past her prime, knowing that the time is brief to win before the edge of daylight touches to pale the candles. A most subtle play, belonging (in the Malvolio business especially) to the highest, most ancient traditions of Comedy—as the very titles of Menander—*The Self-Pitier*, the *Self-Tormentor*—may assure us!

Twelfth Night, too, plays on us the last pretty paradox: that in civilised Comedy, as in the lists of chivalry, civilised woman is ever Queen of Tourney, arbitress of the game: and yet Olivia, president of the lists throughout, with every character in main plot or underplot performing under her eyes, is duped by them all.

Love it or leave it—or 'What you will'—*Twelfth Night* remains the politest of Shakespeare's Comedies.

Q.

Postscript, 1949.

Q's last Introduction but one is left as it stood in 1930. Later discoveries, some of which are referred to in amended or additional notes below, might have led him here and there to reword a passage dealing with matters of fact. No fresh knowledge or new-fangled theory can, however, touch with corruption the perennial charm of style and warm humanity of spirit which breathe from this delightful essay on Shakespeare's finest comedy.

J. D. W.

TO THE READER

The following is a brief description of the punctuation and other typographical devices employed in the text, which have been more fully explained in the *Note on Punctuation* and the *Textual Introduction* to be found in *The Tempest* volume:

An obelisk (†) implies corruption or emendation, and suggests a reference to the Notes.

A single bracket at the beginning of a speech signifies an 'aside.'

Four dots represent a *full-stop* in the original, except when it occurs at the end of a speech, and they mark a long pause. Original *colons* or *semicolons*, which denote a somewhat shorter pause, are retained, or represented as three dots when they appear to possess special dramatic significance. Similarly, significant *commas* have been given as dashes.

Round brackets are taken from the original, and mark a significant change of voice; when the original brackets seem to imply little more than the drop in tone accompanying parenthesis, they are conveyed by commas or dashes.

In plays for which both Folio and Quarto texts exist, passages taken from the text not selected as the basis for the present edition will be enclosed within square brackets. Lines which Shakespeare apparently intended to cancel, have been marked off by frame-brackets.

Single inverted commas (' ') are editorial; double ones (" ") derive from the original, where they are used to draw attention to maxims, quotations, etc.

The reference number for the first line is given at the head of each page. Numerals in square brackets are placed at the beginning of the traditional acts and scenes.

TWELFTH NIGHT:
OR,
WHAT YOU WILL

The scene: Illyria

CHARACTERS IN THE PLAY

ORSINO, *Duke of Illyria*

SEBASTIAN, *brother to Viola*

ANTONIO, *a sea-captain, friend to Sebastian*

Another sea-captain, friend to Viola

VALENTINE
CURIO } *gentlemen attending on the Duke*

SIR TOBY BELCH, *kinsman to Olivia*

SIR ANDREW AGUECHEEK

MALVOLIO, *steward to Olivia*

FABIAN, *a gentleman in the service of Olivia*

FESTE, *fool to Olivia*

OLIVIA, *a rich countess*

VIOLA, *in love with the Duke*

MARIA, *Olivia's gentlewoman (small of stature)*

Lords, priests, sailors, officers, musicians,
and other attendants

TWELFTH NIGHT:
OR,
WHAT YOU WILL

[1. 1.]   *A room in the Duke's palace*

The Duke ORSINO, CURIO *and Lords,
hearing music; the music ceases*

Duke. If music be the food of love, play on,
Give me excess of it; that, surfeiting,
The appetite may sicken, and so die....
That strain again! it had a dying fall:
O, it came o'er my ear like the sweet sound
That breathes upon a bank of violets;
Stealing and giving odour....[*music again*] Enough,
  no more!
'Tis not so sweet now as it was before.
O spirit of love, how quick and fresh art thou,
That, notwithstanding thy capacity   10
Receiveth as the sea, nought enters there,
Of what validity and pitch soe'er,
But falls into abatement and low price,
Even in a minute...So full of shapes is fancy,
That it alone is high fantastical.
 Curio. Will you go hunt, my lord?
 Duke.   What, Curio?
 Curio.   The hart.
 Duke. Why, so I do, the noblest that I have:
O, when mine eyes did see Olivia first,
Methought she purged the air of pestilence;
That instant was I turned into a hart,
And my desires, like fell and cruel hounds,   20
E'er since pursue me....

VALENTINE enters

        How now? what news from her?

Valentine. So please my lord, I might not be admitted,
But from her handmaid do return this answer:
†The element itself, till seven years hence,
Shall not behold her face at ample view;
But like a cloistress she will veiléd walk,
And water once a day her chamber round
With eye-offending brine: all this to season
30 A brother's dead love, which she would keep fresh
And lasting, in her sad remembrance.

 Duke. O, she that hath a heart of that fine frame
To pay this debt of love but to a brother,
How will she love, when the rich golden shaft
Hath killed the flock of all affections else
That live in her; when liver, brain and heart,
These sovereign thrones, are all supplied and filled,
Her sweet perfections, with one self king!
Away before me to sweet beds of flowers—
40 Love-thoughts lie rich when canopied with bowers.

              [they go

[I. 2.]   *Near the sea-coast*

VIOLA, Captain, and sailors

Viola. What country, friends, is this?

Captain. This is Illyria, lady.

Viola. And what should I do in Illyria?
My brother he is in Elysium.
Perchance he is not drowned: what think you, sailors?

Captain. It is perchance that you yourself were saved.

Viola. O my poor brother! and so perchance may he be.

Captain. True, madam, and to comfort you
    with chance,
Assure yourself, after our ship did split,

When you and those poor number saved with you   10
Hung on our driving boat...I saw your brother,
Most provident in peril, bind himself—
Courage and hope both teaching him the practice—
To a strong mast that lived upon the sea;
Where, like Arion on the dolphin's back,
I saw him hold acquaintance with the waves
So long as I could see.

Viola.   For saying so, there's gold:
Mine own escape unfoldeth to my hope,
Whereto thy speech serves for authority,
The like of him. Know'st thou this country?   20

Captain. Ay, madam, well, for I was bred and born
Not three hours' travel from this very place.

Viola. Who governs here?

Captain. A noble duke, in nature as in name.

Viola. What is his name?

Captain. Orsino.

Viola. Orsino: I have heard my father name him.
He was a bachelor then.

Captain. And so is now, or was so very late:
For but a month ago I went from hence,   30
And then 'twas fresh in murmur—as, you know,
What great ones do the less will prattle of—
That he did seek the love of fair Olivia.

Viola. What's she?

Captain. A virtuous maid, the daughter of a count
That died some twelvemonth since—then leaving her
In the protection of his son, her brother,
Who shortly also died: for whose dear love,
They say, she hath abjured the company
And sight of men.

Viola.   O, that I served that lady,   40
And might not be delivered to the world,

Till I had made mine own occasion mellow,
What my estate is.

Captain.   That were hard to compass,
Because she will admit no kind of suit,
No, not the duke's.

Viola. There is a fair behaviour in thee, captain,
And though that nature with a beauteous wall
Doth oft close in pollution, yet of thee
I will believe thou hast a mind that suits
50 With this thy fair and outward character.
I prithee, and I'll pay thee bounteously,
Conceal me what I am, and be my aid
For such disguise as haply shall become
The form of my intent. I'll serve this duke,
Thou shalt present me as an eunuch to him,
It may be worth thy pains: for I can sing,
And speak to him in many sorts of music,
That will allow me very worth his service.
What else may hap to time I will commit,
60 Only shape thou thy silence to my wit.

Captain. Be you his eunuch, and your mute I'll be,
When my tongue blabs, then let mine eyes not see!

Viola. I thank thee: lead me on.   [*they go*

[1. 3.]   *A room in Olivia's house*

*Sir TOBY BELCH seated with drink before him,
and MARIA*

Sir Toby. What a plague means my niece, to take
the death of her brother thus? I am sure care's an
enemy to life.

Maria. By my troth, Sir Toby, you must come in
earlier o' nights: your cousin, my lady, takes great
exceptions to your ill hours.

Sir Toby. Why, let her except before excepted.

Maria. Ay, but you must confine yourself within the modest limits of order.

Sir Toby. Confine? I'll confine myself no finer than 10 I am: these clothes are good enough to drink in, and so be these boots too: an they be not, let them hang themselves in their own straps.

Maria. That quaffing and drinking will undo you: I heard my lady talk of it yesterday: and of a foolish knight, that you brought in one night here, to be her wooer.

Sir Toby. Who? Sir Andrew Aguecheek?

Maria. Ay, he.

Sir Toby. He's as tall a man as any's in Illyria.   20

Maria. What's that to th' purpose?

Sir Toby. Why, he has three thousand ducats a year.

Maria. Ay, but he'll have but a year in all these ducats; he's a very fool and a prodigal.

Sir Toby. Fie, that you'll say so! he plays o'th' viol-de-gamboys, and speaks three or four languages word for word without book, and hath all the good gifts of nature.

Maria. He hath, indeed almost natural: for, besides that he's a fool, he's a great quarreller: and but that he 30 hath the gift of a coward to allay the gust he hath in quarrelling, 'tis thought among the prudent he would quickly have the gift of a grave.

Sir Toby. By this hand, they are scoundrels and sub-stractors that say so of him. Who are they?

Maria. They that add, moreover, he's drunk nightly in your company.

Sir Toby. With drinking healths to my niece: I'll drink to her as long as there is a passage in my throat and drink in Illyria: he's a coward and a coystrill that will not 40

drink to my niece, till his brains turn o'th' toe like a
parish-top....[*he seizes her about the waist and they
dance a turn*] What, wench! †Castiliano vulgo; for here
comes Sir Andrew Agueface.

Sir ANDREW AGUECHEEK enters

Sir Andrew. Sir Toby Belch! how now, Sir Toby
Belch?

Sir Toby. Sweet Sir Andrew!

Sir Andrew. Bless you, fair shrew.

Maria [*curtsies*]. And you too, sir!

50 *Sir Toby.* Accost, Sir Andrew, accost.

Sir Andrew. What's that?

Sir Toby. My niece's chambermaid.

Sir Andrew. Good Mistress Accost, I desire better
acquaintance.

Maria. My name is Mary, sir.

Sir Andrew. Good Mistress Mary Accost,—

Sir Toby. You mistake, knight: 'accost' is front her,
board her, woo her, assail her.

Sir Andrew. By my troth, I would not undertake her
60 in this company. Is that the meaning of 'accost'?

Maria. Fare you well, gentlemen.   [*she turns to go*

Sir Toby. An thou let part so, Sir Andrew, would
thou mightst never draw sword again.

Sir Andrew. An you part so, mistress, I would I might
never draw sword again...Fair lady, do you think you
have fools in hand?

Maria. Sir, I have not you by th'hand

Sir Andrew. Marry, but you shall have—and here's
my hand.   [*he holds it out*

70 *Maria* [*takes it*]. Now, sir, 'thought is free'...[*she
looks at his palm*] I pray you, bring your hand to th'
buttery-bar, and let it drink.

Sir Andrew. Wherefore, sweet-heart? what's your metaphor?

Maria. It's dry, sir.

Sir Andrew. Why, I think so; I am not such an ass, but I can keep my hand dry. But what's your jest?

Maria. A dry jest, sir.

Sir Andrew. Are you full of them?

Maria. Ay, sir; I have them at my fingers' ends: 80 marry, now I let go your hand, I am barren.

[*she drops his hand, curtsies and trips away*

Sir Toby [*sits*]. O knight, thou lack'st a cup of canary: when did I see thee so put down?

Sir Andrew. Never in your life, I think, unless you see canary put me down...[*sits beside him*] Methinks sometimes I have no more wit than a Christian or an ordinary man has: but I am a great eater of beef and I believe that does harm to my wit.

Sir Toby. No question.

Sir Andrew. An I thought that, I'd forswear it. I'll 90 ride home to-morrow, Sir Toby.

Sir Toby. Pourquoi, my dear knight?

Sir Andrew. What is 'pourquoi'? do or not do? I would I had bestowed that time in the tongues, that I have in fencing, dancing and bear-baiting: O, had I but followed the arts!

Sir Toby [*fondles him*]. Then hadst thou had an excellent head of hair.

Sir Andrew. Why, would that have mended my hair?   100

Sir Toby. Past question, for thou seest it will not curl by nature.

Sir Andrew. But it becomes me well enough, does't not?

Sir Toby. Excellent! it hangs like flax on a distaff; and

I hope to see a housewife take thee between her legs and
spin it off.

Sir Andrew. Faith, I'll home to-morrow, Sir Toby.
Your niece will not be seen, or if she be it's four to one
110 she'll none of me: the count himself here hard by
woos her.

Sir Toby. She'll none o'th' count—she'll not match
above her degree, neither in estate, years, nor wit;
I have heard her swear't. Tut, there's life in't, man.

Sir Andrew. I'll stay a month longer....I am a fellow
o'th' strangest mind i'th' world: I delight in masques
and revels sometimes altogether.

Sir Toby. Art thou good at these kickshawses, knight?

Sir Andrew. As any man in Illyria, whatsoever he be,
120 under the degree of my betters, and yet I will not compare with an old man.

Sir Toby. What is thy excellence in a galliard, knight?

Sir Andrew. Faith, I can cut a caper.

(*Sir Toby.* And I can cut the mutton to't.

Sir Andrew. And I think I have the back-trick simply
as strong as any man in Illyria.

Sir Toby. Wherefore are these things hid? wherefore
have these gifts a curtain before 'em? are they like to
take dust, like Mistress Mall's picture? why dost thou
130 not go to church in a galliard and come home in a
coranto? My very walk should be a jig; I would not so
much as make water but in a sink-a-pace. What dost
thou mean? Is it a world to hide virtues in? I did think,
by the excellent constitution of thy leg, it was formed
under the star of a galliard.

Sir Andrew. Ay, 'tis strong, and it does indifferent well
in a †dun-coloured stock. Shall we set about some revels?

Sir Toby. What shall we do else? were we not born
under Taurus?

Sir Andrew. Taurus! That's sides and heart.   140

Sir Toby. No, sir, it is legs and thighs...Let me see thee caper [*Sir Andrew leaps*]....Ha! higher: ha, ha! excellent!   [*they go*

[1. 4.]   *A room in the Duke's palace*

'Enter VALENTINE, and VIOLA in man's attire'

Valentine. If the duke continue these favours towards you, Cesario, you are like to be much advanced. He hath known you but three days, and already you are no stranger.

Viola. You either fear his humour or my negligence, that you call in question the continuance of his love. Is he inconstant, sir, in his favours?

Valentine. No, believe me.

Viola. I thank you. Here comes the count.

'Enter DUKE, CURIO and attendants'

Duke. Who saw Cesario, ho!   10

Viola. On your attendance, my lord, here.

Duke. Stand you awhile aloof....[*Curio and attendants withdraw*] Cesario,
Thou know'st no less but all: I have unclasped
To thee the book even of my secret soul.
Therefore, good youth, address thy gait unto her,
Be not denied access, stand at her doors,
And tell them, there thy fixéd foot shall grow
Till thou have audience.

Viola.   Sure, my noble lord,
If she be so abandoned to her sorrow
As it is spoke, she never will admit me.   20

Duke. Be clamorous and leap all civil bounds
Rather than make unprofited return.

Viola. Say I do speak with her, my lord, what then?

Duke. O, then unfold the passion of my love,
Surprise her with discourse of my dear faith:
It shall become thee well to act my woes;
She will attend it better in thy youth
Than in a nuncio's of more grave aspect.

Viola. I think not so, my lord.

Duke.   Dear lad, believe it;
30 For they shall yet belie thy happy years,
That say thou art a man: Diana's lip
Is not more smooth and rubious; thy small pipe
Is as the maiden's organ, shrill and sound—
And all is semblative a woman's part.
I know thy constellation is right apt
For this affair...[*he beckons attendants*] Some four or
        five attend him,
All if you will; for I myself am best
When least in company...Prosper well in this,
And thou shalt live as freely as thy lord,
40 To call his fortunes thine.

Viola.   I'll do my best,
To woo your lady...[*aside*] Yet, ah! barful strife!
Whoe'er I woo, myself would be his wife.   [*they go*

[1. 5.]   *A room in Olivia's house; at the
        back a chair of state*

MARIA *and* CLOWN

Maria. Nay, either tell me where thou hast been, or
I will not open my lips so wide as a bristle may enter
in way of thy excuse: my lady will hang thee for thy
absence.

Clown. Let her hang me: he that is well hanged in this
world needs to fear no colours.

Maria. Make that good.

Clown. He shall see none to fear.

Maria. A good lenten answer: I can tell thee where that saying was born, of 'I fear no colours.'   10

Clown. Where, good Mistress Mary?

Maria. In the wars—and that may you be bold to say in your foolery.

Clown. Well, God give them wisdom that have it; and those that are fools, let them use their talents.

Maria. Yet you will be hanged for being so long absent; or to be turned away, is not that as good as a hanging to you?

Clown. Many a good hanging prevents a bad marriage; and, for turning away, let summer bear it out.   20

Maria. You are resolute, then?

Clown. Not so neither, but I am resolved on two points—

Maria. That if one break, the other will hold; or if both break, your gaskins fall.

Clown. Apt in good faith, very apt...[*she turns to go*] Well, go thy way—if Sir Toby would leave drinking, thou wert as witty a piece of Eve's flesh as any in Illyria.

Maria. Peace, you rogue, no more o' that: here comes my lady: make your excuse wisely, you were best.   30

[*she goes*

The Lady OLIVIA *enters in black,* MALVOLIO *and attendants following; she sits in her chair of state*

Clown [*feigns not to see them*]. Wit, an't be thy will, put me into good fooling! Those wits that think they have thee, do very oft prove fools; and I, that am sure I lack thee, may pass for a wise man. For what says Quinapalus? 'Better a witty fool than a foolish wit.' [*turns*] God bless thee, lady!

Olivia. Take the fool away.

Clown. Do you not hear, fellows? Take away the lady.

Olivia. Go to, y'are a dry fool: I'll no more of you:
40 besides, you grow dishonest.

Clown. Two faults, madonna, that drink and good
counsel will amend: for give the dry fool drink, then is
the fool not dry: bid the dishonest man mend himself; if
he mend, he is no longer dishonest; if he cannot, let the
botcher mend him: any thing that's mended is but
patched: virtue that transgresses, is but patched with sin,
and sin that amends is but patched with virtue....If that
this simple syllogism will serve, so: if it will not, what
remedy? As there is no true cuckold but calamity, so
50 beauty's a flower: the lady bade take away the fool,
therefore I say again, take her away.

Olivia. Sir, I bade them take away you.

Clown. Misprision in the highest degree! Lady,
'Cucullus non facit monachum'; that's as much to say
as I wear not motley in my brain...Good madonna, give
me leave to prove you a fool.

Olivia. Can you do it?

Clown. Dexteriously, good madonna.

Olivia. Make your proof.

60 *Clown.* I must catechize you for it, madonna. Good
my mouse of virtue, answer me.

Olivia. Well, sir, for want of other idleness, I'll bide
your proof.

Clown. Good madonna, why mourn'st thou?

Olivia. Good fool, for my brother's death.

Clown. I think his soul is in hell, madonna.

Olivia. I know his soul is in heaven, fool.

Clown. The more fool, madonna, to mourn for
your brother's soul, being in heaven....Take away the
70 fool, gentlemen.

Olivia. What think you of this fool, Malvolio? doth he not mend?

Malvolio. Yes, and shall do, till the pangs of death shake him: infirmity, that decays the wise, doth ever make the better fool.

Clown. God send you, sir, a speedy infirmity, for the better increasing your folly! Sir Toby will be sworn that I am no fox, but he will not pass his word for two pence that you are no fool.

Olivia. How say you to that, Malvolio?   80

Malvolio. I marvel your ladyship takes delight in such a barren rascal: I saw him put down the other day with an ordinary fool that has no more brain than a stone. Look you now, he's out of his guard already; unless you laugh and minister occasion to him, he is gagged. I protest, I take these wise men, that crow so at these set kind of fools, no better than the fools' zanies.

Olivia. O, you are sick of self-love, Malvolio, and taste with a distempered appetite. To be generous, guiltless, and of free disposition, is to take those things 90 for bird-bolts that you deem cannon-bullets: there is no slander in an allowed fool, though he do nothing but rail; nor no railing in a known discreet man, though he do nothing but reprove.

Clown. Now Mercury endue thee with leasing, for thou speakest well of fools!

MARIA returns

Maria. Madam, there is at the gate a young gentleman much desires to speak with you.

Olivia. From the Count Orsino, is it?

Maria. I know not, madam—'tis a fair young man, and 100 well attended.

Olivia. Who of my people hold him in delay?

Maria. Sir Toby, madam, your kinsman.

Olivia. Fetch him off, I pray you! he speaks nothing but madman: fie on him....[*Maria hurries away*] Go you, Malvolio: if it be a suit from the count, I am sick, or not at home....what you will, to dismiss it. [*Malvolio goes*] Now you see, sir, how your fooling grows old, and people dislike it.

110 *Clown.* Thou hast spoke for us, madonna, as if thy eldest son should be a fool: whose skull Jove cram with brains! for—here he comes—one of thy kin, has a most weak pia mater.

Sir TOBY BELCH staggers in

Olivia. By mine honour, half drunk....What is he at the gate, cousin?

Sir Toby [*speaks thick*]. A gentleman.

Olivia. A gentleman? What gentleman?

Sir Toby. 'Tis a gentleman here...[*hiccoughs*] A plague o'these pickle-herring....[*Clown laughs*] How 120 now, sot!

Clown. Good Sir Toby—

Olivia. Cousin, cousin, how have you come so early by this lethargy?

Sir Toby. Lechery! I defy lechery...There's one at the gate.

Olivia. Ay, marry, what is he?

Sir Toby. Let him be the devil, an he will, I care not: give me 'faith,' say I....[*he totters to the door*] Well, it's all one.   [*he goes*

130 *Olivia.* What's a drunken man like, fool?

Clown. Like a drowned man, a fool, and a mad man: one draught above heat makes him a fool, the second mads him, and a third drowns him.

Olivia. Go thou and seek the crowner, and let him

sit o' my coz; for he's in the third degree of drink: he's
drowned: go look after him.

Clown. He is but mad yet, madonna, and the fool shall
look to the madman.   [*he follows Sir Toby*

MALVOLIO *returns*

Malvolio. Madam, yon young fellow swears he will
speak with you. I told him you were sick, he takes on 140
him to understand so much, and therefore comes to
speak with you. I told him you were asleep, he seems to
have a foreknowledge of that too, and therefore comes to
speak with you. What is to be said to him, lady? he's
fortified against any denial.

Olivia. Tell him he shall not speak with me.

Malvolio. Has been told so; and he says he'll stand
at your door like a sheriff's post, and be the supporter
to a bench, but he'll speak with you.

Olivia. What kind o' man is he?   150

Malvolio. Why, of mankind.

Olivia. What manner of man?

Malvolio. Of very ill manner; he'll speak with you,
will you, or no.

Olivia. Of what personage and years is he?

Malvolio. Not yet old enough for a man, nor young
enough for a boy; as a squash is before 'tis a peascod, or
a codling when 'tis almost an apple: 'tis with him in
standing water between boy and man. He is very well-
favoured and he speaks very shrewishly; one would 160
think his mother's milk were scarce out of him.

Olivia. Let him approach...Call in my gentlewoman.

Malvolio [*goes to the door*]. Gentlewoman, my lady
calls.   [*he departs*

MARIA returns

Olivia. Give me my veil: come, throw it o'er my face—
We'll once more hear Orsino's embassy. [*Maria veils her*

VIOLA (as Cesario) enters

Viola. The honourable lady of the house, which is
she?

170 *Olivia.* Speak to me, I shall answer for her: your will?

Viola. Most radiant, exquisite, and unmatchable
beauty!—I pray you, tell me if this be the lady of the
house, for I never saw her. I would be loath to cast
away my speech; for besides that it is excellently well
penned, I have taken great pains to con it. Good
beauties, let me sustain no scorn; I am very comptible,
even to the least sinister usage.

Olivia. Whence came you, sir?

Viola. I can say little more than I have studied, and
180 that question's out of my part. Good gentle one, give
me modest assurance if you be the lady of the house,
that I may proceed in my speech.

Olivia. Are you a comedian?

Viola. No, my profound heart: and yet, by the very
fangs of malice I swear, I am not that I play. Are you
the lady of the house?

Olivia. If I do not usurp myself, I am.

Viola. Most certain, if you are she, you do usurp yourself; for what is yours to bestow, is not yours to reserve.
190 But this is from my commission: I will on with my
speech in your praise, and then show you the heart of my
message.

Olivia. Come to what is important in't: I forgive you
the praise.

Viola. Alas, I took great pains to study it, and 'tis
poetical.

Olivia. It is the more like to be feigned, I pray you keep it in. I heard you were saucy at my gates, and allowed your approach rather to wonder at you than to hear you. If you be not mad, be gone; if you have 200 reason, be brief: 'tis not that time of moon with me to make one in so skipping a dialogue.

Maria [*points to the hat in Viola's hand*]. Will you hoist sail, sir? here lies your way.

[*she opens the door to thrust her out*

Viola [*resists*]. No, good swabber; I am to hull here a little longer....Some mollification for your giant, sweet lady!

Olivia. Tell me your mind.

Viola. I am a messenger.

Olivia. Sure, you have some hideous matter to deliver, 210 when the courtesy of it is so fearful. Speak your office.

Viola. It alone concerns your ear. I bring no overture of war, no taxation of homage; I hold the olive in my hand: my words are as full of peace as matter.

Olivia. Yet you began rudely. What are you? what would you?

Viola. The rudeness that hath appeared in me have I learned from my entertainment. What I am, and what I would, are as secret as maidenhead: to your ears, 220 divinity; to any other's, profanation.

Olivia. Give us the place alone: we will hear this divinity....[*Maria and attendants withdraw*] Now, sir, what is your text?

Viola. Most sweet lady,—

Olivia. A comfortable doctrine, and much may be said of it. Where lies your text?

Viola. In Orsino's bosom.

Olivia. In his bosom! In what chapter of his bosom?

230 *Viola.* To answer by the method, in the first of his
heart.

Olivia. O, I have read it; it is heresy. Have you no
more to say?

Viola. Good madam, let me see your face.

Olivia. Have you any commission from your lord to
negotiate with my face? you are now out of your text:
but we will draw the curtain, and show you the picture....
[*she unveils*] Look you, sir, such a one I was—this
present! Is't not well done?

240 *Viola.* Excellently done, if God did all.

Olivia. 'Tis in grain, sir, 'twill endure wind and
weather.

Viola. 'Tis beauty truly blent, whose red and white
Nature's own sweet and cunning hand laid on:
Lady, you are the cruell'st she alive,
If you will lead these graces to the grave,
And leave the world no copy.

Olivia. O, sir, I will not be so hard-hearted; I will
give out divers schedules of my beauty: it shall be in-
250 ventoried, and every particle and utensil labelled to my
will: as, *Item*, Two lips indifferent red; *Item*, Two grey
eyes with lids to them; *Item*, One neck, one chin, and so
forth. Were you sent hither to praise me?

Viola. I see you what you are, you are too proud;
But, if you were the devil, you are fair...
My lord and master loves you; O, such love
Could be but recompensed, though you were crowned
The nonpareil of beauty!

Olivia. How does he love me?

Viola. With adorations, fertile tears,
260 With groans that thunder love, with sighs of fire.

Olivia. Your lord does know my mind, I cannot love
him:

Yet I suppose him virtuous, know him noble,
Of great estate, of fresh and stainless youth;
In voices well divulged, free, learned and valiant,
And in dimension and the shape of nature
A gracious person: but yet I cannot love him;
He might have took his answer long ago.

Viola. If I did love you in my master's flame,
With such a suff'ring, such a deadly life,
In your denial I would find no sense,   270
I would not understand it.

    Olivia.   Why, what would you?

Viola. Make me a willow cabin at your gate,
And call upon my soul within the house,
Write loyal cantons of contemnéd love,
And sing them loud even in the dead of night;
Holla your name to the reverberate hills,
And make the babbling gossip of the air
Cry out 'Olivia!' O, you should not rest
Between the elements of air and earth,
But you should pity me.

    Olivia.   You might do much: 280
What is your parentage?

Viola. Above my fortunes, yet my state is well:
I am a gentleman.

    Olivia.   Get you to your lord;
I cannot love him: let him send no more,
Unless—perchance—you come to me again,
To tell me how he takes it...Fare you well:
I thank you for your pains: spend this for me.

                                  [*offers money*

Viola. I am no fee'd post, lady; keep your purse.
My master, not myself, lacks recompense.
Love make his heart of flint that you shall love,   290
And let your fervour like my master's be

Placed in contempt! Farewell, fair cruelty.   [*she goes*
  Olivia. 'What is your parentage?'
'Above my fortunes, yet my state is well:
I am a gentleman'....I'll be sworn thou art!
Thy tongue, thy face, thy limbs, actions, and spirit,
Do give thee five-fold blazon...Not too fast: soft! soft!
Unless the master were the man....[*she muses*] How now!
Even so quickly may one catch the plague?
300 Methinks I feel this youth's perfections
With an invisible and subtle stealth
To creep in at mine eyes....Well, let it be....
What, ho, Malvolio!

MALVOLIO returns

  Malvolio.   Here, madam, at your service.
  Olivia. Run after that same peevish messenger,
The county's man: he left this ring behind him,
Would I or not; tell him I'll none of it.
Desire him not to flatter with his lord,
Nor hold him up with hopes—I am not for him:
If that the youth will come this way to-morrow,
310 I'll give him reasons for't...Hie thee, Malvolio.
  Malvolio. Madam, I will.   [*he hurries forth*
  Olivia. I do I know not what, and fear to find
Mine eye too great a flatterer for my mind...
Fate, show thy force—ourselves we do not owe—
What is decreed, must be; and be this so!   [*she goes*

[2. 1.]   *At the door of Antonio's house*

ANTONIO and SEBASTIAN

  Antonio. Will you stay no longer? nor will you not
that I go with you?
  Sebastian. By your patience, no: my stars shine darkly

over me; the malignancy of my fate might perhaps distemper yours; therefore I shall crave of you your leave
that I may bear my evils alone: it were a bad recompense for your love, to lay any of them on you.

Antonio. Let me yet know of you whither you are
bound.

Sebastian. No, sooth, sir: my determinate voyage is 10
mere extravagancy. But I perceive in you so excellent a
touch of modesty, that you will not extort from me what
I am willing to keep in; therefore it charges me in
manners the rather to express myself...You must know
of me then, Antonio, my name is Sebastian, which
I called Roderigo. My father was that Sebastian of
Messaline, whom I know you have heard of. He left
behind him myself and a sister, both born in an hour: if
the heavens had been pleased, would we had so ended!
But you, sir, altered that, for some hour before you took 20
me from the breach of the sea was my sister drowned.

Antonio. Alas, the day!

Sebastian. A lady, sir, though it was said she much re-
sembled me, was yet of many accounted beautiful: but,
though I could not with such estimable wonder overfar
believe that, yet thus far I will boldly publish her—she
bore a mind that envy could not but call fair...She is
drowned already, sir, with salt water, though I seem to
drown her remembrance again with more.

Antonio. Pardon me, sir, your bad entertainment.　　30

Sebastian. O, good Antonio, forgive me your trouble.

Antonio. If you will not murder me for my love, let
me be your servant.

Sebastian. If you will not undo what you have done,
that is, kill him whom you have recovered, desire it not.
Fare ye well at once. My bosom is full of kindness, and
I am yet so near the manners of my mother, that upon

the least occasion more mine eyes will tell tales of me...
[*they clasp hands*] I am bound to the Count Orsino's
40 court—farewell!   [*he goes*

Antonio. The gentleness of all the gods go with thee!
I have many enemies in Orsino's court,
Else would I very shortly see thee there:
But, come what may, I do adore thee so,
That danger shall seem sport, and I will go. [*he goes in*

[2. 2.]   *A street near Olivia's house*

        VIOLA *approaches*, MALVOLIO *following after*

Malvolio [*comes up*]. Were not you e'en now with the
Countess Olivia?

Viola. Even now, sir. On a moderate pace I have
since arrived but hither.

Malvolio [*sharply*]. She returns this ring to you, sir;
you might have saved me my pains, to have taken it
away yourself. She adds moreover, that you should put
your lord into a desperate assurance she will none of
him: and one thing more, that you be never so hardy to
10 come again in his affairs, unless it be to report your lord's
taking of this...[*he holds out the ring*] Receive it so.

Viola. She took the ring of me...I'll none of it.

Malvolio. Come, sir, you peevishly threw it to her;
and her will is, it should be so returned: [*he throws it
at her feet*] if it be worth stooping for, there it lies in
your eye; if not, be it his that finds it.   [*he walks off*

Viola. I left no ring with her: what means this lady?
Fortune forbid my outside have not charmed her!
She made good view of me, indeed so much,
20 That as methought her eyes had lost her tongue,
For she did speak in starts distractedly....
She loves me, sure—the cunning of her passion

Invites me in this churlish messenger...
None of my lord's ring! why, he sent her none...
I am the man—if it be so, as 'tis,
Poor lady, she were better love a dream...
Disguise, I see thou art a wickedness,
Wherein the pregnant enemy does much.
How easy is it for the proper-false
In women's waxen hearts to set their forms! 30
Alas, our frailty is the cause, not we,
For such as we are made of, such we be...
How will this fadge? My master loves her dearly,
And I (poor monster!) fond as much on him:
And she, mistaken, seems to dote on me:
What will become of this? As I am man,
My state is desperate for my master's love;
As I am woman—now alas the day!—
What thriftless sighs shall poor Olivia breathe?
O time, thou must untangle this, not I, 40
It is too hard a knot for me t'untie. [*she goes*

[2. 3.] *A room in Olivia's house; a bench and a table
with cold viands and drinking-vessels thereon*

Sir TOBY BELCH *and* Sir ANDREW AGUECHEEK
enter, drunk

Sir Toby [*sits at table*]. Approach, Sir Andrew: [*Sir
Andrew follows with difficulty*] not to be a-bed after
midnight is to be up betimes; and 'diluculo surgere,'
thou know'st,—

Sir Andrew [*sits beside him*]. Nay, by my troth, I
know not: but I know, to be up late is to be up late.
[*he eats*

Sir Toby [*takes up a pot and finds it empty*]. A false
conclusion: I hate it as an unfilled can. To be up after

midnight and to go to bed then, is early; so that to go to
10 bed after midnight is to go to bed betimes. Does not our
life consist of the four elements?

Sir Andrew [*his mouth full*]. Faith, so they say—but
I think it rather consists of eating and drinking.

Sir Toby. Th'art a scholar; let us therefore eat and
drink. [*bawls*] Marian, I say! a stoup of wine!

The CLOWN comes in

Sir Andrew. Here comes the fool, i'faith.

Clown [*sits between them upon the bench*]. How now,
my hearts! Did you never see the picture of 'we
three'?

20 *Sir Toby.* Welcome, ass. Now let's have a catch.

Sir Andrew. By my troth, the fool has an excellent
breast. I had rather than forty shillings I had such a leg,
and so sweet a breath to sing, as the fool has. In sooth,
thou wast in very gracious fooling last night, when thou
spok'st of Pigrogromitus, of the Vapians passing the
equinoctial of Queubus; 'twas very good, i'faith...
I sent thee sixpence for thy leman—hadst it?

Clown. I did impetticoat thy gratillity: for Malvolio's
nose is no whipstock: my lady has a white hand, and the
30 Myrmidons are no bottle-ale houses.

Sir Andrew. Excellent! why, this is the best fooling,
when all is done. Now, a song.

Sir Toby. Come on, there is sixpence for you. Let's
have a song.

Sir Andrew. There's a testril of me too: if one knight
give a—

Clown. Would you have a love-song, or a song of
good life?

Sir Toby. A love-song, a love-song.

40 *Sir Andrew.* Ay, ay. I care not for good life.

Clown [*sings*].

> O mistress mine, where are you roaming?
> O, stay and hear, your true love's coming,
>   That can sing both high and low.
> Trip no further pretty sweeting:
> Journeys end in lovers meeting,
>   Every wise man's son doth know.

Sir Andrew. Excellent good, i'faith!

Sir Toby. Good, good.

Clown [*sings*].

> What is love, 'tis not hereafter,
> Present mirth hath present laughter: 50
>   What's to come is still unsure.
> In delay there lies no plenty,
> Then come kiss me, sweet and twenty:
>   Youth's a stuff will not endure.

Sir Andrew. A mellifluous voice, as I am true knight.

Sir Toby. A contagious breath.

Sir Andrew. Very sweet and contagious, i'faith.

Sir Toby. To hear by the nose, it is dulcet in contagion....But shall we make the welkin dance indeed? 60 Shall we rouse the night-owl in a catch, that will draw three souls out of one weaver? shall we do that?

Sir Andrew. An you love me, let's do't: I am dog at a catch.

Clown. By'r lady, sir, and some dogs will catch well.

Sir Andrew. Most certain...Let our catch be, 'Thou knave.'

Clown. 'Hold thy peace, thou knave,' knight? I shall be constrained in't to call thee knave, knight.

Sir Andrew. 'Tis not the first time I have constrained 70 one to call me knave. Begin, fool; it begins, 'Hold thy peace.'

Clown. I shall never begin if I hold my peace.

Sir Andrew. Good, i'faith! Come, begin.

[*they sing the catch*

MARIA *enters with wine*

Maria. What a caterwauling do you keep here! If my lady have not called up her steward Malvolio and bid him turn you out of doors, never trust me.

Sir Toby. 'My lady''s a Cataian, we are politicians, Malvolio's a Peg-a-Ramsey, and

80   [*sings*] 'Three merry men be we.'
Am not I consanguineous? am I not of her blood? Tillyvally! 'lady'!
    [*sings*] 'There dwelt a man in Babylon,
                    Lady, lady!'

Clown. Beshrew me, the knight's in admirable fooling.

Sir Andrew. Ay, he does well enough, if he be disposed, and so do I too; he does it with a better grace, but I do it more natural.

Sir Toby [*sings*]. 'O' the twelfth day of December,'—

90   *Maria.* For the love o' God, peace.

MALVOLIO *enters*

Malvolio. My masters, are you mad? or what are you? Have you no wit, manners, nor honesty, but to gabble like tinkers at this time of night? Do ye make an alehouse of my lady's house, that ye squeak out your coziers' catches without any mitigation or remorse of voice? Is there no respect of place, persons, nor time in you?

Sir Toby. We did keep time, sir, in our catches. Sneck up!

Malvolio. Sir Toby, I must be round with you. My

100 lady bade me tell you, that, though she harbours you as her kinsman, she's nothing allied to your disorders. If

you can separate yourself and your misdemeanours, you
are welcome to the house; if not, an it would please you
to take leave of her, she is very willing to bid you
farewell.

Sir Toby [*sings to Maria*]. 'Farewell, dear heart, since
I must needs be gone.'   [*he embraces her*
Maria. Nay, good Sir Toby.

Clown [*sings*]. 'His eyes do show his days are almost
done.'   110

Malvolio. Is't even so?

Sir Toby [*sings*]. 'But I will never die.'
                                        [*he falls to the ground*
Clown [*sings*]. Sir Toby, there you lie.

Malvolio. This is much credit to you.

Sir Toby [*rising, sings*]. 'Shall I bid him go?'

Clown [*sings*]. 'What an if you do?'

Sir Toby [*sings*]. 'Shall I bid him go, and spare not?'

Clown [*sings*]. 'O no, no, no, no, you dare not.'

Sir Toby [*to Clown*]. Out o' tune, sir! ye lie...[*to
Malvolio*] Art any more than a steward? Dost thou 120
think because thou art virtuous, there shall be no more
cakes and ale?

Clown. Yes, by Saint Anne, and ginger shall be hot
i'th' mouth too.

Sir Toby. Th'art i'th' right....Go, sir, rub your chain
with crumbs....A stoup of wine, Maria!
                                        [*she fills their vessels*
Malvolio. Mistress Mary, if you prized my lady's
favour at any thing more than contempt, you would not
give means for this uncivil rule; she shall know of it, by
this hand.   [*he departs* 130
Maria. Go shake your ears.

Sir Andrew. 'Twere as good a deed as to drink when
a man's a-hungry, to challenge him the field, and

then to break promise with him and make a fool of
him.

Sir Toby. Do't, knight. I'll write thee a challenge; or
I'll deliver thy indignation to him by word of mouth.

Maria. Sweet Sir Toby, be patient for to-night: since
the youth of the count's was to-day with my lady, she is
140 much out of quiet. For Monsieur Malvolio, let me
alone with him: if I do not gull him into a nayword, and
make him a common recreation, do not think I have wit
enough to lie straight in my bed: I know I can do it.

Sir Toby. Possess us, possess us, tell us something of
him.

Maria. Marry, sir, sometimes he is a kind of puritan.

Sir Andrew. O, if I thought that, I'd beat him like a
dog.

Sir Toby. What, for being a puritan? thy exquisite
150 reason, dear knight?

Sir Andrew. I have no exquisite reason for't, but I have
reason good enough.

Maria. The devil a puritan that he is, or any thing
constantly but a time-pleaser, an affectioned ass, that cons
state without book and utters it by great swarths: the
best persuaded of himself, so crammed, as he thinks, with
excellencies, that it is his ground of faith that all that look
on him love him; and on that vice in him will my revenge
find notable cause to work.

160 *Sir Toby.* What wilt thou do?

Maria. I will drop in his way some obscure epistles of
love, wherein by the colour of his beard, the shape of
his leg, the manner of his gait, the expressure of his eye,
forehead, and complexion, he shall find himself most
feelingly personated. I can write very like my lady your
niece, on a forgotten matter we can hardly make dis-
tinction of our hands.

Sir Toby. Excellent! I smell a device.

Sir Andrew. I have't in my nose too.

Sir Toby. He shall think by the letters that thou wilt 170 drop that they come from my niece, and that she's in love with him.

Maria. My purpose is, indeed, a horse of that colour.

Sir Andrew. And your horse now would make him an ass.

Maria. Ass, I doubt not.

Sir Andrew. O, 'twill be admirable.

Maria. Sport royal, I warrant you: I know my physic will work with him. I will plant you two, and let the fool make a third, where he shall find the letter: observe 180 his construction of it...For this night, to bed, and dream on the event...Farewell.   [*she goes out*

Sir Toby. Good night, Penthesilea.

Sir Andrew. Before me, she's a good wench.

Sir Toby. She's a beagle, true-bred, and one that adores me...what o' that?   [*he sighs*

Sir Andrew. I was adored once too.   [*he sighs also*

Sir Toby. Let's to bed, knight....Thou hadst need send for more money.

Sir Andrew. If I cannot recover your niece, I am a 190 foul way out.

Sir Toby. Send for money knight, if thou hast her not i'th'end, call me cut.

Sir Andrew. If I do not, never trust me, take it how you will.

Sir Toby. Come, come, I'll go burn some sack, 'tis too late to go to bed now: come knight; come knight.

[*they go*

[2. 4.]   *A room in the Duke's palace*

'*Enter* DUKE, VIOLA, CURIO *and others*'

Duke [*to Viola*]. Give me some music...Now—
    [*musicians enter*] good morrow, friends....
Now, good Cesario, but that piece of song,
That old and antic song we heard last night:
Methought it did relieve my passion much,
More than light airs and recollected terms
Of these most brisk and giddy-pacéd times.
Come, but one verse.
    Curio. He is not here, so please your lordship, that
should sing it.
10 *Duke.* Who was it?
    Curio. Feste, the jester, my lord, a fool that the Lady
Olivia's father took much delight in. He is about the
house.
    Duke. Seek him out, and play the tune the while.
                    [*Curio goes; music plays*
Come hither, boy—if ever thou shalt love,
In the sweet pangs of it remember me:
For, such as I am all true lovers are,
Unstaid and skittish in all motions else,
Save in the constant image of the creature
20 That is beloved....How dost thou like this tune?
    Viola. It gives a very echo to the seat
Where Love is throned.
    Duke.   Thou dost speak masterly.
My life upon't, young though thou art, thine eye
Hath stayed upon some favour that it loves:
Hath it not, boy?
    Viola.   A little, by your favour.
    Duke. What kind of woman is't?
    Viola.   Of your complexion.

Duke. She is not worth thee then. What years,
    i'faith?
Viola. About your years, my lord.
Duke. Too old, by heaven: let still the woman take
An elder than herself; so wears she to him,   30
So sways she level in her husband's heart:
For, boy, however we do praise ourselves,
Our fancies are more giddy and unfirm,
More longing, wavering, sooner lost and won,
Than women's are.
Viola.   I think it well, my lord.
Duke. Then let thy love be younger than thyself,
Or thy affection cannot hold the bent:
For women are as roses, whose fair flower
Being once displayed doth fall that very hour.
Viola. And so they are: alas, that they are so;   40
To die, even when they to perfection grow!

Curio re-enters with Clown

Duke. O fellow, come, the song we had last night...
Mark it, Cesario, it is old and plain:
The spinsters and the knitters in the sun,
And the free maids that weave their thread with bones
Do use to chant it; it is silly sooth,
And dallies with the innocence of love,
Like the old age.
Clown. Are you ready, sir?
Duke. Ay, prithee, sing.   [*music* 50
Clown [*sings*].
        Come away, come away death,
          And in sad cypress let me be laid:
            Fly away, fly away breath,
          I am slain by a fair cruel maid:

My shroud of white, stuck all with yew,
　　O, prepare it!
My part of death no one so true
　　Did share it.

Not a flower, not a flower sweet
60　On my black coffin let there be strown:
　　Not a friend, not a friend greet
My poor corpse, where my bones shall be thrown:
A thousand thousand sighs to save,
　　Lay me O where
Sad true lover never find my grave,
　　To weep there.

Duke [*gives money*]. There's for thy pains.

Clown. No pains, sir, I take pleasure in singing, sir.

Duke. I'll pay thy pleasure then.

70　*Clown.* Truly, sir, and pleasure will be paid, one time or another.

Duke. Give me now leave to leave thee.

Clown. Now, the melancholy god protect thee, and the tailor make thy doublet of changeable taffeta, for thy mind is a very opal. I would have men of such constancy put to sea, that their business might be every thing and their intent every where, for that's it that always makes a good voyage of nothing....Farewell. [*he goes*

Duke. Let all the rest give place...
　　　　　　　　　　　　[*Curio and attendants depart*
　　　　　　　　　　　　Once more, Cesario,
80 Get thee to yon same sovereign cruelty:
Tell her, my love, more noble than the world,
Prizes not quantity of dirty lands;
The parts that fortune hath bestowed upon her,
Tell her, I hold as giddily as fortune;
But 'tis that miracle and queen of gems
That nature pranks her in attracts my soul.

Viola. But if she cannot love you, sir?

Duke. I cannot be so answered.

Viola.　　　　　　　　　　　Sooth, but you must.
Say that some lady, as perhaps there is,
Hath for your love as great a pang of heart　　　90
As you have for Olivia: you cannot love her;
You tell her so; must she not then be answered?

Duke. There is no woman's sides
Can bide the beating of so strong a passion
As love doth give my heart: no woman's heart
So big, to hold so much, they lack retention.
Alas, their love may be called appetite—
No motion of the liver, but the palate—
That suffers surfeit, cloyment and revolt;
But mine is all as hungry as the sea,　　　100
And can digest as much. Make no compare
Between that love a woman can bear me
And that I owe Olivia.

Viola.　　　　　　　　Ay, but I know—

Duke. What dost thou know?

Viola. Too well what love women to men may owe:
In faith they are as true of heart as we.
My father had a daughter loved a man,
As it might be, perhaps, were I a woman,
I should your lordship.

Duke.　　　　　　　And what's her history?

Viola. A blank, my lord: she never told her love,　　　110
But let concealment like a worm i'th' bud
Feed on her damask cheek: she pined in thought,
And with a green and yellow melancholy
She sat like Patience on a monument,
Smiling at grief. Was not this love, indeed?
We men may say more, swear more—but indeed
Our shows are more than will; for still we prove

Much in our vows, but little in our love.

Duke. But died thy sister of her love, my boy?

120 *Viola.* I am all the daughters of my father's house,
And all the brothers too...and yet I know not....

                                      [*they muse*

Sir, shall I to this lady?

Duke [*starts and rouses*]. Ay, that's the theme.
To her in haste; give her this jewel; say,
My love can give no place, bide no denay.   [*they go*

[2. 5.] *A walled garden adjoining the house of Olivia;
two doors, one leading out of the garden, the other opening
into the house whence there runs a broad walk with
great box-trees on either side and a stone seat next the
wall*

    *The house-door opens and Sir TOBY BELCH comes
        out with Sir ANDREW AGUECHEEK*

Sir Toby [*turns and calls*]. Come thy ways, Signior
Fabian.

Fabian [*follows through the door*]. Nay, I'll come: if
I lose a scruple of this sport, let me be boiled to death
with melancholy.

Sir Toby. Wouldst thou not be glad to have the nig-
gardly rascally sheep-biter come by some notable shame?

Fabian. I would exult, man: you know, he brought
me out o' favour with my lady about a bear-baiting here.

10 *Sir Toby.* To anger him, we'll have the bear again,
and we will fool him black and blue—shall we not, Sir
Andrew?

Sir Andrew. An we do not, it is pity of our lives.

    MARIA appears, hurrying down the walk

Sir Toby. Here comes the little villain...How now,
my metal of India?

Maria. Get ye all three into the box-tree: Malvolio's coming down this walk, he has been yonder i'the sun practising behaviour to his own shadow this half hour: observe him, for the love of mockery; for I know this letter will make a contemplative idiot of him. Close, in 20 the name of jesting! [*the men hide in a box-tree*] Lie thou there [*throws down a letter*]...for here comes the trout that must be caught with tickling.

[*she goes within*

MALVOLIO, *in plumed hat, comes slowly along the path, musing*

Malvolio. 'Tis but fortune, all is fortune....Maria once told me she did affect me, and I have heard herself come thus near, that should she fancy it should be one of my complexion....Besides, she uses me with a more exalted respect than any one else that follows her....What should I think on't?

(*Sir Toby.* Here's an overweening rogue!   30

(*Fabian.* O, peace! Contemplation makes a rare turkey-cock of him. How he jets under his advanced plumes!

(*Sir Andrew.* 'Slight, I could so beat the rogue!

(*Fabian.* Peace, I say.

Malvolio. To be Count Malvolio!

(*Sir Toby.* Ah, rogue!

(*Sir Andrew.* Pistol him, pistol him.

(*Fabian.* Peace, peace!

Malvolio. There is example for't; the lady of the Strachy married the yeoman of the wardrobe.   40

(*Sir Andrew.* Fie on him, Jezebel!

(*Fabian.* O, peace! now he's deeply in: look, how imagination blows him.

Malvolio. Having been three months married to her, sitting in my state—

(*Sir Toby.* O, for a stone-bow, to hit him in the eye!

Malvolio. Calling my officers about me, in my branched velvet gown; having come from a day-bed, where I have left Olivia sleeping—

50 (*Sir Toby.* Fire and brimstone!

(*Fabian.* O, peace, peace!

Malvolio. And then to have the humour of state: and after a demure travel of regard, telling them I know my place as I would they should do theirs, to ask for my kinsman Toby—

(*Sir Toby.* Bolts and shackles!

(*Fabian.* O, peace, peace, peace! now, now.

Malvolio. Seven of my people, with an obedient start, make out for him: I frown the while, and perchance wind 60 up my watch, or play with my [*touches his steward's chain an instant*]—some rich jewel...Toby approaches; curtsies there to me—

(*Sir Toby.* Shall this fellow live?

(*Fabian.* Though our silence be drawn from us with cars, yet peace.

Malvolio. I extend my hand to him thus; quenching my familiar smile with an austere regard of control—

(*Sir Toby.* And does not 'Toby' take you a blow o'the lips then?

70 *Malvolio.* Saying, 'Cousin Toby, my fortunes having cast me on your niece give me this prerogative of speech'—

Sir Toby. What, what?

Malvolio. 'You must amend your drunkenness.'

(*Sir Toby.* Out, scab! [*Malvolio turns as at a sound*

(*Fabian.* Nay, patience, or we break the sinews of our plot.

Malvolio. 'Besides, you waste the treasure of your time with a foolish knight'—

(*Sir Andrew.* That's me, I warrant you.   80

Malvolio. 'One Sir Andrew'—   [*he sees the letter*

(*Sir Andrew.* I knew 'twas I, for many do call me fool.

Malvolio [*takes up the letter*]. What employment have we here?

(*Fabian.* Now is the woodcock near the gin.

(*Sir Toby.* O, peace! and the spirit of humours intimate reading aloud to him!

Malvolio. By my life, this is my lady's hand: these be her very *c*'s, her *u*'s, and her *t*'s, and thus makes 90 she her great *P*'s. It is, in contempt of question, her hand.

(*Sir Andrew.* Her *c*'s, her *u*'s, and her *t*'s: why that?

Malvolio [*reads the superscription*]. 'To the unknown beloved, this, and my good wishes'...her very phrases! By your leave, wax. Soft!—and the impressure her Lucrece, with which she uses to seal: 'tis my lady...To whom should this be?   [*he opens the letter*

(*Fabian.* This wins him, liver and all.

Malvolio [*reads*]. 'Jove knows I love: 100

But who?

Lips, do not move!

No man must know.'

'No man must know'....What follows? the numbers altered...[*he muses*] 'No man must know'—if this should be thee, Malvolio!

(*Sir Toby.* Marry, hang thee, brock!

Malvolio [*reads*].

'I may command where I adore:

But silence, like a Lucrece knife,

With bloodless stroke my heart doth gore: 110

M, O, A, I, doth sway my life.'

(*Fabian.* A fustian riddle!

(*Sir Toby.* Excellent wench, say I.

Malvolio. 'M, O, A, I, doth sway my life.'—Nay, but first, let me see, let me see, let me see.

(*Fabian.* What dish o' poison has she dressed him!

(*Sir Toby.* And with what wing the stallion checks at it!

Malvolio. 'I may command where I adore'...Why,
120 she may command me; I serve her, she is my lady....
Why, this is evident to any formal capacity. There is no obstruction in this. And the end: what should that alphabetical position portend? If I could make that resemble something in me! Softly! 'M, O, A, I,'—

(*Sir Toby.* O, ay, make up that—he is now at a cold scent.

(*Fabian.* Sowter will cry upon't for all this, though it be as rank as a fox.

Malvolio. 'M,'—Malvolio—'M,'—why, that begins
130 my name.

(*Fabian.* Did not I say he would work it out? the cur is excellent at faults.

Malvolio. 'M'—but then there is no consonancy in the sequel that suffers under probation: 'A' should follow, but 'O' does.

(*Fabian.* And O shall end, I hope.

(*Sir Toby.* Ay, or I'll cudgel him, and make him cry 'O!'

Malvolio. And then 'I' comes behind.

140 (*Fabian.* Ay, an you had any eye behind you, you might see more detraction at your heels, than fortunes before you.

Malvolio. 'M, O, A, I.'...This simulation is not as the former: and yet, to crush this a little, it would bow to me, for every one of these letters are in my name. Soft! here follows prose....

[*reads*] 'If this fall into thy hand, revolve. In my stars I am above thee, but be not afraid of greatness: some are born great, some achieve greatness, and some have greatness thrust upon 'em. Thy Fates open their hands, let thy 150 blood and spirit embrace them; and to inure thyself to what thou art like to be, cast thy humble slough, and appear fresh. Be opposite with a kinsman, surly with servants; let thy tongue tang arguments of state; put thyself into the trick of singularity. She thus advises thee that sighs for thee. Remember who commended thy yellow stockings, and wished to see thee ever cross-gartered: I say, remember. Go to, thou art made, if thou desir'st to be so; if not, let me see thee a steward still, the fellow of servants, and not worthy to touch Fortune's 160 fingers. Farewell. She, that would alter services with thee,

THE FORTUNATE-UNHAPPY.'

Daylight and champian discovers not more: this is open. I will be proud, I will read politic authors, I will baffle Sir Toby, I will wash off gross acquaintance, I will be point-devise the very man. I do not now fool myself, to let imagination jade me; for every reason excites to this, that my lady loves me. She did commend my yellow stockings of late, she did praise my leg being cross- 170 gartered, and in this she manifests herself to my love, and with a kind of injunction drives me to these habits of her liking. I thank my stars, I am happy...I will be strange, stout, in yellow stockings, and cross-gartered, even with the swiftness of putting on. Jove, and my stars be praised! Here is yet a postscript.

[*reads*] 'Thou canst not choose but know who I am. If thou entertain'st my love, let it appear in thy smiling, thy smiles become thee well. Therefore in my presence still smile, dear, O my sweet, I prithee.'
180

Jove, I thank thee! [*he lifts his hands towards heaven*]
I will smile, I will do everything that thou wilt have me.
                                        [*he goes within*

Fabian. I will not give my part of this sport for a
pension of thousands to be paid from the Sophy.

Sir Toby. I could marry this wench for this device—

Sir Andrew. So could I too.

Sir Toby. And ask no other dowry with her but such
another jest.

Sir Andrew. Nor I neither.

MARIA *comes from the house*

190 *Fabian.* Here comes my noble gull-catcher.

Sir Toby. Wilt thou set thy foot o' my neck?

Sir Andrew. Or o' mine either?

Sir Toby. Shall I play my freedom at trey-trip, and
become thy bond-slave?

Sir Andrew. I'faith or I either?

Sir Toby. Why, thou hast put him in such a dream,
that when the image of it leaves him he must run mad.

Maria. Nay, but say true, does it work upon him?

Sir Toby. Like aqua-vitæ with a midwife.

200 *Maria.* If you will then see the fruits of the sport, mark
his first approach before my lady: he will come to her in
yellow stockings, and 'tis a colour she abhors, and cross-
gartered, a fashion she detests; and he will smile upon
her, which will now be so unsuitable to her disposition,
being addicted to a melancholy as she is, that it cannot
but turn him into a notable contempt: if you will see it,
follow me.

Sir Toby. To the gates of Tartar, thou most excellent
devil of wit!

210 *Sir Andrew.* I'll make one too.   [*they enter the house*

[3. 1.] *The CLOWN enters the garden with his pipe and tabor; he plays. VIOLA comes in through the outer door as he finishes*

Viola. Save thee, friend, and thy music: dost thou live by thy tabor?

Clown. No, sir, I live by the church.

Viola. Art thou a churchman?

Clown. No such matter, sir, I do live by the church: for I do live at my house, and my house doth stand by the church.

Viola. So thou mayst say the king lies by a beggar, if a beggar dwell near him: or the church stands by thy tabor, if thy tabor stand by the church.   10

Clown. You have said, sir...To see this age! A sentence is but a cheveril glove to a good wit—how quickly the wrong side may be turned outward!

Viola. Nay, that's certain; they that dally nicely with words may quickly make them wanton.

Clown. I would therefore my sister had had no name, sir.

Viola. Why, man?

Clown. Why, sir, her name's a word, and to dally with that word might make my sister want-one...But indeed 20 words are very rascals since bonds disgraced them.

Viola. Thy reason, man?

Clown. Troth, sir, I can yield you none without words, and words are grown so false I am loath to prove reason with them.

Viola. I warrant thou art a merry fellow and car'st for nothing.

Clown. Not so, sir, I do care for something: but in my conscience, sir, I do not care for you: if that be to care for nothing, sir, I would it would make you invisible.   30

Viola. Art not thou the Lady Olivia's fool?

Clown. No indeed sir, the Lady Olivia has no folly. She will keep no fool, sir, till she be married, and fools are as like husbands as pilchards are to herrings—the husband's the bigger. I am, indeed, not her fool, but her corrupter of words.

Viola. I saw thee late at the Count Orsino's.

Clown. Foolery, sir, does walk about the orb like the sun, it shines every where. I would be sorry, sir, but the
40 fool should be as oft with your master as with my mistress: I think I saw your wisdom there.

Viola. Nay, an thou pass upon me, I'll no more with thee. Hold, there's expenses for thee.

[*she gives him a coin*

Clown [*gazes at the coin in his palm*]. Now Jove, in his next commodity of hair, send thee a beard!

Viola. By my troth I'll tell thee, I am almost sick for one—[*aside*] though I would not have it grow on my chin. Is thy lady within?

Clown [*still gazes at the coin*]. Would not a pair of
50 these have bred, sir?

Viola. Yes, being kept together and put to use.

Clown. I would play Lord Pandarus of Phrygia, sir, to bring a Cressida to this Troilus.

Viola. I understand you, sir, 'tis well begged.

[*she gives another coin*

Clown. The matter, I hope, is not great, sir; begging but a beggar: Cressida was a beggar. My lady is within, sir. I will conster to them whence you come, who you are and what you would are out of my welkin—I might say 'element,' but the word is over-worn. [*he goes within*
60 *Viola.* This fellow is wise enough to play the fool,
And to do that well craves a kind of wit:
He must observe their mood on whom he jests,

The quality of persons, and the time;
And, like the haggard, check at every feather
That comes before his eye. This is a practice,
As full of labour as a wise man's art:
For folly that he wisely shows is fit;
But wise men, folly-fall'n, quite taint their wit.

Sir TOBY BELCH and Sir ANDREW AGUECHEEK
come forth

Sir Toby. Save you, gentleman.
Viola. And you, sir.
Sir Andrew [*bows*]. Dieu vous garde, monsieur.   70
Viola [*bows*]. Et vous aussi; votre serviteur.
Sir Andrew. I hope, sir, you are—and I am yours.
Sir Toby. Will you encounter the house? my niece is
desirous you should enter, if your trade be to her.
Viola. I am bound to your niece, sir. I mean, she is
the list of my voyage.
Sir Toby. Taste your legs, sir, put them to motion.
Viola. My legs do better under-stand me, sir, than I
understand what you mean by bidding me taste my legs. 80
Sir Toby. I mean, to go, sir, to enter.
Viola. I will answer you with gate and entrance—but
we are prevented.

OLIVIA comes from the house with MARIA

Most excellent accomplished lady, the heavens rain
odours on you!
Sir Andrew. That youth's a rare courtier—'Rain
odours'—well!
Viola. My matter hath no voice, lady, but to your own
most pregnant and vouchsafed ear.
Sir Andrew. 'Odours,' 'pregnant,' and 'vouchsafed': 90
I'll get 'em all three all ready.

Olivia. Let the garden door be shut, and leave me to my hearing....

[*Sir Toby, Sir Andrew and Maria depart*

Give me your hand, sir.

Viola [*bows low*]. My duty, madam, and most humble service.

Olivia. What is your name?

Viola. Cesario is your servant's name, fair princess.

Olivia. My servant, sir! 'Twas never merry world,

100 Since lowly feigning was called compliment:
Y'are servant to the Count Orsino, youth.

Viola. And he is yours, and his must needs be yours;
Your servant's servant is your servant, madam.

Olivia. For him, I think not on him: for his thoughts,
Would they were blanks, rather than filled with me!

Viola. Madam, I come to whet your gentle thoughts
On his behalf.

Olivia. O, by your leave, I pray you;
I bade you never speak again of him:
But, would you undertake another suit,

110 I had rather hear you to solicit that
Than music from the spheres.

Viola. Dear lady,—

Olivia. Give me leave, beseech you: I did send,
After the last enchantment you did here,
A ring in chase of you; so did I abuse
Myself, my servant and, I fear me, you:
Under your hard construction must I sit,
To force that on you in a shameful cunning
Which you knew none of yours: what might you think?
Have you not set mine honour at the stake,

120 And baited it with all th'unmuzzled thoughts
That tyrannous heart can think?
To one of your receiving enough is shown,

A cypress, not a bosom, hides my heart:
So let me hear you speak.

Viola.   I pity you.

Olivia. That's a degree to love.

Viola.   No, not a grise;
For 'tis a vulgar proof,
That very oft we pity enemies.

Olivia. Why then methinks 'tis time to smile again:
O world, how apt the poor are to be proud!
If one should be a prey, how much the better   130
To fall before the lion than the wolf?   ['*clock strikes*'
The clock upbraids me with the waste of time...
Be not afraid, good youth, I will not have you:
And yet, when wit and youth is come to harvest,
Your wife is like to reap a proper man:
There lies your way, due west.

Viola.   Then westward-ho!
Grace and good disposition attend your ladyship!
You'll nothing, madam, to my lord by me?

Olivia. Stay:
I prithee, tell me what thou think'st of me.   140

Viola. That you do think you are not what you are.

Olivia. If I think so, I think the same of you.

Viola. Then think you right; I am not what I am.

Olivia. I would you were as I would have you be!

Viola. Would it be better, madam, than I am,
I wish it might, for now I am your fool.

Olivia. O, what a deal of scorn looks beautiful
In the contempt and anger of his lip!
A murd'rous guilt shows not itself more soon
Than love that would seem hid: love's night is noon.   150
Cesario, by the roses of the spring,
By maidhood, honour, truth, and every thing,
I love thee so, that, maugre all thy pride,

Nor wit nor reason can my passion hide.
Do not extort thy reasons from this clause,
For that I woo, thou therefore hast no cause:
But rather reason thus with reason fetter,
Love sought is good...but given unsought is better.

Viola. By innocence I swear, and by my youth,
160 I have one heart, one bosom, and one truth,
And that no woman has, nor never none
Shall mistress be of it, save I alone.
And so adieu, good madam! never more
Will I my master's tears to you deplore.

Olivia. Yet come again: for thou perhaps mayst move
That heart, which now abhors, to like his love.

                                           [they go

[3. 2.]   *A room in Olivia's house*

     Sir TOBY BELCH, Sir ANDREW AGUECHEEK,
                   and FABIAN

Sir Andrew. No, faith, I'll not stay a jot longer.

Sir Toby. Thy reason, dear venom, give thy reason.

Fabian. You must needs yield your reason, Sir Andrew.

Sir Andrew. Marry, I saw your niece do more favours to the count's serving-man than ever she bestowed upon me; I saw't i'th'orchard.

Sir Toby. Did she see thee the while, old boy? tell me that.

10 *Sir Andrew.* As plain as I see you now.

Fabian. This was a great argument of love in her toward you.

Sir Andrew. 'Slight! will you make an ass o' me?

Fabian. I will prove it legitimate, sir, upon the oaths of judgement and reason.

Sir Toby. And they have been grand-jurymen since before Noah was a sailor.

Fabian. She did show favour to the youth in your sight, only to exasperate you, to awake your dormouse valour, to put fire in your heart, and brimstone in your liver: you should then have accosted her, and with some excellent jests, fire-new from the mint, you should have banged the youth into dumbness: this was looked for at your hand, and this was balked: the double gilt of this opportunity you let time wash off, and you are now sailed into the north of my lady's opinion, where you will hang like an icicle on a Dutchman's beard, unless you do redeem it by some laudable attempt, either of valour or policy.

Sir Andrew. An't be any way, it must be with valour, for policy I hate: I had as lief be a Brownist, as a politician.

Sir Toby. Why then, build me thy fortunes upon the basis of valour. Challenge me the count's youth to fight with him, hurt him in eleven places—my niece shall take note of it, and assure thyself there is no love-broker in the world can more prevail in man's commendation with woman than report of valour.

Fabian. There is no way but this, Sir Andrew.

Sir Andrew. Will either of you bear me a challenge to him?

Sir Toby. Go, write it in a martial hand, be curst and brief; it is no matter how witty, so it be eloquent and full of invention: taunt him with the license of ink: if thou 'thou'st' him some thrice, it shall not be amiss; and as many lies as will lie in thy sheet of paper, although the sheet were big enough for the bed of Ware in England, set 'em down—go, about it. Let there be gall enough in thy ink, though thou write with a goose-pen, no matter: about it.

QTN   4

50 *Sir Andrew.* Where shall I find you?

Sir Toby. We'll call thee at thy †cubicle: go.

[*Sir Andrew goes*

Fabian. This is a dear manakin to you, Sir Toby.

Sir Toby. I have been dear to him, lad—some two thousand strong, or so.

Fabian. We shall have a rare letter from him...but you'll not deliver't?

Sir Toby. Never trust me then; and by all means stir on the youth to an answer. I think oxen and wainropes cannot hale them together. For Andrew, if he were 60 opened and you find so much blood in his liver as will clog the foot of a flea, I'll eat the rest of th'anatomy.

Fabian. And his opposite, the youth, bears in his visage no great presage of cruelty.

MARIA comes tripping in, holding
her sides for laughter

Sir Toby. Look, where the youngest wren of nine comes.

Maria. If you desire the spleen, and will laugh yourselves into stitches, follow me...Yon gull Malvolio is turned heathen, a very renegado; for there is no Christian, that means to be saved by believing rightly, 70 can ever believe such impossible passages of grossness....
[*overcome with laughter*] He's in yellow stockings!

Sir Toby [*shouts*]. And cross-gartered?

Maria. Most villainously; like a pedant that keeps a school i'th' church...I have dogged him like his murderer. He does obey every point of the letter that I dropped to betray him: he does smile his face into more lines than is in the new map, with the augmentation of the Indies: you have not seen such a thing as 'tis...I can hardly forbear hurling things at him, I know my lady

will strike him: if she do, he'll smile and take't for a great 80
favour.

Sir Toby. Come, bring us, bring us where he is.

[*they rush forth*

[3. 3.]   *A street*

ANTONIO *and* SEBASTIAN *approach*

Sebastian. I would not by my will have troubled you,
But since you make your pleasure of your pains,
I will no further chide you.

Antonio. I could not stay behind you: my desire,
More sharp than filéd steel, did spur me forth;
And not all love to see you, though so much
As might have drawn one to a longer voyage,
But jealousy what might befall your travel,
Being skilless in these parts; which to a stranger,
Unguided and unfriended, often prove   10
Rough and unhospitable: my willing love,
The rather by these arguments of fear,
Set forth in your pursuit.

Sebastian.   My kind Antonio,
I can no other answer make but thanks,
†And thanks, and ever thanks; and oft good turns
Are shuffled off with such uncurrent pay:
But, were my worth as is my conscience firm,
You should find better dealing...What's to do?
Shall we go see the relics of this town?

Antonio. To-morrow sir—best first go see your lodging. 20

Sebastian. I am not weary, and 'tis long to night:
I pray you, let us satisfy our eyes
With the memorials and the things of fame
That do renown this city.

Antonio.   Would you'ld pardon me;
I do not without danger walk these streets.

Once in a sea-fight 'gainst the count his galleys
I did some service, of such note indeed
That were I ta'en here it would scarce be answered.
   Sebastian. Belike you slew great number of his people.
30 *Antonio.* Th'offence is not of such a bloody nature,
Albeit the quality of the time and quarrel
Might well have given us bloody argument:
It might have since been answered in repaying
What we took from them, which for traffic's sake
Most of our city did: only myself stood out,
For which, if I be lapséd in this place,
I shall pay dear.
   Sebastian.   Do not then walk too open.
   Antonio. It doth not fit me...Hold, sir, here's my
          purse.   [*he gives it*
In the south suburbs, at the Elephant,
40 Is best to lodge: I will bespeak our diet,
Whiles you beguile the time and feed your knowledge
With viewing of the town; there shall you have me.
   Sebastian. Why I your purse?
   Antonio. Haply your eye shall light upon some toy
You have desire to purchase; and your store,
I think, is not for idle markets, sir.
   Sebastian. I'll be your purse-bearer, and leave you for
an hour.
   Antonio. To th'Elephant.
50 *Sebastian.* I do remember.
                      [*they go off in different directions*

[3. 4.]   *Olivia's garden*

OLIVIA enters musing, followed by MARIA;
Olivia sits

Olivia. I have sent after him, he says he'll come;
How shall I feast him? what bestow of him?
For youth is bought more oft than begged or borrowed.
I speak too loud...
[*to Maria*] Where's Malvolio? he is sad and civil,
And suits well for a servant with my fortunes—
Where is Malvolio?

Maria. He's coming, madam; but in very strange
manner. He is, sure, possessed, madam.

Olivia. Why, what's the matter? does he rave?   10

Maria. No, madam, he does nothing but smile: your
ladyship were best to have some guard about you, if he
come, for sure the man is tainted in's wits.

Olivia. Go, call him hither....

MALVOLIO, in yellow stockings and with awkward
gait, is seen coming down the walk

                                I am as mad as he,
If sad and merry madness equal be.
How now, Malvolio?

Malvolio. Sweet lady, ho, ho.

Olivia. Smil'st thou?
I sent for thee upon a sad occasion.

Malvolio. Sad, lady? I could be sad: this does make   20
some obstruction in the blood, this cross-gartering—but
what of that? if it please the eye of one, it is with me as
the very true sonnet is: 'Please one and please all.'

Olivia. Why, how dost thou, man? what is the matter
with thee?

Malvolio. Not black in my mind, though yellow in my legs...It did come to his hands, and commands shall be executed. I think we do know the sweet Roman hand.

30   *Olivia.* Wilt thou go to bed, Malvolio?

Malvolio. To bed! ay, sweet-heart, and I'll come to thee.

Olivia. God comfort thee! Why dost thou smile so, and kiss thy hand so oft?

Maria. How do you, Malvolio?

Malvolio [*disdainful*]. At your request! yes, nightingales answer daws.

Maria. Why appear you with this ridiculous boldness before my lady?

40   *Malvolio* [*to Olivia*]. 'Be not afraid of greatness': 'twas well writ.

Olivia. What mean'st thou by that, Malvolio?

Malvolio. 'Some are born great,'—

Olivia. Ha?

Malvolio. 'Some achieve greatness,'—

Olivia. What say'st thou?

Malvolio. 'And some have greatness thrust upon them.'

Olivia. Heaven restore thee!

50   *Malvolio.* 'Remember, who commended thy yellow stockings'—

Olivia. Thy yellow stockings!

Malvolio. 'And wished to see thee cross-gartered.'

Olivia. Cross-gartered?

Malvolio. 'Go to, thou art made, if thou desir'st to be so'—

Olivia. Am I made?

Malvolio. 'If not, let me see thee a servant still.'

Olivia. Why, this is very midsummer madness.

A servant comes from the house

Servant. Madam, the young gentleman of the Count 60
Orsino's is returned—I could hardly entreat him back:
he attends your ladyship's pleasure.

Olivia. I'll come to him. [*the servant goes*]   Good
Maria, let this fellow be looked to. Where's my cousin
Toby? let some of my people have a special care of
him, I would not have him miscarry for the half of my
dowry.   [*she enters the house followed by Maria*

Malvolio. O, ho! do you come near me now? no worse
man than Sir Toby to look to me! This concurs directly
with the letter—she sends him on purpose, that I may 70
appear stubborn to him; for she incites me to that in the
letter. 'Cast thy humble slough,' says she; 'be opposite
with a kinsman, surly with servants, let thy tongue tang
with arguments of state, put thyself into the trick of
singularity'; and consequently sets down the manner
how; as, a sad face, a reverend carriage, a slow tongue,
in the habit of some sir of note, and so forth. I have
limed her, but it is Jove's doing, and Jove make me
thankful! And when she went away now, 'Let this
fellow be looked to': fellow! not Malvolio, nor after 80
my degree, but 'fellow.' Why, every thing adheres
together, that no dram of a scruple, no scruple
of a scruple, no obstacle, no incredulous or unsafe
circumstance—what can be said?—nothing that can be,
can come between me and the full prospect of my hopes.
Well, Jove, not I, is the doer of this, and he is to be
thanked.

Maria returns with Sir Toby Belch *and* Fabian

Sir Toby. Which way is he, in the name of sanctity?
If all the devils of hell be drawn in little, and Legion
himself possessed him, yet I'll speak to him.   90

Fabian. Here he is, here he is…How is't with you, sir?

†*Sir Toby.* How is't with you, man?

Malvolio. Go off, I discard you; let me enjoy my private: go off.

Maria. Lo, how hollow the fiend speaks within him! did not I tell you? Sir Toby, my lady prays you to have a care of him.

Malvolio. Ah, ha! does she so!

Sir Toby. Go to, go to: peace, peace, we must deal
100 gently with him: let me alone. How do you, Malvolio? how is't with you? What, man! defy the devil: consider, he's an enemy to mankind.

Malvolio. Do you know what you say?

Maria. La you! an you speak ill of the devil, how he takes it at heart! Pray God, he be not bewitched!

Fabian. Carry his water to th'wise woman.

Maria. Marry, and it shall be done to-morrow morning, if I live. My lady would not lose him for more than I'll say.

110 *Malvolio.* How now, mistress!

Maria [*chokes*]. O Lord!

Sir Toby. Prithee, hold thy peace, this is not the way: do you not see you move him? let me alone with him.

Fabian. No way but gentleness, gently, gently: the fiend is rough, and will not be roughly used.

Sir Toby. Why, how now, my bawcock! how dost thou, chuck?

Malvolio. Sir!

Sir Toby. Ay, Biddy, come with me. What, man! 'tis
120 not for gravity to play at cherry-pit with Satan. Hang him, foul collier!

Maria. Get him to say his prayers, good Sir Toby, get him to pray.

Malvolio. My prayers, minx!

Maria. No, I warrant you, he will not hear of godliness.

Malvolio. Go, hang yourselves all! you are idle shallow things—I am not of your element—you shall know more hereafter.

> [*he goes; they gaze after him in amazement*

Sir Toby. Is't possible?   130

Fabian. If this were played upon a stage now, I could condemn it as an improbable fiction.

Sir Toby. His very genius hath taken the infection of the device, man.

Maria. Nay, pursue him now, lest the device take air and taint.

Fabian. Why, we shall make him mad indeed.

Maria. The house will be the quieter.

Sir Toby. Come, we'll have him in a dark room and bound. My niece is already in the belief that he's mad; 140 we may carry it thus, for our pleasure and his penance, till our very pastime, tired out of breath, prompt us to have mercy on him: at which time we will bring the device to the bar and crown thee for a finder of madmen...But see, but see.

> *Sir ANDREW AGUECHEEK comes forth,
> a letter in his hand*

Fabian. More matter for a May morning!

Sir Andrew. Here's the challenge, read it: I warrant there's vinegar and pepper in't.

Fabian. Is't so saucy?

Sir Andrew. Ay, is't! I warrant him: do but read.   150

Sir Toby. Give me. [*he reads*] 'Youth, whatsoever thou art, thou art but a scurvy fellow.'

Fabian. Good, and valiant.

Sir Toby. 'Wonder not, nor admire not in thy mind,

why I do call thee so, for I will show thee no reason
for't.'

Fabian. A good note, that keeps you from the blow
of the law.

Sir Toby. 'Thou com'st to the Lady Olivia, and in my
160 sight she uses thee kindly: but thou liest in thy throat,
that is not the matter I challenge thee for.'

Fabian. Very brief, and to exceeding good sense—
[*aside*] less.

Sir Toby. 'I will waylay thee going home, where if it
be thy chance to kill me,'—

Fabian. Good.

Sir Toby. 'Thou kill'st me like a rogue and a villain.'

Fabian. Still you keep o'th' windy side of the law:
good.

170 *Sir Toby.* 'Fare thee well, and God have mercy upon
one of our souls! He may have mercy upon mine, but
my hope is better, and so look to thyself. Thy friend, as
thou usest him, and thy sworn enemy,

ANDREW AGUECHEEK.'

If this letter move him not, his legs cannot: I'll give't
him.

Maria. You may have very fit occasion for't: he is now
in some commerce with my lady, and will by and by
depart.

180 *Sir Toby.* Go, Sir Andrew; scout me for him at the
corner of the orchard like a bum-baily: so soon as ever
thou seest him, draw, and as thou draw'st, swear
horrible; for it comes to pass oft that a terrible oath, with
a swaggering accent sharply twanged off, gives manhood
more approbation than ever proof itself would have
earned him. Away!

Sir Andrew. Nay, let me alone for swearing.

[*he leaves the garden by the outer door*

Sir Toby. Now will not I deliver his letter: for the behaviour of the young gentleman gives him out to be of good capacity and breeding; his employment between 190 his lord and my niece confirms no less; therefore this letter, being so excellently ignorant, will breed no terror in the youth: he will find it comes from a clodpole. But, sir, I will deliver his challenge by word of mouth; set upon Aguecheek a notable report of valour; and drive the gentleman, as I know his youth will aptly receive it, into a most hideous opinion of his rage, skill, fury and impetuosity. This will so fright them both, that they will kill one another by the look, like cockatrices.

OLIVIA and VIOLA come from the house

Fabian. Here he comes with your niece—give them 200 way till he take leave, and presently after him.

Sir Toby. I will meditate the while upon some horrid message for a challenge.

[*Sir Toby, Fabian and Maria go off into the garden*

Olivia. I have said too much unto a heart of stone,
And laid mine honour too unchary out:
There's something in me that reproves my fault;
But such a headstrong potent fault it is,
That it but mocks reproof.

Viola. With the same 'haviour that your passion bears
Goes on my master's grief.   210

Olivia. Here, wear this jewel for me, 'tis my picture;
Refuse it not, it hath no tongue to vex you:
And I beseech you come again to-morrow.
What shall you ask of me, that I'll deny,
That honour saved may upon asking give?

Viola. Nothing but this—your true love for my master.

Olivia. How with mine honour may I give him that
Which I have given to you?

Viola.   I will acquit you.

Olivia. Well, come again to-morrow: fare thee well.
220 A fiend, like thee, might bear my soul to hell.

[*she goes within; Viola walks toward the outer gate*

Sir TOBY BELCH and FABIAN come up

Sir Toby. Gentleman, God save thee.

Viola [*turns*]. And you, sir.

Sir Toby. That defence thou hast, betake thee to't: of
what nature the wrongs are thou hast done him, I know
not; but thy intercepter, full of despite, bloody as the
hunter, attends thee at the orchard-end: dismount thy
tuck, be yare in thy preparation, for thy assailant is
quick, skilful and deadly.

Viola. You mistake, sir. I am sure no man hath any
230 quarrel to me; my remembrance is very free and clear
from any image of offence done to any man.

Sir Toby. You'll find it otherwise, I assure you: therefore, if you hold your life at any price, betake you to
your guard; for your opposite hath in him what youth,
strength, skill and wrath can furnish man withal.

Viola. I pray you, sir, what is he?

Sir Toby. He is knight, dubbed with unhatched rapier
and on carpet consideration, but he is a devil in private
brawl: souls and bodies hath he divorced three, and his
240 incensement at this moment is so implacable, that satis-
faction can be none but by pangs of death and sepulchre...
Hob, nob, is his word; give't or take't.

Viola. I will return again into the house and desire
some conduct of the lady. I am no fighter. I have heard
of some kind of men that put quarrels purposely on others,
to taste their valour: belike this is a man of that quirk.

Sir Toby. Sir, no; his indignation derives itself out of
a very competent injury, therefore get you on and give

him his desire. Back you shall not to the house, unless
you undertake that with me which with as much safety 250
you might answer him: therefore on, or strip your sword
stark naked; for meddle you must, that's certain, or forswear to wear iron about you.

Viola. This is as uncivil as strange. I beseech you, do
me this courteous office, as to know of the knight what
my offence to him is; it is something of my negligence,
nothing of my purpose.

Sir Toby. I will do so. Signior Fabian, [*he winks*] stay
you by this gentleman till my return.

> [*he departs by the outer door*

Viola. Pray you, sir, do you know of this matter?　260

Fabian. I know the knight is incensed against you,
even to a mortal arbitrement, but nothing of the
circumstance more.

Viola. I beseech you, what manner of man is he?

Fabian. Nothing of that wonderful promise, to read
him by his form, as you are like to find him in the proof
of his valour. He is indeed, sir, the most skilful, bloody
and fatal opposite that you could possibly have found in
any part of Illyria...[*he takes her by the arm*] Will you
walk towards him? I will make your peace with him 270
if I can.

Viola. I shall be much bound to you for't: I am one,
that had rather go with sir priest than sir knight: I care
not who knows so much of my mettle.

> [*they leave the garden*

*A quiet street at the back of Olivia's walled garden,
with a gate leading thereto; trees and shrubs*

Sir TOBY and Sir ANDREW

Sir Toby. Why, man, he's a very devil, I have not
seen such a firago...I had a pass with him, rapier,

scabbard and all, and he gives me the stuck in with such
a mortal motion that it is inevitable; and on the answer,
he pays you as surely as your feet hit the ground they
280 step on. They say he has been fencer to the Sophy.

Sir Andrew. Pox on't, I'll not meddle with him.

Sir Toby. Ay, but he will not now be pacified: Fabian
can scarce hold him yonder.

Sir Andrew. Plague on't, an I thought he had been
valiant and so cunning in fence, I'd have seen him
damned ere I'd have challenged him. Let him let the
matter slip, and I'll give him my horse, grey Capilet.

Sir Toby. I'll make the motion: stand here, make a good
show on't—this shall end without the perdition of souls.
290 [*aside*] Marry, I'll ride your horse as well as I ride you.

FABIAN and VIOLA come from the garden;
Sir Toby beckons Fabian aside

I have his horse to take up the quarrel; I have persuaded
him the youth's a devil.

(*Fabian.* He is as horribly conceited of him; and pants
and looks pale, as if a bear were at his heels.

Sir Toby [*to Viola*]. There's no remedy, sir, he will
fight with you for's oath sake: marry, he hath better be-
thought him of his quarrel, and he finds that now scarce
to be worth talking of: therefore draw for the supportance of his vow, he protests he will not hurt you.
300 (*Viola.* Pray God defend me! A little thing would
make me tell them how much I lack of a man.

Fabian. Give ground, if you see him furious.

Sir Toby. Come, Sir Andrew, there's no remedy, the
gentleman will for his honour's sake have one bout with
you: he cannot by the duello avoid it: but he has promised
me, as he is a gentleman and a soldier, he will not hurt
you. Come on, to't!

Sir Andrew. Pray God, he keep his oath!

Viola. I do assure you, 'tis against my will.

They make ready to fight; ANTONIO comes up

Antonio [to Sir Andrew]. Put up your sword: if this
    young gentleman   310
Have done offence, I take the fault on me;
If you offend him, I for him defy you.

Sir Toby. You, sir! why, what are you?

Antonio. One, sir, that for his love dares yet do more
Than you have heard him brag to you he will.

Sir Toby. Nay, if you be an undertaker, I am for you.
                                 [they draw

Two officers approach

Fabian. O good Sir Toby, hold; here come the
    officers.

Sir Toby [to Antonio]. I'll be with you anon.
        [he hides from the officers behind a tree

Viola [to Sir Andrew]. Pray, sir, put your sword up,
if you please.   320

Sir Andrew. Marry, will I, sir; and, for that I
promised you, I'll be as good as my word. [*he sheathes his
sword*] He will bear you easily, and reins well.

1 Officer. This is the man, do thy office.

2 Officer. Antonio, I arrest thee at the suit
Of Count Orsino.

Antonio.   You do mistake me, sir.

1 Officer. No, sir, no jot; I know your favour well:
Though now you have no sea-cap on your head...
Take him away, he knows I know him well.

Antonio. I must obey. [*to Viola*] This comes with
    seeking you;   330
But there's no remedy, I shall answer it...

What will you do, now my necessity
Makes me to ask you for my purse? it grieves me
Much more for what I cannot do for you
Than what befalls myself…You stand amazed,
But be of comfort.

    2 Officer. Come, sir, away.

    Antonio. I must entreat of you some of that money.

    Viola. What money, sir?

340 For the fair kindness you have showed me here,
And part being prompted by your present trouble,
Out of my lean and low ability
I'll lend you something…[*opens her purse*] My having
    is not much,
I'll make division of my present with you:
Hold, there's half my coffer.   [*she proffers coin*

    Antonio [*refuses it*].   Will you deny me now?
Is't possible that my deserts to you
Can lack persuasion? Do not tempt my misery,
Lest that it make me so unsound a man
As to upbraid you with those kindnesses
350 That I have done for you.

    Viola.   I know of none,
Nor know I you by voice or any feature:
I hate ingratitude more in a man,
Than lying vainness, babbling drunkenness,
Or any taint of vice whose strong corruption
Inhabits our frail blood.

    Antonio.   O heavens themselves!

    2 Officer. Come, sir, I pray you, go.

    Antonio.   Let me speak a little.
This youth that you see here
I snatched one half out of the jaws of death,
Relieved him with such sanctity of love,
360 And to his image, which methought did promise

Most venerable worth, did I devotion.

I Officer. What's that to us? The time goes by: away!

Antonio. But, O, how vile an idol proves this god!
Thou hast, Sebastian, done good feature shame.
In nature there's no blemish but the mind;
None can be called deformed but the unkind:
Virtue is beauty, but the beauteous evil
Are empty trunks o'erflourished by the devil.

I Officer. The man grows mad, away with him!
Come, come, sir.   370

Antonio. Lead me on.   [*they carry him off*
Viola. Methinks his words do from such passion fly,
That he believes himself—so do not I?
Prove true, imagination, O prove true,
That I, dear brother, be now ta'en for you!

Sir Toby [*peeps from behind the tree*]. Come hither,
knight—come hither, Fabian; we'll whisper o'er a
couplet or two of most sage saws.

Viola. He named Sebastian; I my brother know
Yet living in my glass; even such and so   380
In favour was my brother, and he went
Still in this fashion, colour, ornament,
For him I imitate: O, if it prove,
Tempests are kind and salt waves fresh in love!

[*she goes*

Sir Toby. A very dishonest paltry boy, and more a
coward than a hare. His dishonesty appears in leaving
his friend here in necessity and denying him; and for his
cowardship, ask Fabian.

Fabian. A coward, a most devout coward, religious
in it.   390

Sir Andrew. 'Slid, I'll after him again and beat him.

Sir Toby. Do, cuff him soundly, but never draw thy
sword.

Sir Andrew. An I do not,—
               [*he draws his sword and hurries after Viola*
Fabian. Come, let's see the event.
Sir Toby. I dare lay any money, 'twill be nothing yet.
                         [*they follow Sir Andrew*

[4. 1.]   *A square before Olivia's house*

SEBASTIAN and CLOWN

Clown. Will you make me believe that I am not sent
for you?

Sebastian. Go to, go to, thou art a foolish fellow;
Let me be clear of thee.

Clown. Well held out, i'faith! No, I do not know you,
nor I am not sent to you by my lady to bid you come
speak with her, nor your name is not Master Cesario,
nor this is not my nose neither: nothing that is so, is so.

Sebastian. I prithee, vent thy folly somewhere else,
10 Thou know'st not me.

Clown. Vent my folly! He has heard that word of some
great man and now applies it to a fool. Vent my folly!
I am afraid this great lubber, the world, will prove a
cockney...I prithee now, ungird thy strangeness and
tell me what I shall vent to my lady: [*whispers, winking*]
shall I vent to her that thou art coming?

Sebastian. I prithee, foolish Greek, depart from me.
There's money for thee [*he gives a coin*]—if you tarry
        longer
I shall give worse payment.

20 *Clown.* By my troth, thou hast an open hand...These
wise men that give fools money get themselves a good
report—after fourteen years' purchase.

*Sir ANDREW with drawn sword enters the square,
    Sir TOBY and FABIAN following*

Sir Andrew. Now, sir, have I met you again? there's
for you.   [*he strikes wide*
    Sebastian [*replies with his fists*]. Why, there's for thee,
        and there, and there!   [*he knocks him down*
Are all the people mad?   [*his hand upon his dagger*
    Sir Toby [*seizes him from behind*]. Hold, sir, or I'll
throw your dagger o'er the house.
    Clown. This will I tell my lady straight: I would not
be in some of your coats for two pence. [*he goes within* 30
    Sir Toby. Come on, sir! hold!   [*Sebastian struggles*
    Sir Andrew [*rubbing his bruises*]. Nay, let him alone,
I'll go another way to work with him: I'll have an action
of battery against him, if there be any law in Illyria:
though I struck him first, yet it's no matter for that.
    Sebastian. Let go thy hand!
    Sir Toby. Come, sir, I will not let you go. [*to Sir
Andrew*] Come, my young soldier, put up your iron:
you are well fleshed...[*to Sebastian*] Come on.
    Sebastian. I will be free from thee....[*he throws him
        off*] What wouldst thou now?   [*he draws* 40
If thou dar'st tempt me further, draw thy sword.
    Sir Toby. What, what? [*he also draws*] Nay, then I
must have an ounce or two of this malapert blood from
you.   [*they begin to fight*

OLIVIA comes from the house

Olivia. Hold, Toby! on thy life, I charge thee, hold!
    Sir Toby. Madam!   [*they break off*
Olivia. Will it be ever thus? Ungracious wretch,
Fit for the mountains and the barbarous caves,
Where manners ne'er were preached! out of my sight!

50 Be not offended, dear Cesario...
Rudesby, be gone!
                    [*Sir Toby, Sir Andrew and Fabian slink off*
                    I prithee, gentle friend,
Let thy fair wisdom, not thy passion, sway
In this uncivil and unjust extent
Against thy peace. Go with me to my house,
And hear thou there how many fruitless pranks
This ruffian hath botched up, that thou thereby
Mayst smile at this...[*he draws back*] Thou shalt not
        choose but go;
Do not deny. Beshrew his soul for me,
He started one poor heart of mine in thee.
60 (*Sebastian.* What relish is in this? how runs the stream?
Or I am mad, or else this is a dream:
Let fancy still my sense in Lethe steep—
If it be thus to dream, still let me sleep!
    Olivia. Nay, come, I prithee: would thou'dst be
        ruled by me!
    Sebastian. Madam, I will.
    Olivia.   O, say so, and so be!
                                    [*they go in*

[4. 2.] *A room in Olivia's house; at the back a closet
        with a curtain before it*

CLOWN *and* MARIA, *holding a black gown and
        a false beard in her hand*

    Maria. Nay, I prithee, put on this gown and this
beard, make him believe thou art Sir Topas the curate,
do it quickly. I'll call Sir Toby the whilst. [*she goes out*
    Clown. Well, I'll put it on, and I will dissemble myself
in't, and I would I were the first that ever dissembled in
such a gown. [*he dons the gown and the beard*] I am not
tall enough to become the function well, nor lean

enough to be thought a good student: but to be said an honest man and a good housekeeper goes as fairly as to say a careful man and a great scholar. The competitors 10 enter.

MARIA returns with Sir TOBY

Sir Toby. Jove bless thee, Master Parson!

Clown [in feigned voice]. Bonos dies, Sir Toby: for as the old hermit of Prague, that never saw pen and ink, very wittily said to a niece of King Gorboduc, 'That that is, is': so I, being Master Parson, am Master Parson; for what is 'that' but that? and 'is' but is?

Sir Toby. To him, Sir Topas.

Clown [draws near the curtain]. What, ho, I say! peace in this prison!   20

Sir Toby. The knave counterfeits well; a good knave.

Malvolio [from the closet]. Who calls there?

Clown. Sir Topas the curate, who comes to visit Malvolio the lunatic.

Malvolio. Sir Topas, Sir Topas, good Sir Topas, go to my lady.

Clown. Out, hyperbolical fiend! how vexest thou this man? talkest thou nothing but of ladies?

Sir Toby. Well said, Master Parson.

Malvolio. Sir Topas, never was man thus wronged— 30 good Sir Topas, do not think I am mad; they have laid me here in hideous darkness.

Clown. Fie, thou dishonest Satan! I call thee by the most modest terms, for I am one of those gentle ones that will use the devil himself with courtesy: say'st thou that house is dark?

Malvolio. As hell, Sir Topas.

Clown. Why, it hath bay windows transparent as barricadoes, and the clerestories toward the south-north

40 are as lustrous as ebony; and yet complainest thou of
obstruction?

Malvolio. I am not mad, Sir Topas. I say to you, this
house is dark.

Clown. Madman, thou errest: I say, there is no darkness but ignorance, in which thou art more puzzled than
the Egyptians in their fog.

Malvolio. I say, this house is as dark as ignorance,
though ignorance were as dark as hell; and I say, there
was never man thus abused. I am no more mad than
50 you are—make the trial of it in any constant question.

Clown. What is the opinion of Pythagoras concerning
wild fowl?

Malvolio. That the soul of our grandam might haply
inhabit a bird.

Clown. What think'st thou of his opinion?

Malvolio. I think nobly of the soul, and no way
approve his opinion.

Clown. Fare thee well: remain thou still in darkness.
Thou shalt hold th'opinion of Pythagoras ere I will
60 allow of thy wits, and fear to kill a woodcock, lest thou
dispossess the soul of thy grandam. Fare thee well.

[*he turns back from before the curtain*

Malvolio [*calls*]. Sir Topas, Sir Topas!

Sir Toby. My most exquisite Sir Topas!

Clown. Nay, I am for all waters.

[*he puts off the disguise*

Maria. Thou mightst have done this without thy
beard and gown, he sees thee not.

Sir Toby. To him in thine own voice, and bring me
word how thou find'st him…[*to Maria*] I would we
were well rid of this knavery. If he may be conveniently
70 delivered, I would he were, for I am now so far in
offence with my niece, that I cannot pursue with any

safety this sport to the upshot. Come by and by to my
chamber. [*Sir Toby and Maria go out by different doors*
   Clown [*sings*]. 'Hey Robin, jolly Robin,
               Tell me how thy lady does.'
Malvolio. Fool,—
Clown [*sings*]. 'My lady is unkind, perdy.'
Malvolio. Fool,—
Clown [*sings*]. 'Alas, why is she so?'
Malvolio. Fool, I say,—
Clown [*sings*]. 'She loves another'—Who calls, ha?   80
Malvolio. Good fool, as ever thou wilt deserve well at
my hand, help me to a candle, and pen, ink and paper;
as I am a gentleman, I will live to be thankful to thee for't.
Clown. Master Malvolio!
Malvolio. Ay, good fool.
Clown. Alas, sir, how fell you besides your five wits?
Malvolio. Fool, there was never man so notoriously
abused: I am as well in my wits, fool, as thou art.
Clown. But as well? then you are mad indeed, if you   90
be no better in your wits than a fool.
Malvolio. They have here propertied me; keep me in
darkness, send ministers to me, asses, and do all they can
to face me out of my wits.
Clown. Advise you what you say; the minister is
here....[*he changes his voice*] Malvolio, Malvolio, thy
wits the heavens restore! endeavour thyself to sleep, and
leave thy vain bibble babble.
Malvolio. Sir Topas,—
Clown. Maintain no words with him, good fellow.— 100
Who, I, sir? not I, sir. God buy you, good Sir Topas.—
Marry, amen.—I will, sir, I will.
Malvolio. Fool, fool, fool, I say,—
Clown. Alas, sir, be patient. What say you, sir? I am
shent for speaking to you.

Malvolio. Good fool, help me to some light and some paper. I tell thee, I am as well in my wits, as any man in Illyria.

Clown. Well-a-day that you were, sir!

110 *Malvolio.* By this hand, I am...Good fool, some ink, paper and light: and convey what I will set down to my lady; it shall advantage thee more than ever the bearing of letter did.

Clown. I will help you to't. But tell me true, are you not mad indeed? or do you but counterfeit?

Malvolio. Believe me, I am not—I tell thee true.

Clown. Nay, I'll ne'er believe a madman till I see his brains. I will fetch you light and paper and ink.

Malvolio. Fool, I'll requite it in the highest degree: 120 I prithee, be gone.

Clown [*sings as he dances from the room*].
> I am gone, sir, and anon, sir,
> I'll be with you again:
>   In a trice, like to the old Vice,
> Your need to sustain.
> Who with dagger of lath,
> In his rage and his wrath,
>   Cries ah ha, to the devil:
> Like a mad lad,
> Pare thy nails dad,
130   Adieu goodman devil.   [*he goes*

[4. 3.]   *Olivia's garden*

SEBASTIAN *comes from the house*

Sebastian. This is the air, that is the glorious sun,
This pearl she gave me, I do feel't and see't,
And though 'tis wonder that enwraps me thus,
Yet 'tis not madness. Where's Antonio then?

I could not find him at the Elephant,
Yet there he was, and there I found this credit,
That he did range the town to seek me out.
His counsel now might do me golden service,
For though my soul disputes well with my sense,
That this may be some error, but no madness,   10
Yet doth this accident and flood of fortune
So far exceed all instance, all discourse,
That I am ready to distrust mine eyes
And wrangle with my reason, that persuades me
To any other trust but that I am mad,
Or else the lady's mad; yet, if 'twere so,
She could not sway her house, command
            her followers,
Take and give back affairs and their dispatch,
With such a smooth, discreet, and stable bearing
As I perceive she does: there's something in't   20
That is deceivable. But here the lady comes.

OLIVIA comes forth with a priest

Olivia. Blame not this haste of mine...If you
            mean well,
Now go with me and with this holy man
Into the chantry by: there, before him,
And underneath that consecrated roof,
Plight me the full assurance of your faith,
That my most jealous and too doubtful soul
May live at peace. He shall conceal it,
Whiles you are willing it shall come to note,
What time we will our celebration keep   30
According to my birth. What do you say?
    Sebastian. I'll follow this good man and go
            with you,
And having sworn truth, ever will be true.

Olivia. Then lead the way, good father, and heavens
        so shine,
That they may fairly note this act of mine!   [*they go*

[5. 1.]   *The square before Olivia's house*

CLOWN and FABIAN

Fabian. Now, as thou lov'st me, let me see his letter.

Clown. Good Master Fabian, grant me another
request.

Fabian. Any thing.

Clown. Do not desire to see this letter.

Fabian. This is, to give a dog, and in recompense
desire my dog again.

The DUKE *and* VIOLA (*as Cesario*) *enter
        the square with attendants*

Duke. Belong you to the Lady Olivia, friends?

Clown. Ay, sir, we are some of her trappings.

10 *Duke.* I know thee well: how dost thou, my good
fellow?

Clown. Truly, sir, the better for my foes and the worse
for my friends.

Duke. Just the contrary; the better for thy friends.

Clown. No, sir, the worse.

Duke. How can that be?

Clown. Marry, sir, they praise me and make an ass
of me; now my foes tell me plainly I am an ass: so that
by my foes, sir, I profit in the knowledge of myself, and
20 by my friends I am abused: so that, conclusions to be as
kisses, if your four negatives make your two affirmatives,
why then—the worse for my friends and the better for
my foes.

Duke. Why, this is excellent.

Clown. By my troth, sir, no; though it please you to be one of my friends.

Duke. Thou shalt not be the worse for me—there's gold.   [*he gives him money*

Clown. But that it would be double-dealing, sir, I would you could make it another.   30

Duke. O, you give me ill counsel.

Clown. Put your grace in your pocket, sir, for this once, and let your flesh and blood obey it.

Duke. Well, I will be so much a sinner, to be a double-dealer; there's another.   [*he gives more money*

Clown. Primo, secundo, tertio, is a good play, and the old saying is, the third pays for all: the triplex, sir, is a good tripping measure, or the bells of St Bennet, sir, may put you in mind—one, two, three!

Duke. You can fool no more money out of me at this   40 throw: if you will let your lady know I am here to speak with her, and bring her along with you, it may awake my bounty further.

Clown. Marry, sir, lullaby to your bounty till I come again. I go, sir, but I would not have you to think that my desire of having is the sin of covetousness: but, as you say, sir, let your bounty take a nap, I will awake it anon.   [*he goes within*

Officers approach with ANTONIO *bound*

Viola. Here comes the man, sir, that did rescue me.

Duke. That face of his I do remember well,   50
Yet when I saw it last it was besmeared
As black as Vulcan in the smoke of war:
A baubling vessel was he captain of,
For shallow draught and bulk unprizable,
With which such scathful grapple did he make

With the most noble bottom of our fleet,
That very envy and the tongue of loss
Cried fame and honour on him. What's the matter?

  1 *Officer.* Orsino, this is that Antonio
60 That took the Phœnix and her fraught from Candy,
And this is he that did the Tiger board,
When your young nephew Titus lost his leg:
Here in the streets, desperate of shame and state,
In private brabble did we apprehend him.

  Viola. He did me kindness, sir, drew on my side,
But in conclusion put strange speech upon me,
I know not what 'twas but distraction.

  Duke. Notable pirate! thou salt-water thief!
What foolish boldness brought thee to their mercies,
70 Whom thou, in terms so bloody and so dear,
Hast made thine enemies?

  Antonio.   Orsino, noble sir,
Be pleased that I shake off these names you give me;
Antonio never yet was thief or pirate,
Though I confess, on base and ground enough,
Orsino's enemy. A witchcraft drew me hither:
That most ingrateful boy there by your side,
From the rude sea's enraged and foamy mouth
Did I redeem; a wrack past hope he was:
His life I gave him and did thereto add
80 My love, without retention or restraint,
All his in dedication. For his sake
Did I expose myself—pure for his love!—
Into the danger of this adverse town,
Drew to defend him when he was beset:
Where being apprehended, his false cunning,
Not meaning to partake with me in danger,
Taught him to face me out of his acquaintance,
And grew a twenty years removéd thing

While one would wink; denied me mine own purse,
Which I had recommended to his use   90
Not half an hour before.
   Viola.   How can this be?
   Duke. When came he to this town?
   Antonio. To-day, my lord; and for three
          months before,
No interim, not a minute's vacancy,
Both day and night did we keep company.

     OLIVIA comes from her house, attended

   Duke. Here comes the countess! now heaven walks
         on earth...
But for thee, fellow—fellow, thy words are madness,
Three months this youth hath tended upon me.
But more of that anon....Take him aside.
                           [the officers obey
   Olivia [*draws near*]. What would my lord, but that
         he may not have,   100
Wherein Olivia may seem serviceable?
Cesario, you do not keep promise with me.
   Viola. Madam?
   Duke. Gracious Olivia,—
   Olivia. What do you say, Cesario?—Good my lord,—
   Viola. My lord would speak, my duty hushes me.
   Olivia. If it be aught to the old tune, my lord,
It is as fat and fulsome to mine ear
As howling after music.
   Duke.   Still so cruel?
   Olivia. Still so constant, lord.   110
   Duke. What, to perverseness? you uncivil lady,
To whose ingrate and unauspicious altars
My soul the faithfull'st off'rings hath breathed out,
That e'er devotion tendered! What shall I do?

Olivia. Even what it please my lord, that shall
   become him.
   Duke. Why should I not, had I the heart to do it,
Like to th'Egyptian thief, at point of death,
Kill what I love?—a savage jealousy
That sometime savours nobly. But hear me this:
120 Since you to non-regardance cast my faith,
And that I partly know the instrument
That screws me from my true place in your favour,
Live you, the marble-breasted tyrant, still;
But this your minion, whom I know you love,
And whom, by heaven I swear, I tender dearly,
Him will I tear out of that cruel eye,
Where he sits crownéd in his master's spite....
Come boy with me. My thoughts are ripe in mischief:
I'll sacrifice the lamb that I do love,
130 To spite a raven's heart within a dove. [*he turns away*
   Viola [*follows*]. And I, most jocund, apt and willingly,
To do you rest, a thousand deaths would die.
   Olivia. Where goes Cesario?
   Viola.   After him I love
More than I love these eyes, more than my life,
More, by all mores, than e'er I shall love wife.
If I do feign, you witnesses above
Punish my life for tainting of my love!
   Olivia. Ay me, detested! how am I beguiled!
   Viola. Who does beguile you? who does do
       you wrong?
140 *Olivia.* Hast thou forgot thyself? is it so long?
Call forth the holy father.   [*an attendant goes within*
   Duke [*to Viola*].   Come, away!
   Olivia. Whither, my lord? Cesario, husband, stay.
   Duke. Husband?
   Olivia.   Ay, husband. Can he that deny?

Duke. Her husband, sirrah?

Viola.   No, my lord, not I.

Olivia. Alas, it is the baseness of thy fear,
That makes thee strangle thy propriety:
Fear not, Cesario, take thy fortunes up,
Be that thou know'st thou art, and then thou art
As great as that thou fear'st.

The priest comes forth

                              O, welcome, father!
Father, I charge thee, by thy reverence,   150
Here to unfold—though lately we intended
To keep in darkness, what occasion now
Reveals before 'tis ripe—what thou dost know
Hath newly passed between this youth and me.

Priest. A contract of eternal bond of love,
Confirmed by mutual joinder of your hands,
Attested by the holy close of lips,
Strength'ned by interchangement of your rings,
And all the ceremony of this compact
Sealed in my function, by my testimony: 160
Since when, my watch hath told me, toward my grave,
I have travelled but two hours.

Duke. O, thou dissembling cub! what wilt thou be
When time hath sowed a grizzle on thy case?
Or will not else thy craft so quickly grow,
That thine own trip shall be thine overthrow?
Farewell, and take her, but direct thy feet
Where thou and I henceforth may never meet.

Viola. My lord, I do protest—

Olivia.   O, do not swear!
Hold little faith, though thou hast too much fear.   170

*Sir ANDREW AGUECHEEK comes up
with his head broke*

Sir Andrew. For the love of God, a surgeon! Send one
presently to Sir Toby.

Olivia. What's the matter?

Sir Andrew. H'as broke my head across and has given
Sir Toby a bloody coxcomb too: for the love of God,
your help! I had rather than forty pound I were at home.

                              [*he sinks to the ground*

Olivia. Who has done this, Sir Andrew?

Sir Andrew. The count's gentleman, one Cesario: we
took him for a coward, but he's the very devil incardi-
180 nate.

Duke. My gentleman, Cesario?

Sir Andrew. 'Od's lifelings, here he is! You broke
my head for nothing, and that that I did, I was set on to
do't by Sir Toby.

Viola. Why do you speak to me? I never hurt you:
You drew your sword upon me without cause,
But I bespake you fair, and hurt you not.

Sir Andrew. If a bloody coxcomb be a hurt, you have
hurt me; I think you set nothing by a bloody coxcomb.

Sir TOBY approaches bleeding, led by the CLOWN

190 Here comes Sir Toby halting, you shall hear more: but
if he had not been in drink, he would have tickled you
othergates than he did.

Duke. How now, gentleman! how is't with you?

Sir Toby. That's all one—has hurt me, and there's
th'end on't...[*to Clown*] Sot, didst see Dick surgeon,
sot?

Clown. O he's drunk, Sir Toby, an hour agone; his
eyes were set at eight i'th' morning.

Sir Toby. Then he's a rogue, and a passy-measures
pavin: I hate a drunken rogue.   200

Olivia. Away with him! Who hath made this havoc
with them?

Sir Andrew [rises]. I'll help you, Sir Toby, because
we'll be dressed together.

Sir Toby. Will you help? an ass-head, and a coxcomb,
and a knave! a thin-faced knave, a gull!

Olivia. Get him to bed, and let his hurt be looked to.
          [Clown, Sir Toby, and Sir Andrew go within

          SEBASTIAN *enters the square*

Sebastian. I am sorry, madam, I have hurt
          your kinsman;
But, had it been the brother of my blood,
I must have done no less with wit and safety.   210
                    [all stand in amaze
You throw a strange regard upon me, and by that
I do perceive it hath offended you;
Pardon me, sweet one, even for the vows
We made each other but so late ago.

Duke. One face, one voice, one habit, and
          two persons,
A natural perspective, that is and is not.

Sebastian. Antonio! O my dear Antonio!
How have the hours racked and tortured me,
Since I have lost thee!

Antonio. Sebastian are you?

Sebastian.   Fear'st thou that, Antonio? 220

Antonio. How have you made division of yourself?
An apple, cleft in two, is not more twin
Than these two creatures. Which is Sebastian?

Olivia. Most wonderful!

Sebastian. Do I stand there? I never had a brother:

Nor can there be that deity in my nature,
Of here and every where. I had a sister,
Whom the blind waves and surges have devoured...
Of charity, what kin are you to me?
230 What countryman? what name? what parentage?
    Viola. Of Messaline: Sebastian was my father—
Such a Sebastian was my brother too:
So went he suited to his watery tomb:
If spirits can assume both form and suit,
You come to fright us.
    Sebastian.   A spirit I am indeed,
But am in that dimension grossly clad,
Which from the womb I did participate.
Were you a woman, as the rest goes even,
I should my tears let fall upon your cheek,
240 And say 'Thrice-welcome, drownéd Viola!'
    Viola. My father had a mole upon his brow.
    Sebastian. And so had mine.
    Viola. And died that day when Viola from
            her birth
Had numb'red thirteen years.
    Sebastian. O, that record is lively in my soul!
He finishéd indeed his mortal act,
That day that made my sister thirteen years.
    Viola. If nothing lets to make us happy both,
But this my masculine usurped attire,
250 Do not embrace me till each circumstance
Of place, time, fortune, do cohere and jump
That I am Viola—which to confirm,
I'll bring you to a captain in this town,
Where lie my maiden weeds; by whose gentle help
I was preserved to serve this noble count...
All the occurrence of my fortune since
Hath been between this lady and this lord.

Sebastian [*to Olivia*]. So comes it, lady, you have
      been mistook;
But nature to her bias drew in that.
You would have been contracted to a maid,   260
Nor are you therein, by my life, deceived,
You are betrothed both to a maid and man.
  Duke. Be not amazed—right noble is his blood...
If this be so, as yet the glass seems true,
I shall have share in this most happy wrack.
[*to Viola*] Boy, thou hast said to me a thousand times
Thou never shouldst love woman like to me.
  Viola. And all those sayings will I over-swear,
And all those swearings keep as true in soul,
As doth that orbéd continent the fire   270
That severs day from night.
  Duke.   Give me thy hand,
And let me see thee in thy woman's weeds.
  Viola. The captain that did bring me first on shore,
Hath my maid's garments: he upon some action
Is now in durance, at Malvolio's suit,
A gentleman and follower of my lady's.
  Olivia. He shall enlarge him...Fetch Malvolio
      hither—
And yet, alas, now I remember me,
They say, poor gentleman, he's much distract.

The CLOWN *returns with a letter in his hand,*
FABIAN following

A most extracting frenzy of mine own   280
From my remembrance clearly banished his.
How does he, sirrah?
  Clown. Truly, madam, he holds Belzebub at the
stave's end as well as a man in his case may do: has here
writ a letter to you, I should have given't you to-day

morning: but as a madman's epistles are no gospels, so
it skills not much when they are delivered.

Olivia. Open't, and read it.

Clown. Look then to be well edified, when the fool
290 delivers the madman. [*he shrieks*] 'By the Lord,
madam,'—

Olivia. How now! art thou mad?

Clown. No, madam, I do but read madness: an your
ladyship will have it as it ought to be, you must allow
Vox.

Olivia. Prithee, read i'thy right wits.

Clown. So I do, madonna; but to read his right wits,
is to read thus: therefore perpend, my princess, and
give ear.

300   *Olivia* [*snatches the letter and gives it to Fabian*]. Read
it you, sirrah.

Fabian ['*reads*']. 'By the Lord, madam, you wrong me,
and the world shall know it: though you have put me
into darkness, and given your drunken cousin rule over
me, yet have I the benefit of my senses as well as your
ladyship. I have your own letter that induced me to the
semblance I put on; with the which I doubt not but to
do myself much right, or you much shame. Think of
me as you please. I leave my duty a little unthought of,
310 and speak out of my injury.

THE MADLY-USED MALVOLIO.'

Olivia. Did he write this?

Clown. Ay, madam.

Duke. This savours not much of distraction.

Olivia. See him delivered, Fabian, bring him hither...
                          [*Fabian goes within*

My lord, so please you, these things further thought on,
To think me as well a sister as a wife,
One day shall crown th'alliance on't, so please you,
Here at my house and at my proper cost.

Duke. Madam, I am most apt t'embrace your offer... 320
[*to Viola*] Your master quits you; and for your service
    done him,
So much against the mettle of your sex,
So far beneath your soft and tender breeding,
And since you called me master for so long,
Here is my hand—you shall from this time be
Your master's mistress.

   Olivia.   A sister! you are she.

          FABIAN returns with MALVOLIO

   Duke. Is this the madman?

   Olivia.   Ay, my lord, this same:
How now, Malvolio?

   Malvolio.   Madam, you have done me wrong,
Notorious wrong.

   Olivia.   Have I, Malvolio? no!

   Malvolio. Lady, you have. Pray you, peruse
         that letter....   [*he takes a letter from his bosom* 330
You must not now deny it is your hand,
Write from it, if you can, in hand or phrase,
Or say 'tis not your seal, not your invention:
You can say none of this. Well, grant it then,
And tell me, in the modesty of honour,
Why you have given me such clear lights of favour,
Bade me come smiling and cross-gartered to you,
To put on yellow stockings and to frown
Upon Sir Toby and the lighter people:
And, acting this in an obedient hope,   340
Why have you suffered me to be imprisoned,
Kept in a dark house, visited by the priest,
And made the most notorious geck and gull
That e'er invention played on? tell me why.

   Olivia. Alas, Malvolio, this is not my writing,
Though, I confess, much like the character:

But, out of question, 'tis Maria's hand.
And now I do bethink me, it was she
First told me thou wast mad; then cam'st in smiling,
350 And in such forms which here were presupposed
Upon thee in the letter...Prithee, be content—
This practice hath most shrewdly passed upon thee;
But, when we know the grounds and authors of it,
Thou shalt be both the plaintiff and the judge
Of thine own cause.

    Fabian.   Good madam, hear me speak;
And let no quarrel nor no brawl to come
Taint the condition of this present hour,
Which I have wond'red at. In hope it shall not,
Most freely I confess, myself and Toby
360 Set this device against Malvolio here,
Upon some stubborn and uncourteous parts
We had conceived in him: Maria writ
The letter at Sir Toby's great importance,
In recompense whereof he hath married her...
How with a sportful malice it was followed,
May rather pluck on laughter than revenge,
If that the injuries be justly weighed
That have on both sides passed.

    Olivia. Alas, poor fool! how have they baffled thee!
370 *Clown.* Why, 'Some are born great, some achieve
greatness, and some have greatness thrown upon them.'
I was one, sir, in this interlude, one Sir Topas, sir—but
that's all one...'By the Lord, fool, I am not mad!' But
do you remember? 'Madam, why laugh you at such a
barren rascal? an you smile not, he's gagged'...And thus
the whirligig of time brings in his revenges.

    Malvolio. I'll be revenged on the whole pack of you.
                 [he turns upon his heel and goes
    Olivia. He hath been most notoriously abused.

Duke. Pursue him, and entreat him to a peace:
He hath not told us of the captain yet.   380
When that is known, and golden time convents,
A solemn combination shall be made
Of our dear souls...Meantime, sweet sister,
We will not part from hence. Cesario, come!
For so you shall be, while you are a man;
But, when in other habits you are seen,
Orsino's mistress and his fancy's queen.

                           [*all save the Clown go within*

Clown [*sings*].

     When that I was and a little tiny boy,
         With hey, ho, the wind and the rain:
     A foolish thing was but a toy,   390
         For the rain it raineth every day.

     But when I came to man's estate,
         With hey, ho, the wind and the rain:
     'Gainst knaves and thieves men shut their gate,
         For the rain it raineth every day.

     But when I came alas to wive,
         With hey, ho, the wind and the rain:
     By swaggering could I never thrive,
         For the rain it raineth every day.

     But when I came unto my beds,   400
         With hey, ho, the wind and the rain:
     With toss-pots still had drunken heads,
         For the rain it raineth every day.

     A great while ago the world begun,
         With hey, ho, the wind and the rain:
     But that's all one, our play is done,
         And we'll strive to please you every day.

                               [*he goes*

THE COPY FOR
TWELFTH NIGHT, 1623

Stage-directions like 'Enter Viola and Maluolio, at seuerall doores' (2. 2. head) and 'Maluolio within' (4. 2. 22 S.D.) suggest that the manuscript from which *Twelfth Night* was printed in 1623 was, as we have found with most other texts hitherto issued in this edition, either itself a theatrical prompt-book or a transcript therefrom. This original, moreover, must have been a fine example of its kind, since the transmitted text contains very few verbal cruxes, most of them long ago solved, is furnished with stage-directions and punctuation which are on the whole both adequate and competent, and gives no serious trouble either in the arrangement of its verse or—except for some natural confusion between the speech-headings *Fab.* and *Tob.*—in the distribution of its speeches. In short, the Folio text is on the whole happy and well-ordered like the exquisite comedy it has preserved, and the task of an editor is light indeed in comparison with that presented him in *All's Well*, the play last issued in this edition. Yet there is one respect in which the editorial problems of the two plays are surprisingly alike. We found that *All's Well* had been neglected and that much work needed doing on its exegetic side. *Twelfth Night*, one of the most popular of all Shakespeare's productions, would have attracted, one might suppose, a full measure of attention from commentators. And in many ways it has. Yet much remained still to do. One character, in particular, has been strangely passed over, that of Feste, possibly in accordance with the unavowed principle of most Shakespearian editors that what the Clown says is mostly nonsense and may be disregarded. A perusal of the notes that follow dealing with Feste's sallies will, I hope, help to disabuse readers of this illusion. Indeed, having now edited thirteen out of the fifteen comedies, I am bold to say that Shakespeare never places pointless remarks in the mouths of his characters, and that where they appear pointless, that is generally because we have missed the point, though occasionally it may be because someone has been tampering with Shakespeare's text. And what is true of Feste is true also of Toby in his cups. 'Sir Toby's drunken repartees,' says Aldis Wright, 'are intentionally not much to the point.' To which I can only reply that Sir Toby drunk is at his best[1].

Fine specimen of good playhouse copy as the Folio *Twelfth Night* gives us, we cannot feel certain that it was in Shakespeare's own handwriting. On the contrary, the cleanness of the text suggests that the printers handled a very readable manuscript, and if we are to judge from texts like *Love's Labour's Lost, Hamlet* (Q2), *Coriolanus* and *Antony and Cleopatra*, all of which seem to have been set up from autograph MSS, Shakespeare's papers were not at all easy reading for contemporary compositors. His archaic spelling they apparently found especially puzzling. Now though there are a certain number of spellings and abbreviated forms in *Twelfth Night* which might be called Shakespearian, they are not striking or frequent; and the impression which a study of the text leaves is that the copy used by the Folio compositors was a careful transcript of the original, perhaps an alternative prompt-book of a play which must have been much in demand.

A tidy text tells us little about its history, since all or most of the irregularities of the original will have been removed; and as a matter of fact the Folio *Twelfth Night* is remarkably free from bibliographical clues, the most interesting of the few that exist being the appearance of Violenta for Viola in the S.D. at 1. 5. 167[2] which strangely enough seems to link the text of *Twelfth*

---

[1] E.g. v. note 1. 5. 128.   [2] v. note 1. 5. 167.

Night with that of *All's Well.* There are however one or two dramatic points which may be noted here and which seemed weighty enough to persuade Fleay and some others that the text is a revised one. Fleay indeed argued that while the prose was written by Shakespeare for the performance at the Middle Temple, Feb. 1602, all the verse-scenes had originally been composed somewhere about 1593[1]; and he bases this theory upon his metrical verse-tests, which no one now takes very seriously, and upon certain similarities with early plays like *The Two Gentlemen* and *The Comedy of Errors*[2]. But when all is said, he can point to only one unmistakable sign of revision, and that is the evidence which the text affords that Feste has been substituted for Viola as the singer of the song before the Duke. Of this substitution there can be no reasonable doubt. Viola was clearly intended to be a singer, else why does she say to the Captain at 1. 2. 55–7, when offering to take service with Orsino:

> Thou shalt present me as an eunuch to him,
> It may be worth thy pains: for I can sing,
> And speak to him in many sorts of music.

And again the scene (2. 4.) to which the song itself belongs opens thus oddly:

Duke. Giue me some Musick; Now good morrow frends.
Now good Cesario, but that peece of song,
That old and Anticke song we heard last night;
Come, but one verse.
Curio. He is not heere (so please your lordshippe) that should sing it.
Duke. Who was it?
Curio. Feste the Iester my Lord, a foole that the Ladie Oliuiaes Father tooke much delight in. He is about the house.

First, as Fleay notes, we have a request (in verse) that Cesario should sing the song, followed by Curio's strange

---

[1] *Shakespeare Manual,* pp. 227–29.
[2] Cf. note 4. 1. 61–3.

answer (in prose) that the singer is not present and the,
to my mind, still stranger or at least lamer, explanation
(also in prose) of how Olivia's fool comes to be in
Orsino's house. Furthermore, as Fleay adds, the Duke
'afterwards points out the special character of the song
(ll. 43–48) to Cesario, who had also heard it, and who
had been just asked to sing it.' Both adaptation and
substitution are palpable.

A recent critic, Mr Richmond Noble, has revived
Fleay's thesis while giving it a different turn. After re-
marking upon the substitution just noticed, he continues:

If all were known, it is not improbable that in this change
is contained an interesting piece of theatrical history. From
Hamlet and *Othello* we know that Shakespeare's company
had from about 1601 until 1604 a leading boy available
capable both of playing upon the lute[1] and of singing
ballads of the plaintive kind alluded to by Orsino. Probably on the occasion of a revival there was no boy available
capable both of taking such a part as Viola's and of
singing[2]. Also the comedian, who personated Feste, may
have proved such an excellent 'draw' as a singer, that it
was good business not only to allot him all the songs but
actually to increase their number. As the play now stands,
Feste is not only a witty fool and a plausible beggar, but
domestic minstrelsy is his profession, and Malvolio dis-
tinguishes him from Sir Topas by his breaking into song[3].

And later in the same chapter he throws out the interesting suggestion that

'in all probability' *Twelfth Night* 'in its original form was
no longer than *The Comedy of Errors*, and hence its suita-
bility to be performed at the feast in the Middle Temple...
I believe, judging from the character of "Come away,

[1] 'See the 1603 Quarto of *Hamlet*, where Ophelia is indi-
cated as playing on a lute' (R.N.).
[2] 'In *Othello* the discrepancy between the Quarto and
Folio suggests a similar problem relative to Desdemona'
(R.N.).
[3] *Shakespeare's Use of Song*, pp. 80–1.

come away death" and "When that I was and a little tiny boy," that the final substantial revision, to which the comedy was very evidently subjected, occurred between the years 1603 and 1606. The reference to the latter song in *King Lear* would suggest that it was, at the time of the production of that tragedy, a newly popular song—the allusion is obviously topical[1].'

Before considering these two theories and the question of dates which they raise, one or two further points must be brought forward which have, I think, hitherto escaped notice. First of all, if (as seems indisputable) Feste has been foisted into 2. 4. and into Orsino's palace in order that he might sing 'Come away, come away death' in place of the boy who played Viola, then the change, though a little clumsily effected in the scene in question, is cleverly led up to in 1. 5. where at the Fool's first entrance he is accused of truancy, so that the audience may be prepared to find him impetticoating gratillities in other houses than Olivia's. Moreover, seeing that Feste's presence in the Duke's palace is referred to at 3. 1. 37–41, and again at the opening of 5. 1. when Orsino and the Fool encounter, it is clear that the substitution in 2. 4. was not just an isolated change in the cast for the sake of a single song, but involved changes affecting several scenes at least. Again, the striking thing about Feste, a feature not found in any clown in Shakespeare's earlier plays, is that he is a singing Fool, and something of a musician as well. *Twelfth Night* contains four songs, an unusually large number for one play, and all are sung by Feste. Furthermore, it seems obvious, though no previous editor has noticed it[2], that he is commissioned to carry out some kind of musical performance, perhaps accompanied by dancing, at the beginning of Act 3, for which the reader may be referred to the notes

[1] *Shakespeare's Use of Song*, p. 87.
[2] Mr Granville-Barker, however, did not overlook it in his 1912 production of *Twelfth Night.*

that follow. It would appear also that these musical gifts which have led to the amplification of his part in one direction have been compensated by reductions in another, since though Maria announces that the Fool is to 'make a third' with Sir Toby and Sir Andrew as eavesdroppers from the box-tree in the letter-scene (2. 3. 180), when we get to the scene itself we find his place unexpectedly taken by Fabian, a retainer of whom previously we have heard nothing. The truth is surely that it was necessary to lighten Feste's part, and that a fresh character had to be created to carry the burden. Incidentally, it should be noted, the letter-scene comes immediately before 3. 1., and had Feste 'made a third' in the Malvolio plot his performance with the tabor at the opening of the following scene would have been theatrically exceedingly awkward if not impossible.

Is it not a fair inference from all this that the text of *Twelfth Night*, as we have it, has been revised, and revised primarily to give scope for a Clown with a voice? Mr Richmond Noble thinks the revision took place between 1603 and 1606, but new clowns did not join Shakespeare's company every year, and since William Kemp left the Chamberlain's Men in c. 1599 it is difficult to escape the conclusion that the singing Fool in question was Robert Armin, Kemp's successor at the Globe. Indeed, it looks as if, probably after winning his spurs (or earning his cap and bells) as Touchstone, Armin may have been Shakespeare's chief inspiration in the composition of *Twelfth Night* as we know it, for Viola's speech (3. 1. 60–8), beginning

> This fellow is wise enough to play the fool,
> And to do that well craves a kind of wit,

reads like an official diploma. Armin seems to have been a much subtler player than Kemp, and Shakespeare paid him the high compliment of creating the Fool in *King Lear* for him, a character as 'full of songs'——to use

Lear's own words—as Feste himself. We possess little external evidence as to Armin's character and qualifications, but he remained principal clown to Shakespeare's company until 1610, when he was playing in Ben Jonson's *Alchemist,* if not later[1].

There are also other reasons for keeping to Manningham's date, for the play as we have it. In the first place, the prose-scenes are full of legal jests, much fuller than has hitherto been recognised, and these jests were clearly penned expressly for performance at the Inns of Court. Furthermore, as Miss Violet Wilson (*Society Women of Shakespeare's Time,* 1924, pp. 238–56) has recently pointed out, the famous drinking-scene in which the 'puritan' Malvolio rebukes the roistering Sir Toby in his hostess's name for disturbing the household, has undoubtedly some relation to a Star Chamber case which was the talk of London during the years 1600–2, a case brought by the strait-laced and ridiculous Sir Posthumus Hoby against a party of gentlemen who, having invited themselves, while on a hunting expedition, to stay the night at his house at Hackness in Yorkshire, disturbed the household with their toping, especially during family prayers. The names Orsino and Valentine, again, were probably suggested to Shakespeare by the visit of an Italian Duke, Don Valentino Orsino, to the English court in Jan. 1600 (v. pp. 103–104 below), while there are other links with the period, such as the famous mention of 'the new map with the augmentation of the Indies' (3. 2. 77–8, v. note). One of the most interesting of these, of which sufficient notice has not yet, I think, been taken, is the double reference to the Sophy or Shah of Persia (2. 5. 184; 3. 4. 280), which has been rightly connected by editors with the exploits of Sir Anthony Shirley and his two brothers. But none, I fancy, has observed how pat the reference is. Shirley's stay at the Sophy's court was for a limited period, less than a year;

[1] v. Chambers, *Eliz. Stage,* ii. 299–300.

he reached Persia in 1599 or the beginning of 1600, and was back again in Venice before 1601. The journey created a great stir in London, partly because of its adventurous character, but partly because Shirley was a strong adherent of the Essex party, and his exploits were looked upon with no favour by the government. A testimony both to this interest and this disfavour was the issue and the suppression by authority in 1600 of *A true Report of Sir A. Shierlies iourney*. But the book was re-issued in Sept. of 1601, and was followed before the end of that year by a second book on the same theme, by William Parry, entitled *A new and large discourse of the trauels of Sir A. Sherly*. Talk then of 'a pension of thousands to be paid from the Sophy' would be highly topical in Feb. 1602.

Yet though the ties with 1601-2 are many and strong, there are also clues, far less definite but not on that account to be summarily dismissed, pointing to the year 1606. Mr Richmond Noble, for instance, is assuredly right in insisting upon some connexion between *King Lear* and the song at the end of *Twelfth Night*, the common refrain being a palpable reference to a wet season. We can, of course, only speculate, but for my part I join with Warburton, Capell, Farmer, Steevens, Aldis Wright and others in refusing to believe that Shakespeare can have been personally responsible for the song as a whole, even if Dr A. C. Bradley be allowed his plea on behalf of the last stanza (v. note 5. 1. 388–407). And if the first four verses are not Shakespeare's then the most likely author for them is Armin himself, who was writing ballads as early as 1592, and having, I suggest, scored a theatrical hit with the Shakespearian 'He that has and a little tiny wit' in *King Lear* hoped to repeat it with a variation of his own on the same theme. In other words, I believe that the song at the end of *Twelfth Night* may have been written after the production of *King Lear*, which took place, if we adopt the

generally accepted date, in the year 1606. The alternative
is to assume that Shakespeare was not only complacent
enough to allow Armin to add the song to *Twelfth Night*
in 1602, but himself admired it so much as to write a
variant of it for *King Lear*.

We can at any rate be certain that alterations of some
kind were made in the text after May 27, 1606, since
that was the date of the passage of the statute against the
'abuse of the Holy Name of God in Stage-plays[1]' etc.
The frequent use of 'Jove' in the play where we should
naturally expect 'God' has been almost universally explained as due to the influence of this statute. But may
not Shakespeare himself have been partly responsible?
The absurd law would be likely to tempt him to multiply
examples; the spectacle of the 'puritan' Malvolio offering
thanks to Jove, so as to 'keep o'th' windy side of the law,'
adds an additional touch of humour to his figure; and
one can imagine that with the right emphasis Sir Toby's
ludicrous 'Jove bless thee, *Master Parson*!' (4. 2. 12)
would raise a great laugh. Such a theory of course
assumes that Shakespeare himself was handling the text
after May 27, 1606. This assumption would find support in a hitherto unexplained passage, if the following
account of it be sound.

The passage in question occurs at 3. 1. 20–30, and
runs:

Clo. But indeed words are very rascals since bonds disgraced them.

Vio. Thy reason, man?

Clo. Troth, sir, I can yield you none without words, and
words are grown so false I am loath to prove reason with
them.

Vio. I warrant thou art a merry fellow and car'st for
nothing.

Clo. Not so, sir, I do care for something: but in my conscience, sir, I do not care for you: if that be to care for
nothing, sir, I would it would make you invisible.

[1] v. Chambers, *Eliz. Stage*, iv. 338.

Now if 'bonds' be taken as oaths sworn by conspira-
tors (cf. *Jul. Caes.* 2. 1. 124), then Feste's remark
seems to point straight to the doctrine of equivocation,
held by Jesuits in England at this period, a doctrine
which, resting on the argument of the Schoolmen that
in certain circumstances 'mixed propositions' were
allowable, declared that when a Catholic was being
questioned on oath by a Protestant magistrate, he might
make a verbal proposition in one sense and at the same
time a mental proposition in another, or, in other words,
he might *say* on oath one thing and *mean* something
different. The doctrine was elaborated in a *Treatise of
Equivocation*, which circulated privately among recu-
sants and had been expressly composed to ease the
consciences of those who, suspected by the authorities
of harbouring Roman priests in secret rooms in their
houses, were required to say on oath whether such priests
were there and where they were hid. The sub-title of
the *Treatise* makes this quite clear. Thus it runs, according to the reprint in 1851 by David Jardine:

> Whether a Catholicke or any other person before a
> magistrate beyng demaunded vppon his oath whether a
> Preiste were in such a place, may (notw^{th}standing his
> perfect knowledge to the contrary) w^{th}out Periury and
> securely in conscience answere, No, wth this secreat meaning
> reserued in his mynde, That he was not there so that any
> man is bounde to detect it.

Here we have the clue to Feste's talk of his 'conscience'
and of invisibility. Furthermore, the *Treatise* being
concerned with the question of oaths, naturally begins
by elaborating 'the conditions required in every lawful
oath' and chap. i. opens as follows:

> Thou shalt swear (sayeth the Prophett Hieremy) our
> Lord liueth, in trewth and in iudgement, and in iustice.
> Vppon wch place the holy doctour St. Hierom. noteth that
> there must be three companions of euery oath, truth, iudge-
> ment, and iustice. Of whome all the deuines have learned

the same, requiring these three conditions in euery lawfull oath, and condemning all oathes wᶜʰ are made without all or any one of them.

These sentences connect themselves with yet another passage from *Twelfth Night*, viz. 3. 2. 11–15:

> *Fab.* This was a great argument of love in her toward you.
> *Sir And.* 'Slight! will you make an ass o' me?
> *Fab.* I will prove it legitimate, sir, upon the oaths of judgement and reason.

In other words, 'I will not prove it at all, since I omit the condition of truth'—just as the Jesuits did in their oaths. The jest was of course lost upon Sir Andrew, as it has been lost upon all modern commentators, but Shakespeare's audience, with the doctrine of equivocation in their minds, would catch it readily enough.

Now there is only one occasion when jests of this character would easily get across, to use a modern theatrical term. In other words there was one period when the views of the Jesuits upon oaths were being eagerly debated among all classes of people in London, and that was in 1606 when Henry Garnett the Superior of the English Jesuits was on trial for complicity in the Gunpowder Plot, when he openly and candidly admitted that he and his fellow-recusants subscribed to the doctrine of equivocation, and when the notorious *Treatise* itself was discovered by authority and aroused almost as much abhorrence in the nation as the discovery of the Plot. At such a time well might Feste remark that words had become 'very rascals since bonds [conspiracy] disgraced them,' and that they had 'grown so false' that he was 'loath to prove reason with them.' Shakespeare alludes to all this in the well-known passage in *Macbeth*:

> Here's an equivocator, that could swear in both the scales against either scale; who committed treason enough for God's sake, yet could not equivocate to heaven;

and it is natural to suppose that the passages quoted

above from *Twelfth Night* were written at much the same time[1].

What then must be our final conclusion from all this as regards the history of the text before us? At first I was inclined to think that the revision dated from 1602 and that the revival of 1606 accounted at most for one or two topical jokes. But apart from the absence of any real evidence for the existence of an original *Twelfth Night* before 1602, there are serious difficulties in supposing Armin to be the singer of the four songs in 1602. If he was so excellent a singer, why did not Shakespeare provide the Clowns in other plays of the period with a similar repertory of song? The Clown in *Hamlet* had a voice, it is true, and Touchstone can also sing, but theirs is lenten entertainment compared with what Feste provides. On the other hand in 1602 there was no need to take the songs from Viola since it was just at that time, i.e. 1600–1604, that Shakespeare's company, on Mr Richmond Noble's showing, possessed a leading boy with a good singing voice. And this consideration carries with it a still further consequence: the first draft of the play, in which the songs belonged to Viola, must have been made between those dates. Somewhere about 1604 however the boy's voice cracked or it ceased for some other reason to be available and those songs written for him had, on the revival of the plays containing them, either to be cut out or transferred to another character. In the case of *Othello* the omission of the Willow-song from the quarto points to excision; in *Twelfth Night* the company 'made content with its fortunes fit' and gave the songs to Feste. To sum up, *Twelfth Night* was, I take it, originally drafted for the performance at the Inns of

[1] For a fuller treatment of this matter, v. an article on *'Twelfth Night' and the Gunpowder Plot* in the *Times Literary Supplement* for June 13, 1929, where, however, I placed an interpretation upon the word 'bonds' which I now believe to be incorrect.

Court in February 1602, with Robert Armin as Feste, a part specially written for the company's new and clever stage-fool, and with the boy doing the singing, except for the catches in 2. 3. and 'Hey Robin, jolly Robin' in 4. 2. In 1606, however, when the play was called for again—possibly for the visit of King Christian of Denmark before whom Shakespeare's company played twice between July 17 and August 11—it had to be adapted to the changed conditions of the cast. Armin, who had perhaps recently scored a success as a singing fool in *Lear*, took the songs, with some new ones added, and changes in the dialogue were made accordingly. All this is conjecture, of course, but it seems the most economical hypothesis to account for the facts as we know them. I have only to add that if it prove to have life in it, it will be largely owing to Dr A. W. Pollard and Mr Richmond Noble, under whose helpful criticisms it took shape.

D. W.

Postscript, 1949.

The theory of a revision of the text in or soon after 1606 is further supported by Prof. Sisson's discovery relating to "the lady of the Strachy" (v. note 2. 5. 39–40) and by Mr Fitzroy Pyle's article on "*Twelfth Night*", "*King Lear*", *and* "*Arcadia*" in the *Modern Language Review* of Oct. 1948.

NOTES

All significant departures from the Folio text, including emendations in punctuation, are recorded; the name of the critic who first suggested or printed an accepted reading being placed in brackets. Illustrative spellings and misprints are quoted from the Good Quarto texts, or from the Folio where no Good Quarto exists. The line-numeration for reference to plays not yet issued in this edition is that used in Bartlett's *Concordance*.

F., unless otherwise specified, stands for the First Folio; T.I. for the Textual Introduction, to be found in the *Tempest* volume; Ham. Sp. and Misp. for *Spellings and Misprints in the Second Quarto of Hamlet* (Essays and Studies: English Assoc. vol. x); N.E.D. for *The New English Dictionary*; Sh. Eng. for *Shakespeare's England*; Luce for the edition of the play by Morton Luce in *The Arden Shakespeare*; Furness for the edition in the American *Variorum Shakespeare*; Aldis Wright for the edition in *The Clarendon Shakespeare*; Tilley for *Elizabethan Proverb Lore* by M. P. Tilley; S.D. for stage-direction; G. for Glossary.

Title. The twelve days between Christmas and Epiphany formed the 'season of high revels' at Elizabeth's and James's court, which culminated in Twelfth Night (cf. Chambers, *Eliz. Stage*, i. 19). Thus *Twelfth Night* may mean either a play written for this feast or one full of jollity and light-heartedness typical of the season. For '*What you will*' cf. the titles *As you like it*, and *Much ado about nothing*; Shakespeare at this period affected a carelessness in his choice of titles.

Characters in the Play. A list was first supplied by Rowe. (i) *Orsino.* Mr G. B. Harrison draws my attention to Winwood's *Memorials*, i. 292, which records the visit of one Don Valentino Orsino, Duke of Bracciano, to Queen Elizabeth in Jan. 1600 (cf. Sarrazin, *Shak. Jahrb.* xxxii. 168). The coincidence of name can hardly be accidental, and the date of the visit helps to determine the date of the play. (ii) *Valentine*. Perhaps Shakespeare borrowed this name also from the Italian Duke. (iii) *Curio* is a shadowy character and has only four short speeches in the whole play. It looks as if he may have taken a larger place at some stage in the history of the text: cf. note 5. 1. 7 S.D. (iv) *Sir Toby Belch*. Rowe describes him as 'uncle to Olivia.' The word 'uncle' does not occur in the play, and though Olivia is often called his 'niece' this is a vaguer term in Shakespeare's day than ours and she herself addresses him as 'cousin,' a vaguer term still. (v) *Malvolio*. Farmer suggests this is a transposition of 'Malivolo'; cf. Benvolio in *R. & J.* (vi) *Fabian*. Mr Richmond Noble points out (privately) that Fabian is addressed as Signior (v. note 2. 5. 1) and Master, and that his position is sufficiently assured to enable him to take on blame in 5. 1. that was not his. It is therefore misleading to describe him as 'a servant' as Rowe does. (vii) *Feste*. It has not hitherto apparently been noticed that this name = the contemporary Fr. for 'fête' = feast, festival—most appropriate for one who is the life and soul of *Twelfth Night*. We have, somewhat reluctantly, preserved the F. designation, Clown, in the speech-headings. It is characteristic of this tidy text that, except for 'Enter Violenta' at 1. 5. 167 (v. note), there is almost perfect consistency in the treatment of names in S.D.s and speech-headings.

Acts and Scenes. The F. not only divides into acts and scenes but prints 'Finis Actus primus,' 'Finis Actus secundus,' 'Finis Actus Quartus' at the appropriate points. The only parallel to this in Shakespearian texts is 'Finis' at the end of Act 1 of *Two Gent*. and 'Finis Actus Primus' in the same position in the F. text of *L.L.L.* As the headings 'Actus Secundus, Scaena prima' and so on, follow in every case, there seems to be no

reason for these 'Finis' entries from the editorial point
of view. It is more likely that they belong to the prompt-
book, and may have been inserted after Shakespeare's
retirement or death to mark the act-pauses at the Black-
friars Theatre (cf. J. Dover Wilson, *Act and scene divi-
sions in Shakespeare*, Review of Eng. Studies, iii. no. 12).

If the scenes were marked by the printers with the
help of a theatrical 'plot' (v. T.I. pp. xxxvi-xxxvii),
they missed one of the 'exeunt omnes' at 3. 4. 274
(v. note). The act-divisions, as Spedding (Furness, p. 57)
points out, are likewise open to question, though here
the blame must rest with the theatre not the printing-
office. At the end of Act 1 Malvolio runs after Viola;
at the beginning of Act 2 Sc. 2 he overtakes her with the
question 'Were not you e'en now with the Countess
Olivia?' Similarly at the end of Act 3 Aguecheek runs
after Viola, with Sir Toby and Fabian following; at
4. 1. 22 they overtake her. As Spedding says, these
pauses 'interrupt what was evidently meant for a con-
tinuous and rapid action, and so spoil the fun.'

Punctuation. Excellent, of the ordinary playhouse
type; it seldom needs emendation, but is very free with
the full-stop, which is too frequent to be noted.

Stage-directions. All original S.D.s are quoted in the
notes. There are none of special interest, except 'Enter
Violenta' (1. 5. 167).

1. 1.

S.D. F. 'Enter Orſino Duke of Illyria, Curio, and
other Lords.' The Duke's speech indicates that music
is being played as the scene opens, that it ceases while
he utters ll. 1–7, and that then the last strain is repeated
at his command.

1–3. *If music...so die.* Almost universally interpreted as an expression by Orsino of the wish that his
love might die of a surfeit and so cease to trouble him—
the last thing he would desire. The speech should be

taken as a whole (ll. 1–15). Orsino acclaims the tyranny
of love, which accepts all offerings but at the same time
makes them seem worthless (ll. 9–14). 'Appetite'
means, not 'love' as is generally assumed, but 'love's
appetite for music'; and Orsino does not value music
for itself but as a temporary food for his love, which is
'all as hungry as the sea,/And can digest as much'
(2. 4. 100–1)—a hunger he is always seeking to allay.
Cf. *A. & C.* 2. 5. 1–2 'music, moody food Of us that
trade in love.'

4. *a dying fall* v. G. 'fall.'

5. *sound* Sound as such cannot 'breathe upon a bank
of violets,' nor can it steal and give odour. Rowe therefore read 'wind' and Pope 'south,' which latter reading,
though graphically inadmissible, was accepted by all
edd. until questioned by Knight in 1840, who pointed
out that the south-wind in Shakespeare is generally
anything but 'sweet' (cf. *A.Y.L.* 3. 5. 50 'foggy south,'
Temp. 1. 2. 322–24, *R. & J.* 1. 4. 103, *Cymb.* 2. 3.
136). But *sough* (anon. conj. apud Clark and Wright),
which in the contemporary sp. 'sowe' might (by combined minim and *e : d* confusion) be misread 'sound,'
would give the sense of sound and wind and softness,
which fits the context perfectly. N.E.D. describes the
word as 'almost exclusively Sc. and north dial.' from
16th to 19th centuries, but quotes examples of its use
from Stanyhurst and from Ben Jonson's *Epigrams*.

Steevens cites Sidney's *Arcadia* 'Her breath is more
sweete than a gentle south-west wind, which comes
creping over flowrie fieldes and shadowed waters in the
extreame heate of sommer,' which is almost certainly the
source of Shakespeare's simile; cf. note 1. 1. 35–6.

7. *no more!* F. 'no more.'

8. *'Tis not so sweet...before* The 'appetite' is beginning to 'sicken.'

9. *how quick...art thou* i.e. what a keen appetite
thou hast! Cf. G. 'quick,' and 'fresh.' The connexion

of these words with 'capacity' does not seem hitherto
to have been noticed.

11. *sea, nought* F. 'Sea. Nought'—which is de-
fensible, there being a natural pause at 'sea.'

12. *validity and pitch* v. G.

14–15. *So full of shapes...fantastical* Cf. *M.N.D.*
5. 1. 4–17. Orsino claims for the lover alone the faculty
which Theseus attributes also to the lunatic and the poet.
Cf. G. 'shape.'

14. *fancy* i.e. love, v. G.

16. *Curio* (F2) F. 'Cnrio'

18–20. *O, when mine eyes...That instant* The
notion of love at first sight, as something akin to a
sudden physical seizure, is the constant theme of Shakespeare and the Elizabethans. Cf. *Shrew*, 1. 1. 149–50
'But see, while idly I stood looking on,/I found the
effect of love in idleness.'

19. *Methought...pestilence* The point of this has
escaped notice. Orsino implies that, though she seemed to
'purge the air,' the very sight of her smote him with the
pestilence—of love. Cf. below, 1. 5. 299 'Even so quickly
may one catch the plague?' and *L.L.L.* 5. 2. 419–21.

20. *turned into a hart* In reference to the story of
Actaeon, which Shakespeare may have read in his
favourite Ovid (*Met.* iii. 138 sqq.). Cf. *M.W.W.* 2. 1.
108; 3. 2. 39. 'Actaeon, who saw Diana naked, and
was torn in pieces by his hounds, represents a man, who
indulging his eyes, or his imagination, with the view of
a woman that he cannot gain, has his heart torn with
incessant longing' (Johnson).

22. S.D. F. 'Enter Valentine'—after 'news from
her.'

25. *element* v. G. and cf. 3. 1. 59 (note).
years hence (Rowe) F. 'yeares heate' Some explain
'heat' as 'heated,' though they cannot explain why
'seven years' (winters and summers) should 'heat the
element,' i.e. the sky. Others take it as a sb. meaning

'course.' There is little doubt that Rowe and Dyce were right to read *years hence*, the F. 'heate' being readily accounted for as a combined *a* : *n*, *t* : *c* misreading (v. Ham. Sp. and Misp. pp. 43, 45).

28. *And water...round* i.e. and pace about her chamber in tearful meditation.

29. *to season* lit. to preserve as by salting. A quibble. v. G. and cf. *All's Well*, 1. 1. 44.

30. *A brother's dead love* i.e. the memory of her brother's love for her (Furness).

34. *golden shaft* Cupid had two arrows, one of gold to arouse love, the other with a leaden head to blunt or dispel it. Cf. *M.N.D.* 1. 1. 170.

35–6. *the flock...in her* Edd. quote 'no more all that our eyes can see of her...is to be matched with the flocke of vnspeakable virtues, laid vp delightfully in that best builded folde' [her body], from the same passage in *Arcadia* already referred to in note, l. 5 above. The double parallel seems to make Shakespeare's knowledge of the passage certain.

36. *her; when* F. 'her. When'

36–8. *when liver, brain and heart...self king* A much discussed passage. 'Liver, brain and heart' are in the old physiology the seats, or "sovereign thrones", of the passions, the judgement, and the sentiments respectively. The "rich golden shaft" = Cupid's arrow, and the "one self King" = the one and only lover, Orsino himself he hopes, who will occupy all these thrones and reign alone in her heart [1949].

40. S.D. F. 'Exeunt.'

I. 2.

S.D. F. 'Enter Viola, a Captaine, and Saylors.' The locality of this scene is undefined and of no importance. Rowe read 'the Street,' Capell, followed by all mod. edd., 'the Sea-coast.' The action must take place somewhere near the latter, for the wreck is clearly recent, it being

apparently the first conversation between Viola and the
Captain since it took place.

4. *Elysium* an antithesis to Illyria suggested by the
similar sound.

6. *It is perchance* i.e. it is only by chance. He
catches up Viola's 'perchance' For 'chance' (l. 8) v. G.

14. *strong* (F2) F. 'ſttong'

15. *Arion* (Pope) F. 'Orion' The mistake may be
Shakespeare's.

39–40. *company And sight* (Hanmer). F. 'ſight And
company' The change is accepted by all.

41–3. *And might...estate is* i.e. and that my real
station might not be discovered to the world until an
appropriate time. Cf. G. 'deliver' and *L.L.L.* 4. 2.
74–5 'delivered upon the mellowing of occasion.'
Viola's conduct in this scene is described by Dr Johnson
as that of 'an excellent schemer'; Spedding holds that
she takes the only course open to 'a beautiful, high-bred
girl alone in a foreign country,' i.e. she first enquires
about the Court as a place where she might look for
protection, but a bachelor ruler makes things difficult;
then she thinks of Olivia's service, but the Captain
dashes her hopes there also; finally, as a last resort, she
falls back upon male disguise. Readers must take their
choice.   48. *pollution,* F. 'pollution:'

49. *I will believe* S. Walker conj. 'I well believe'
—which is attractive.

55–7. *as an eunuch...music* Cf. pp. 91–2. For
'eunuch' cf. *M.N.D.* 5. 1. 45, *Cor.* 3. 2. 114, *Cym.*
2. 3. 34–5, and R. Noble, *Shakespeare's Use of Song,*
pp. 133–35.

63. S.D. F. 'Exeunt.'

I. 3.

S.D. F. 'Enter Sir Toby, and Maria.'

7. *except before excepted* A quibble, as Malone
noted, on *exceptis excipiendis* 'the usual language of

leases'; appropriate in a play performed at the Middle Temple. But it has a personal point too, apparently not yet observed. 'Let her leave me alone' implies Sir Toby, 'she has already taken enough exception to my behaviour.' Maria's next speech 'Ay, but you must' etc. follows naturally on this.

10. *confine myself* i.e. dress myself. This is clear from the context, but N.E.D. quotes no other example in support. Is it another legal quibble?

20. *as tall a man* The surface meaning is 'as fine a man,' but Maria takes it literally as referring to height. The jest is also made about Slender in *M.W.W.* (1. 4. 23), who was probably played by the same actor; and there are other similarities between the two characters (v. notes below 1. 3. 120; 2. 3. 22; 5. 1. 182, 206). The reference to money shows that with Sir Toby 'tall' meant eminent, well-to-do.

23–4. *he'll have...ducats* Not satisfactorily explained; perhaps another quibble. Maria seems to mean that his whole fortune will be exhausted within a twelvemonth.

26. *speaks three or four languages* For the substance behind these claims v. ll. 92–6 below.

29. *almost natural* Upton conj. 'all, most natural.' In either case, the meaning is that Sir Andrew has all the gifts of nature much as an idiot has them; v. G. 'natural.'

31. *gust* E. A. Meredith's conj. 'gift' is attractive; it would convert Maria's speech into a catalogue of 'good gifts,' while the common sp. 'guift' would account for the F. 'gust'

34–5. *scoundrels and substractors* Shakespeare is careful to give Sir Toby words which are difficult for the Belch family to articulate.

36. *moreover* (F2) F. 'moreour'

40. *a coward and a coystrill* words again likely to induce hiccough.

41. *niece, till* F. 'Neece. till'

42. *a parish-top* 'A large top formerly kept in every village, to be whipped in frosty weather, that the peasants may be kept warm by exercise, and out of mischief, while they could not work' (Steevens). Cf. Chambers, *Med. Stage*, i. 128; Sh. Eng. ii. 481.

S.D. Derived from a suggestion of Brinsley Nicholson. The words 'What, wench!' etc. require some such business.

43. *Castiliano vulgo* Unexplained, and many editors follow the reading of Hanmer who emended to 'Castiliano volto,' by which, he says, Sir Toby 'means her best, her most civil and worthy looks, which he bids her put on because Sir Andrew is coming.' But this sense, which is excellent, seems possible without any change in the second word: for 'vulgo' = med. L. 'in public' and if so then 'Castiliano' is probably the corrupt word. I have, however, no suggestions to offer, unless it be that the final syllable may stand for 'nō' (= non). Anyhow the general meaning is pretty clear, viz. 'What, wench! Company manners in public! for here comes Sir Andrew Solemnface.' Cf. p. 172.

44. S.D. F. 'Enter Sir Andrew.'

48. *fair shrew*. An auspicious beginning.

49. *And you too, sir!* Mockingly polite.

50. *Accost* v. G. Sir Andrew shows himself ignorant of one of the latest coinages of polite parlance. Malone cites *The English Dictionary* by H. C. 1655 (pt ii.) which gives 'accost' as 'a more refined and elegant' word for 'draw near.'

52. *chambermaid* i.e. lady's maid; cf. 1. 5. 162–63 'my gentlewoman.'

59. *By my troth* etc. Even Sir Andrew cannot have intended this to be overheard by Maria, and her 'Fare you well, gentlemen' comes naturally with the two men whispering aside together.

60. *company*. So F. The 'company' is the audience in the theatre.

70. *thought is free* Tilley (625) quotes *Euphues* '"Why then," quoth he, "dost thou think me a fool?" "Thought is free, my lord," quoth she.' The retort goes back to Cicero (*Pro Mil.* 29, 79).

71–2. *bring your hand...drink* 'A proverbial expression among forward Abigails to ask at once for a kiss and a present' (Kenrick). All these hints are lost upon Sir Andrew.

75. *It's dry, sir.* Dryness of hand betokens (a) meanness, and (b) lack of amorousness; cf. *V.A.* 25–6 'his sweating palm, The precedent of pith and livelihood.' Both meanings appear in *Oth.* 3. 4. 36–8 'This hand is moist...This argues fruitfulness and liberal heart.'

77. *I can keep my hand dry* Referring to the proverb 'Fools have wit enough to keep themselves out of the rain' (Tilley, 253).

78. *A dry jest* = (a) a stupid meaningless jest; cf. *L.L.L.* 5. 2. 373 'This jest is dry to me' and v. below 1. 5. 42, (b) an ironical jest; cf. *Art of English Poesie* 'The figure Ironia, which we call the drye mock' (N.E.D. 'dry' 14).

80. *at my fingers' ends* i.e. (a) ready, (b) referring to his hand which lies open across her fingers.

81. *barren* i.e. of jests. v. G.

S.D. F. 'Exit Maria.'

83, 85. *put down* v. G.

87–8. *a great eater of beef* etc. R. G. White quotes *The Hauen of Health*, 1584, p. 114 'Galen affirmeth yt [that] biefe maketh grosse bloude and engendreth melancholie, especially if such as doe eat it be of melancholy complexion.' Cf. *Troil.* 2. 1. 14 'Thou mongrel, beef-witted lord.' 92. *Pourquoi* F. 'Pur-quoy'

97–8. *Then...head of hair* Sir Toby puns upon 'tongues' and 'tongs' which were at that period pronounced alike (cf. rhyme 'tongues-songs' *V.A.* 775, 'tongue-long' *Luc.* 1465, etc.). Sir Andrew's long straight tow-like hair was part of his make-up.

101–2. *curl by nature* ('Theobald) F. 'coole my nature'—possibly the compositor was misled by the sp. 'corle' or 'courle' and altered 'by' to 'my' accordingly. When Theobald made this brilliant emendation, he was unaware of the 'tongues-tongs' quibble, which was first pointed out by Rann in 1787.

103. *becomes me* (F2) F. 'becoms we'
does't (Rowe) F. 'dost'

115–17. *I'll stay a month longer* etc. It has been suggested that this points to the play's first production as being early in December, about a month before the Twelfth-night festivities, cf. note 2. 3. 89.

116–17. *I delight in masques and revels* etc. This speech and the galliard which follows (no doubt highly ridiculous to an Elizabethan audience which knew how a galliard should be danced) were appropriate in a play performed as part of the 'masques and revels' at the Middle Temple, Feb. 2, 1602.

120. *under the degree of my betters* Cf. *M.W.W.* 3. 4. 47 'Under the degree of a squire' and v. note l. 20 above.

121. *an old man* Possibly = 'an old hand'; v. G. 'old.' But the expression is clearly meant to be ludicrous, and there may be some topical allusion.

123. *a caper* The galliard was a dance of five steps ending in a caper.

124. *cut the mutton to't* This is generally taken as referring in some way to 'mutton' = a woman of low character. Yet it is doubtful whether Sir Toby means to imply more than that the only kind of 'capers' Sir Andrew could cut were those served up with a leg of mutton.

125. *back-trick* v. G.

128. *a curtain before 'em* Cf. below 1. 5. 237; *Troil.* 3. 2. 49 'Come, draw this curtain, and let's see your picture.'

129. *Mistress Mall's picture* Undoubtedly a topical

allusion. If 'Mistress Mall' be, as Steevens suggested, the notorious Moll Cutpurse alias Mary Frith (who became the heroine of Middleton and Dekker's *Roaring Girl*, 1611) the then supposed date of her birth, 1584, would make her too young for this jest in 1602. Such a reference may have been added to the prompt-copy any time between then and 1623 (cf. pp. 96–101); yet this identification would not carry us far, since it does not explain why the picture should 'take dust,' and there are other possible candidates. There is for example a certain Mall Newberry who was making herself 'infamous' in 1600 (v. *Letters of Philip Gawdy*, Roxburghe Club, p. 99).

137. *dun-coloured* (Collier) F. 'dam'd colour'd' Most edd. read 'flame-coloured' with Rowe, which lacks all graphical support. But 'dunne' or 'donne' might easily become 'damd' through the common *e* : *d* confusion (cf. T.I. pp. xli–xlii), while Sir Andrew is more likely to affect some ugly colour for his stockings than the bright hue in which Rowe dresses him.

set about (Rowe) F. 'ſit about' Cf. *All's Well*, 1. 1. 120.

139–41. *Taurus...legs and thighs* The old medical astrology supposed that the twelve signs of the Zodiac controlled the various organs of the human body. 'Sir Andrew makes a mistake. It is Leo that governs "sides and heart."...Taurus is "legs and thighs." The quality of Taurus is "nocturnal and bestial." In the authoritative astrological treatise *Liber Novem Iudicum* (1509) Taurus is stated to govern "crura et pedes," almost the very words Sir Toby uses. All is in harmony with the character of the two knights' (Sh. Eng. i. 460). Most critics have imagined that both knights go astray.

140. *That's sides* (F3) F. 'that ſides' Cf. note 2. 4. 99.

143. S.D. F. 'Exeunt.'

1. 4.

S.D. F. 'Enter Valentine, and Viola in man's attire.'

9. S.D. F. 'Enter Duke, Curio, and Attendants.'—at l. 8.

17. *thy fixèd foot shall grow* Cf. 1. 5. 147–48.

21. *leap all civil bounds* Cf. 1. 5. 210–16.

33. *shrill and sound* Explained as 'high-pitched and clear or uncracked,' and Aldis Wright quotes *Ham.* 2. 2. 448. But N.E.D. gives no support for this meaning of 'sound,' and Hudson plausibly conj. 'shrill of sound'

41. *ah! barful strife!* (P. A. Daniel) F. 'a barrefull ſtrife' 'Ah' was commonly spelt 'a' at this period; cf. the ballad quoted in note 4. 2. 74. For 'strife' v. G.

42. S.D. F. 'Exeunt.'

1. 5.

S.D. F. 'Enter Maria, and Clowne.'

1. *where thou hast been* etc. By thus stressing Feste's truancy, Shakespeare prepares his audience for the rather awkward presence of Olivia's Fool at Orsino's palace (2. 4.); cf. p. 93.

6. *fear no colours* i.e. fear no foe (v. G. 'colours'), with a quibble upon 'collars' of the hangman's type; cf. 2 *Hen. IV*, 5. 5. 91–3.

8. *He shall see none to fear* This 'lenten answer' (i.e. poor retort) is not pointless, as has been supposed. Unless he was 'well hanged,' the criminal in this period had only too much cause to 'fear colours,' since the skilful hangman would delight the spectators by cutting the halter so swiftly after 'turning off' his victim that the latter might live to see the whole scaffold red with his own blood. The Jesuit, Edward Jennings, executed Dec. 10, 1591, had a prayer on his lips while the hangman was cutting out his heart. Cf. G. B. Harrison, *Elizabethan Journal*, pp. 83–4.

12. *In the wars* Cf. G. 'colours.' The connexion between this and the excuse Feste asks for has strangely passed unnoticed. 'Say you have been in the wars;' suggests Maria, 'that's an excuse your Foolship may venture upon.' Feste's reply expresses contempt for such an excuse, and the 'Yet' in Maria's next speech indicates that the excuse will hardly serve.

14–15. *Well...talents* Feste expands this in ll. 31–6.

17. *absent; or to be turned away,* (Malone) F. 'abſent, or to be turn'd away:'

19. *Many...marriage* This leads on to ll. 27–8. 'He enters, and at once we know that Maria's secret is no secret to him' (A. C. Bradley, *Feste the Jester*; v. Gollancz, *Book of Homage,* p. 164).

20. *let summer bear it out* i.e. no one minds being turned out of doors in summer-time.

24–5. *if one break...fall* Quibbling on the commonplace that 'it is best to ride at two anchors, since if one fail, the other may hold' (Tilley, 7). One of the stock jokes of the Eliz. theatre; cf. 1 *Hen. IV*, 2. 4. 238–39.

27–8. *if Sir Toby...Illyria* Cf. note, l. 19 above. 'Eve's flesh' makes the reference to marriage clear.

30. S.D. F. gives no 'exit'; Feste's 'Well, go thy way' supplies it.

S.D. F. 'Enter Lady Oliuia, with Maluolio.' Capell added 'attended,' cf. 'fellows' (l. 38), 'gentlemen' (l. 70). Most edd. transfer the S.D. to l. 36, in spite of Maria's announcement 'here comes my lady' at l. 29. Feste's patter occupies the time during which Olivia and the attendants dispose themselves, while his sudden 'God bless thee, lady!' (= why, there you are all the time!) implies that he intends his soliloquy to be overheard. This is important since Dr A. C. Bradley, for instance, bases a theory of Feste's 'inward gaiety' on the supposition that 'he is alone when he invents that aphorism of Quinapalus' (v. Gollancz, *Book of Homage*, p. 166).

31–6. *Wit, an't be thy will* etc. The Fool's prayer to Wit is in correct form, and is even garnished with a text.

35. *Quinapalus* The Fool is full of mock learning, after the manner of Rabelais; cf. 2. 3. 25–6.

39. *dry fool* i.e. a stupid fool. v. G. 'dry.'

41. *madonna* The term only occurs in this play and is only used by Feste.

43. *himself; if* F. 'himfelf, if'

46. *patched* 'alluding to the patched or particoloured garment of the fool' (Malone). Probably Feste suits the action to the word, by pointedly displaying his motley. His 'simple syllogism' implies that no man is either absolutely good or bad, but of motley morality.

49–50. *As there...flower* i.e. Olivia has wedded calamity by taking her vow, and has proved herself a fool, since women are proverbially unfaithful to their weeds and beauty fades like the flower. The hit, unnoticed hitherto, is as subtle as the reference to Maria's marriage in ll. 27–8 above.

53. *Misprision* It is clear that Shakespeare (without legal warrant apparently) took this word to mean 'arresting or imprisoning one person in mistake for another' and more vaguely 'mistake of identity' or 'confusion of persons,' cf. *M.N.D.* 3. 2. 90; *Ado*, 4. 1. 184; *All's Well*, 2. 3. 155.

54–5. *as much to say as* A common turn of phrase; cf. *2 Hen. VI*, 4. 2. 18.

58. *Dexteriously* Not a comic perversion; v. G.

61. *my mouse of virtue* He is catechizing, as a parson would a small girl, and begins 'my good little dear.' But 'mouse of virtue' also implies that Olivia's virtue was small. Luce quotes Breton, *Miseries of Mamillia*, 'My father would call me good gyrle, sweet mouse, own wench and dad's bird' (Works, ed. Grosart, iii. 37).

71–2. *doth he not mend?* Olivia means 'make amends'; Malvolio takes the word in the sense of 'improve,' 'grow more perfect' (as a fool).

77–9. *Sir Toby...no fool* i.e. in Sir Toby's eyes you are both fox (= a sly ingratiating knave) and fool. Feste brings in Sir Toby because he knows that Malvolio hates him.

83. *an ordinary fool* Probably the common sort of fool paid to jest in an ordinary or tavern (Staunton).

84. *out of his guard* Not 'off his guard,' as N.E.D. suggests, but 'he has used up all his tricks of fence.' The words probably have reference to some action of Feste's, e.g. shrugging his shoulders, or turning away. The Fool treats Malvolio with silent contempt, but he remembers everything; cf. 5. 1. 374–76.

86. *these wise men* etc. Malvolio is impudent, and Olivia retorts in kind.

86–7. *these set kind of fools* i.e. artificial fools of this kind—implying that Feste's wit had to be whipped up for the occasion, so that if anyone put him out of his stride he was brought to silence. Armin (*Nest of Ninnies*, Shak. Soc. rep. p. 12) compares the 'foole naturall' with the 'foole artificiall' to the detriment of the latter.

89–93. *To be generous...but rail* Cf. *A.Y.L.* 2. 7. 47–87.   90. *guiltless* (F3) F. 'guitlesse'

92. *an allowed fool* v. G. 'allowed.' A technical expression; cf. *L.L.L.* 5. 2. 478, *Lear*, 1. 4. 220 and the term 'allowed book' for a MS play licensed by the Censor.   93–4. *no railing...reprove* Olivia is ironical.

95–6. *Now Mercury...fools!* 'May Mercury teach thee to lie, since thou liest in favour of fools' (Johnson). Mercury is the god of lies.

96. S.D. F. 'Enter Maria.'

105. S.D. F. gives no 'exit.'

107. *home....* The F. pause may denote a silent protest from the precise Malvolio at the lie expected of him. S.D. F. 'Exit Maluo.'

108. *grows old* i.e. becomes stale.

112–13. *brains! for—here he comes—one...pia mater* (Clark and Wright). F. prints:

> braines, for heere he comes. *Enter Sir Toby.*
> One of thy kin has a moſt weake Pia-mater.

113. S.D. F. 'Enter Sir Toby.'

118. S.D. Capell reads 'hiccups'

119. *pickle-herring* Notorious as a cause of indigestion. 'Robert Greene died of a surfet taken at pickeld herrings and Rhenish wine' (Meres, *Palladis Tamia*); 'Hee had...shortened his dayes by keeping company with pickle herrings' (Dekker, *A Knight's Conjuring*; quoted N.E.D.).

120. *sot* = both 'fool' and 'drunkard.' It was probably a title which Armin affected himself; cf. his *Foole upon Foole, or Six Sortes of Sottes* (1600).

121. *Good Sir Toby—* Feste here probably mimics Malvolio's manner and speech.

128. *give me 'faith,' say I* Hitherto explained as 'maudlin' nonsense. On the contrary, it is theology! Faced with the Devil, Sir Toby puts his trust in 'faith'; his 'works' would scarce serve his turn.

129. S.D. F. 'Exit.'

132. *above heat* i.e. which raises him above the natural heat of the body.

138. S.D. F. 'Enter Maluolio.' F. gives no 'exit' for Clown.

158–9. *in standing water* i.e. at turn of tide. Cf. *Temp.* 2. 1. 218 '*Seb.* I am standing water. *Ant.* I'll teach you how to flow.' Capell plausibly conj. 'e'en' for 'in' (a common Shak. sp.); cf. *All's Well*, 3. 2. 18 (note).

162–63. *gentlewoman* Important as fixing Maria's social standing. She is also 'chambermaid' (1. 3. 52), and—more rudely—'swabber' (1. 5. 205); but a waiting-gentlewoman in the service of a countess might have menial duties. Sir Toby was socially a catch for her, but they were of the same class, if different in rank.

165. S.D. F. 'Exit.'/'Enter Maria.'

167. S.D. F. 'Enter Violenta.' This might be taken as a mere compositor's slip were it not that an entry to a mysterious 'Violenta' is given at the beginning of 3. 5. in F. *All's Well* (v. pp. 115–16). Possibly the double error is due to a playhouse scribe who with the actor in mind who played Viola and Diana inadvertently employed the name of a character he took in some non-Shakespearian play.

176–77. *comptible...usage* i.e. sensitive to the least discourtesy.

181. *modest assurance if you be* i.e. enough assurance to satisfy me that you are.

182. *that I may* (F2) F. 'that may' The words occur at the turn of the leaf; F. gives 'I' as catchword at foot of p. 258 but omits it at beginning of p. 259.

183. *comedian* i.e. stage-player. Olivia is insulting, but the word follows naturally upon Viola's talk of conning her speech and studying her part.

184. *my profound heart* A mocking compliment to Olivia's penetration.

184–85. *by the very fangs of malice* i.e. by the very poison of malice itself. If you insist on being malicious, says Viola, I will confess etc.

188–89. *you do usurp yourself* Olivia means by 'usurp' 'act as an impostor'; Viola employs it in another sense: 'You are certainly misappropriating yourself,' she says, 'by refusing to marry.'

190. *from my commission* i.e. beyond my instructions.

200. *If you be not mad* A little puzzling; some suspect corruption. But probably 'if you be not quite mad' is meant. Staunton conj. 'but' for 'not'

201. *'tis not that...me* i.e. I am not myself sufficiently lunatic. The emphatic word is 'me.'

205. *swabber...hull* Continuing the metaphor of the ship and implying that Maria's function is to scrub the floors. Perhaps the latter has seized a broom to help her expel Cesario.

206. *Some mollification for your giant* i.e. please keep your giant within bounds—a hit at Maria's diminutive size; cf. 'little villain' (2. 5. 14).

208. *Tell me your mind* F. assigns this to Viola; Warburton first restored it to Olivia, followed by most mod. edd. except Clark and Wright. There has been a scuffle of some kind between 'Cesario' and Maria, in which the former, following instructions (v. 1. 4. 21–2), acts with vigour. Olivia is left a little tremulous and suddenly drops her haughty tone. 'Tell me your mind' is almost beseeching, and when Cesario retorts that 'his' mind has nothing to do with it since 'he' is only a messenger, Olivia meekly follows with 'Speak your office.' The change of tone is significant, and is due to the handling of Maria.

211. *when the courtesy...fearful* This and 'Yet you began rudely' (l. 216) make it clear that Viola has dealt drastically with Maria.

223. S.D. F. gives no 'exeunt' for Maria, etc. Possibly Maria herself goes out after the scuffle at l. 207.

224. *text* Referring to 'divinity,' as do 'comfortable doctrine' (l. 226), 'chapter' (l. 229) and 'heresy' (l. 232).

226. *comfortable doctrine* i.e. doctrine full of comfort. Viola's words mean peace and sound pleasantly in the ears of Olivia, already in love.

229. *In his bosom!*—with a slight emphasis on 'his' and a note of disappointment in Olivia's voice.

230. *by the method* (*a*) to adopt your style, (*b*) according to the table of contents. Cf. 1 *Hen. VI*, 3. 1. 13 [1949].

238–39. *such a one I was—this present!* Much debated; many emendations offered. Olivia is pretending to unveil a portrait, and portraits at this period were usually inscribed with the age of the sitter and the date of the painting. Thus on Federigo Zuccaro's magnificent picture of Sir Walter Raleigh in the National Gallery appears the following: 'Ætatis Suæ 34: An° 1588.' Similarly Olivia dates her own portrait, 'this present' being common form in dating letters, while 'such a one I was' are words that any woman might use in pointing to her own picture. Cf. frontispiece.

241. *in grain* v. G. 'grain.'

247. *leave the world no copy* Cf. *Son.* 3 and 11, ll. 13–14.

249. *beauty: it* F. 'beautie. It'

250. *particle and utensil* Terms applicable to an inventory of household goods.

labelled i.e. added as a codicil, v. G.

253. *praise* Cf. ll. 190–94; but with a quibble on 'praise' = appraise, like a valuer of property.

264. *well divulged* v. G.

269. *deadly* i.e. death-like. *life,* F. 'life:'

272. *willow* The emblem of forlorn love.

273. *my soul* i.e. Olivia (Luce).

280. *You might do much* The accent is on 'you'— but very slight!

285. *perchance* F. encloses this in brackets, denoting a drop in the voice before 'you,' which is once again accented.

292. S.D. F. 'Exit.'

297. *blazon* v. G.

303. S.D. F. 'Enter Maluolio.'

305. *county's* (Capell) F. 'Countes'

311. S.D. F. 'Exit.'

314–15. *Fate, show thy force* etc. Cf. head-note to following scene. *owe* = own.

315. S.D. F. gives no 'exit' but prints 'Finis, Actus primus.' Cf. pp. 104–105.

2. 1.

S.D. F. 'Enter Antonio & Sebaftian.' Capell and
mod. edd. head this scene 'the Sea-coast' like 1. 2. (q.v.),
but the dialogue makes it clear that Antonio, after rescuing
Sebastian, has taken him home and given him 'entertainment' (l. 30).

The prose of this scene does not read like Shakespeare's. On the other hand it strongly resembles the
prose in *Meas.* which we assigned to a collaborator;
and it is noteworthy that the preceding scene closes with
a stiff couplet very much in the style of those discussed
in the Notes of *Meas.* (v. pp. 110–11) and *All's Well*
(v. pp. 108–9). It looks then as if Shakespeare may
have handed over this little interim scene, which con-
veys information and allows Malvolio to catch up Viola,
to be worked up by some dramatic journeyman at the
Globe. There would be nothing to interest him in it.

3–5. *stars...malignancy...distemper* Medical and
astrological language, v. G. 'malignancy.'

6. *alone: it* F. 'alone. It'

10–11. *my...extravagancy* A stilted way of saying
'I have no object but travel.' v. G. 'determinate.'

16. *Roderigo* (Collier) F. 'Rodorigo'

17. *Messaline* A town unknown to geography; cf.
5. 1. 231. Capell conj. 'Mitylene'

19. *heavens* (F2) F. 'Heanens'

25. *estimable wonder* i.e. esteem and wonder. Cf.
Abbott, *Shak. Gram.* § 3, and 'deceivable' 4. 3. 21.
Adj.s in -ble were often used in an active sense at this
period.

32–3. *If you...servant* i.e. 'I shall die if you refuse
to let me serve you' (Deighton).

40. S.D. F. 'Exit.'

45. S.D. F. 'Exit.'

2. 2.

S.D. F. 'Enter Viola and Maluolio, at feuerall doores.'

1. *e'en now* Cf. p. 105.

5–6. *sir; you* F. '(fir) you'

9. *him: and* F. 'him. And'

12. *She took the ring of me* Viola of course had left no ring. But 'though taken quite by surprise, and not knowing at first what exactly it meant, she saw at once this much—that the message contained a secret of some kind which had not been confided to the messenger; and with her quick wit and sympathetic delicacy suppressed the surprise which might have betrayed it' (Spedding).

16. S.D. F. 'Exit'

20. *That as methought* (S. Walker; Dyce) F. 'That me thought' F2 'That sure methought'—which most edd. follow.

lost i.e. lost company with. Cf. Overbury, *Characters* (Melancholy Man) 'Speake to him; he heares with his eyes, eares follow his minde, and that's not at leysure.'

27–8. *Disguise...much* A commonplace, connected with the accepted demonology which held that devils could masquerade as departed spirits (cf. note 5. 1. 234–35 and *L.L.L.* 4. 3. 253 'Devils soonest tempt, resembling spirits of light'), and also perhaps with the puritan dislike of disguise of any kind, based upon *Deut.* xxii. 5.

29. *proper-false* (Malone) F. 'proper falfe' The coiner's die or stamp looks 'proper' (v. G.) enough. Viola refers of course to men, 'deceivers ever.'

30. *women's waxen hearts* Cf. *Lucr.* 1240 'For men have marble, women waxen, minds.'

31. *our frailty* (F2) F. 'O frailtie'—probably misreading of 'o^r' the contracted form of 'our.'

32. *made of* (Tyrwhitt) F. 'made, if'

34. *monster* i.e. both man and woman.

41. S.D. F. gives no 'exit.'

2. 3.

S.D. F. 'Enter Sir Toby, and Sir Andrew.' It is clear that they have been spending the evening at a neighbouring tavern, 'the Myrmidons' or some other. Maria no doubt had been charged to prepare them a repast on their return.

3. *diluculo surgere* (Rowe) F. 'Deliculo furgere,' v. G. A tag from Lilly's *Grammar*; every schoolboy knew it.

10–11. *Does not our life* (Rowe) F. 'Does not our liues'

11. *the four elements* v. G. 'elements.' Sir Toby is not without the ruins of learning. He speaks Spanish (1. 3. 43) and French (1. 3. 92); he knows more about contemporary physiology than most edd. (note 1. 3. 139–41); he talks theology in his cups (1. 5. 128); and here we find him prepared to discuss 'philosophy,' i.e. science—there being no drink to discuss.

14. *Th'art a scholar* Sir Toby's flattery is full of contempt; cf. ll. 3–6 above.

15. S.D. F. 'Enter Clowne.'

18–19. *the picture of 'we three'* i.e. a sign-board representing two fools or two ass-heads and inscribed 'we three,' the spectator being the third. Feste refers to fools; Sir Toby retaliates by referring to asses (Furness).

22. *I had rather than forty shillings* Cf. 5. 1. 176 'I had rather than forty pound' and *M.W.W.* 1. 1. 184–85 'I had rather than forty shillings I had my Book of Songs and Sonnets here.' For other resemblances between Slender and Aguecheek v. note 1. 3. 20.

25–6. *Pigrogromitus...Queubus* Feste's mock astrology. Pigrogromitus we may take to be a great doctor, rival to Paracelsus, while the Vapians must either be some yet undiscovered constellation or the thirteenth sign of the Zodiac. v. G. 'equinoctial.'

27. *leman* (Theobald) F. 'Lemon'

28–30. *I did…houses.* Most edd. have given this up as 'mere fooling,' though Steevens earned Aldis Wright's contempt for trying 'to make sense out of what even Sir Andrew saw was nonsense.' Sir Andrew, however, is not a reliable witness on a question of sense, especially when being handled by Feste, who here as usual deliberately sets himself to bamboozle him. What he says, in paraphrase, is as follows: 'I pocketed your miserable tip myself, for Malvolio was keenly on the watch (after my late truancy, cf. 1. 5. 1–13); moreover the lady of my choice drinks something better than ale, and the Myrmidons, the tavern we patronise, is no common drink-shop.' Taking the passage in detail, 'impetticoat' = to pocket, in reference, as Johnson noted, to the professional long coat of the fool (cf. note 4. 2. 123); 'gratillity' = wretched little gratuity; 'whip-stock' = a whipping-post, the type of stupidity and insentience; 'my lady' = the girl who honours him with her 'white hand'; 'the Myrmidons' we take, with Hutson, to be the name of a high-class tavern, probably well-known to the nobility in Shakespeare's audience; and 'bottle-ale house' = a low-class inn, such as that Christopher Sly frequented in *The Shrew* (cf. note, Ind. ii. 87–8).

28. *impetticoat* (Johnson) F. 'impeticos' Edd. are rightly chary of emending Feste's speeches, but while 'gratillity' is clearly a coinage (= poor little gratuity), 'impeticos' would be a pointless perversion of a coinage. There can be little doubt that it is a misreading of 'impeticot,' 'cot' being a common 16th cent. sp. of 'coat.' For *t : s* (final) misreading cf. 'possesse' for 'posset' *Ham.* 1. 5. 68.

29. *whipstock:* F. 'whipstock.'

35. *testril* Sir Andrew's form of 'tester' (= six-pence), in unconscious imitation of Feste's 'gratillity.'

36. *give a—* F. prints no dash, and as the words occur right at the end of a line, it is pretty clear that the compositor has missed something out. Sir Andrew like Slender is always boasting of his position in life.

37–8. *a song of good life* That Sir Andrew interprets this as a song of sober moral character is evidence that Feste meant something quite different; probably, then, 'good life' = jollification (cf. 'good company').

40. S.D. F. 'Clowne sings.'

41. *O mistress mine* These three words form the title of a 'consort' by Thomas Morley (*Consort Lessons*, 1599—a volume containing music only), and the same tune is also used by Byrd as a theme for the virginals. Again there is a song called *Mistress Mine* in another book of Morley's, *A short book of Ayres* (1600), of which there is only one copy extant, now in the possession of Mr Folger of New York. The words of this song, how-ever, were examined before it left England and were found to be quite unlike Shakespeare's. Moreover, as Dr Fellowes points out, Morley's setting to *O Mistress Mine* in his *Consort Lessons* does not exactly fit Shake-speare's words. The probability is, therefore, that Feste's song is a re-writing of a popular song of the day, and that both Morley and Byrd used the tune for this popular song as a theme for their compositions. Cf. Richmond Noble, *Shakespeare's Use of Song*, pp. 81–2.

53. *sweet and twenty* v. G.

55. *mellifluous* It is interesting to find Shakespeare laughing at this word in 1600 when Meres (*Palladis Tamia*) was writing in 1598 'the sweet wittie soule of Ouid liues in mellifluous and honey-tongued Shake-speare with his *Venus and Adonis*, his *Lucrece*, his sugred *Sonnets* among his private friends.'

57. *A contagious breath* i.e. a catchy song—with a

quibble on 'catching'; at this period 'contagion' almost always has some reference to the plague.

59–60. *To hear...contagion* Sir Toby elaborates Sir Andrew's collocation of epithets: 'If we could hear with our nose, we might call it sweet in stench.'

61–2. *draw three souls out of one weaver* Cf. *Ado*, 2. 3. 58. It is as much as to say 'draw nine souls out of one tailor,' tailors and weavers being incompletely human. Further, as Aldis Wright notes, weavers were given to psalm-singing, so that to affect them by a drinking-song would be a great triumph; cf. 1 *Hen. IV*, 2. 4. 147.

63. *I am dog at* v. G. 'dog at.'

65. *some...catch well* Cf. *Ado*, 5. 2. 11–12 'Thy wit is as quick as the greyhound's mouth; it catches.' v. G. 'catch.'

66–7. *'Thou knave'* A contemporary catch of this name with its music is extant; v. Furness, p. 118. The point of the catch (v. G.) is that each of the singers calls the other 'knave' in turn.

74. S.D. F. 'Catch ſung.'/'Enter Maria.'

78. *'My lady''s* F. 'My Lady's' v. next note.

78–9. *'My lady' 's...Peg-a-Ramsey* Hitherto unexplained. The clue is 'Tillyvally! "lady"!' which refers (as Furness notes) to Maria's use of the word 'lady' to intimidate Sir Toby into better behaviour. But 'My lady' refers to this also, and if it be remembered that 'Cataian' (v. G.) means a cheat, then the sense of the whole is tolerably clear. To paraphrase: 'This "my lady" of yours is a mere trick to put us off. So we (i.e. you) are up to our little schemes, are we? Your talk of Malvolio is all moonshine.' No one has yet discovered what exactly a 'Peg-a-Ramsey' may be, though it occurs as the title both of a song (acc. to Bp Percy 'a very obscene old song') and a dance (v. McKerrow, *Nashe*, iii. p. 122). Sir Toby seems to use it here as more or less equivalent to 'scarecrow.' Ramsey is a town in Huntingdonshire.

80. *Three merry men be we* Furness again gives words and music.

83-4. *There dwelt a man* etc. From the *Ballad of Constant Susanna*. Percy (*Reliques*, ii. x) gives the opening stanza which is so apt to the situation between Sir Toby and Maria that Shakespeare probably intended him to sing it all, substituting 'Maria' for 'Susanna.' Thus it runs:

> There dwelt a man in Babylon
>   Of reputation great by fame;
> He took to wife a faire woman,
>   Susanna she was called by name:
> A woman faire and vertuous:
>   Lady, lady:
> Why should we not of her learn thus
>   To live godly?

Such highly proper sentiments invite jocular treatment, which they receive again from Mercutio in *R. & J.* 2. 4. 151.

89. *'O' the twelfth* (Walker) F. 'O the twelfe' The rest of this ballad has been lost. It is conceivable that the words may give us a clue to the actual date of the first performance; cf. note on 'Ill stay a month longer' 1. 3. 115-17.

90. S.D. F. 'Enter Maluolio.'

93. *like tinkers* Cf. 1 *Hen. IV*, 2. 4. 20 'I can drink with any tinker in his own language.'

106. *Farewell, dear heart*, etc. This ballad (Corydon's Farewell to Phillis) is quoted in Percy's *Reliques*, ii. x. The first two stanzas explain the dialogue that follows.

> Farewell, dear love; since thou wilt needs be gone,
> Mine eyes do show my life is almost done.
>   Nay I will never die, so long as I can spie
> There may be many mo, though that she doe goe,
>   There may be many mo, I fear not:
>   Why then let her goe, I care not.

Farewell, farewell; since this I find is true,
I will not spend more time in wooing you;
  But I will seek elsewhere if I may find love there.
  Shall I bid her goe? what an if I doe?
    Shall I bid her goe and spare not?
    O no, no, no, I dare not.

107. S.D. 'From Maria's "Nay, good Sir Toby" it is to be inferred that the knight addresses his "Farewell, dear heart" personally to her, accompanied with some tipsy demonstrations of affection' (Furness).

109–10. *His eyes...done* Cf. note, l. 106 above, and 5. 1. 198 (note).

112. S.D. Halliwell suggests 'Falls down drunkenly.'

113. *Sir Toby, there you lie.* The words do not belong to the ballad, but the rhyme is maintained and Feste is no doubt meant to sing them.

119. *Out o' tune, sir! ye lie...* Furness points out that Feste has added an extra 'no' (and an extra note) to the line of the ballad and is so 'out o' tune,' while he has earned the 'ye lie' by changing 'I dare not' into 'you dare not.' Sir Toby then turns to Malvolio and does what Feste has dared him to do.

121–22. *because thou...cakes and ale* 'Cakes and ale' = proverbial symbol of jollity, e.g. *Hen. VIII*, 5. 4. 11 'do you look for ale and cakes here?' (cf. the later 'beer and skittles'); but the reference is also to the puritan hatred of church-ales, bride-ales and the sort of feasting that took place between Christmas and Twelfth Night (v. Stubbes, *Anatomie of Abuses*, ed. Furnivall, pp. 150 sqq.). Cf. the description of Zeal-of-the-land Busy in *Bartholomew Fair* (Gifford's *Jonson*, p. 308, ed. 1858), a reformed baker who took 'a scruple...in a spiced conscience' that 'those cakes he made were served to bridals, Maypoles, morrices and such profane feasts and meetings.'

123. *ginger* used to spice the ale; but Feste also hints

at the contemporary notion that ginger was an aphro-
disiac (Furness quotes Gerard, *Herball*, 1633, p. 62).

125–26. *rub your chain with crumbs* i.e. polish up
your steward's chain.

129. *give means* etc. referring to the wine she has
just provided.

130. S.D. F. 'Exit.'

131. *Go shake your ears* Not satisfactorily explained;
perhaps has reference to some dog's trick of the period,
cf. Chapman, *Mons. D'Olive*, II. ii. 234–35 'Shooke
mine eares And lickt my lipps, as if I begg'd attention.'
Other contemporary occurrences of the phrase suggest
begging, e.g. Cotgrave (1611) '*Il est au bout de sa
corde:* he may...go shake his ears,' Howell, *Letters*
(1645) 'They shut their gates against him, and made
him go shake his ears, and to shift for his lodging,' and
Jul. Caes. 4. 1. 26. N.E.D. ('ear' 1. c) confuses 'Go
shake...ears' with 'shake one's ears at' (= defy,
threaten)—a very different thing. Maria implies, I
think, that Malvolio is Olivia's pet dog; 'go wag your
tail' might be a modern equivalent. See p. 172.

132. *as good a deed as to drink* Cf. 1 *Hen. IV*,
2. 1. 32.

133. *challenge him the field* The regular expression,
v. N.E.D. 'challenge' 8. c.

141. *a nayword* (Rowe) F. 'an ayword' *v.* G.

149–50. *thy exquisite...knight?* The barrenness
of Sir Andrew's mind is a source of infinite attraction
to Sir Toby.

154–55. *cons state without book* i.e. learns polite
conversation by heart; cf. G. 'con,' 'state,' 'book.'

155. *swarths:* F. 'fwarths.'

156. *himself,* F. 'himfelfe:'

157. *ground* (F2) F. 'grounds' i.e. the foundation
of his faith; cf. *L.L.L.* 4. 3. 296, 298. 'Grounds'
would mean 'elements' or 'principles'; but Maria's
point is that Malvolio possesses only one principle.

166. *on a forgotten matter* i.e. in a writing, the occasion of which has been forgotten.

173. *a horse of that colour* Cf. *A.Y.L.* 3. 2. 403–404 'boys and women are for the most part cattle of this colour.'

174–75. *And your horse . . . ass* Some think this too smart for Sir Andrew, but as Halliwell notes it gives Maria an opportunity of calling him an ass.

176. *Ass, I doubt not* The quibble upon 'as' and the hit at Sir Andrew are both patent.

179–80. *let the fool make a third* It is Fabian and not the Fool who makes the third; cf. p. 94.

182. S.D. F. 'Exit.'

183. *Penthesilea* Queen of the Amazons—half in admiration, half in jest at Maria's diminutive size; cf. 1. 5. 206, note.

185. *beagle* Another reference to Maria's stature. Furness quotes Markham, *Countrey Contentments*, 1611, 'The little beagle, which may be carried in a man's glove and bred in many countries for delight onely, being of curious scents and passing cunning in their hunting'; and adds that Sir Toby in calling her a 'beagle' means to compliment Maria upon 'her keenness and sagacity.'

188–89. *Thou hadst need send for more money* Here is the material ground of Sir Toby's partiality for Sir Andrew: he could borrow from him upon his 3000 ducats a year. Cf. 3. 2. 53–4.

190–91. *If I cannot recover . . . out* v. G. 'recover,' 'out.'

196. *burn some sack* v. G. 'sack.'

197. S.D. F. 'Exeunt.'

2. 4.

S.D. F. 'Enter Duke, Viola, Curio, and others.'
1–2. F. prints thus:

Du. Giue me fome Mufick; Now good morrow frends.
Now good Cefario, but that peece of fong,

Our arrangement is Furness's based upon Johnson's;
but I do not feel at all confident that it embodies
Shakespeare's intentions; cf. pp. 91–2. It is clear that
Orsino expects Cesario to sing. *but* = only.

3. *old and antic* F. 'old and Anticke' Pope and all
later edd. read 'old and antique' I return to the F. form
to avoid apparent pleonasm; v. G. 'antic.'

4. *passion* i.e. suffering 'the pangs of despised love'
(Wright and Furness).

5. *recollected terms* studied phrases, v. G. 'recollected.'

8–14. *He is not here* etc. Note how the scene drops
into prose when the reference to Feste is introduced.
Note too that this is the only point in the play where
the clown is given a name. The anomaly of Feste's
presence in Orsino's house is cleverly concealed; nothing
wrong is felt in the theatre; but in the study the subter-
fuge is patent enough. Cf. pp. 91–4.

14. S.D. F. 'Muficke playes.' No 'exit' for Curio
is given.

21–2. *It gives...throned* i.e. 'it is an exact echo
to the deepest feelings of the heart' (Luce).

29–30. *let still...than herself* Many see a reference
here to Shakespeare's (supposedly unhappy) marriage
to Anne Hathaway, 7½ years his elder. But Orsino is
hardly an authority on marriage, and he contradicts
himself: at ll. 33–5 man is the fickle sex; at ll. 97–9
woman is.

30. *herself;* F. 'her felfe,' *him,* F. 'him;'

31. *sways...level* A quibble, 'sways' = (*a*) holds

sway, (*b*) swings. Hence 'level' which means in perfect equipoise.

34. *won* (Hanmer) F. 'worne'—probably 'wonne' misread, an *n : r* error, cf. Ham. Sp. and Misp. p. 41. Capell notes that 'won' 'seems wanted to sort with "giddy" and "longing," as "lost" does with the other two.' Malone, Aldis Wright and Furness (a strong combination) support F., the last-named because of the triteness of 'lost and won.' It is this very triteness, or rather this proverbial character, which convinces us that it is the true reading, since 'worn' after 'lost and' would be so violent a wrench from the expected as to constitute affectation.

37. *hold the bent* i.e. stand the strain; v. G. 'bent.'

41. S.D. F. 'Enter Curio & Clowne.'

45. *the free maids...bones* i.e. lace-makers using bone bobbins. Lace-making was a new art in Shakespeare's England, and was popularly supposed to have been introduced by Katherine of Aragon. It spread rapidly through the counties of Bedford, Bucks and Northampton in the 17th cent. (Sh. Eng. i. 327). For 'free' v. G.

46. *silly sooth* i.e. 'plain, simple truth' (Johnson).

47. *dallies...love* Many have doubted whether the song that follows answers to this description, but if 'dally with' (v. G.) be taken as 'dwell upon sentimentally' there seems less difficulty. On the other hand, Mr Richmond Noble points out (privately) that while the context indicates 'a traditional song rendered as plainsong,' we are actually given 'a highly finished product, a lute-song.' It is likely therefore that the song was changed for the performance of 1606. v. pp. 100–1.

48. *the old age* i.e. 'the antique world' (*A.Y.L.* 2. 3. 57). Cf. *Son.* 127. 1.

50. S.D. F. 'Muſicke.'

51. *Come away* etc. F. heads this 'The Song' and gives it no speech-heading. 'Come away' = come hither.

52. *cypress* i.e. 'either a coffin of cypress wood or a bier strewn with branches or garlands of cypress' (Aldis Wright). *laid:* F. 'laide.'

53. *Fly away, fly away* (Rowe) F. 'Fye away, fie away'

55. *yew* F. 'Ew'

57. *My part of death* i.e. my allotted portion—death; v. G. 'part.' Dr Johnson takes 'part' as 'player's part,' but no reference to the theatre seems to be intended.

59–60. *Not a flower...strown* 'Coffins...were covered in black with bunches of yew and rosemary tied to the sides' (Sh. Eng. i. 150).

63. *A thousand thousand sighs* etc. This line would appeal especially to the love-sick Orsino. The song 'with its humourously playful pity for the Duke's sad love-grief' is not of course intended to be taken seriously (Richmond Noble, *Shakespeare's Use of Song*, p. 83).

67. *pains* Orsino characteristically emphasises the word a little, and so evokes Feste's rejoinder.

70. *pleasure will be paid* i.e. with pain. Cf. 'Pleasure must be purchased with the price of pain' Pettie, *Petite Pallace* (Tilley, 493).

73. *the melancholy god protect thee* A broad hint that Orsino, like Jaques, took pleasure in his melancholy. The two characters represent two well recognised Elizabethan types of melancholy; cf. G. B. Harrison's ed. of Breton, *Melancholike Humours*.

74. *changeable taffeta* i.e. shot silk, v. G. 'taffeta.'

75–8. *I would have...voyage of nothing* This has puzzled all. But Feste's argument seems to be ironical as usual. To paraphrase: 'These opal-minded "constant" men should go to sea, for there they can put in at any port and tack with every breeze, which is the best way of bringing a great expedition to nought.' N.B. The opal-minded Essex 'made a good voyage of nothing' in just this fashion when he undertook the Islands Voyage of 1597.

76–7. *their business...every where* Cf. 'my determinate voyage is mere extravagancy' 2. 1. 10–11.

78. S.D. F. 'Exit.'

79. S.D. F. gives no 'exit.'

82–3. *lands;...her*, F. 'lands,...her:'—trans-
posing the pointing.

85. *miracle...gems* i.e. her beauty.

88. *I cannot* (Hanmer) F. 'It cannot'

96. *retention* v. G. After 'woman's sides' and
'woman's heart' Orsino uses a physiological term.

99. *suffers* (Rowe) F. 'suffer' The final *s* is omitted
before 'surfeit'; cf. note 1. 3. 140. *revolt;* F. 'reuolt,'

100–1. *as hungry...much* Cf. 1. 1. 9–14.

112. *thought* i.e. brooding.

124. S.D. F. 'exeunt.'

2. 5.

S.D. F. 'Enter Sir Toby, Sir Andrew, and Fabian.'

1–2. *Signior Fabian* Note Sir Toby's ceremonious
form of address: cf. p. 104.

4–5. *boiled...melancholy* Fabian jests; melancholy
being a 'cold' humour.

9. *bear-baiting* Malvolio's disapproval is a puritan
trait. The sport is thus condemned in Stubbes's *Anatomie of Abuses*, 1583:

Is not the baiting of a Bear, besides that it is a filthie,
stinking, and lothsome game, a dangerous & perilous
exercyse? wherein a man is in daunger of his life euery
minut of an houre; which thing, though it weare not so,
yet what exercyse is this meet for any Christian? what
christen heart can take pleasure to see one poore beast to
rent, teare, and kill another, and all for his foolish pleasure?
And although they be bloody beasts to mankind, & seeke

his distruction, yet we are not to abuse them, for his sake
who made them, and whose creatures they are (ed. Furnivall,
pp. 177–78)

—sentiments worthy of a modern humanitarian.

11. *fool him black and blue* Hitherto taken as referring to Malvolio, but not explained. Surely the 'him'
is the bear, who is to be 'fooled' or worried.

13. S.D. F. 'Enter Maria.'

15. *metal of India* i.e. pure gold. Cf. 1 *Hen. IV*,
2. 4. 307; 3. 1. 169.

20. *contemplative idiot* i.e. the type of idiot who
says nothing but gazes into vacancy, or at his own
shadow.

23. *trout...tickling* 'Trusty trout'=confidential
servant (N.E.D.), and 'tickle'=flatter. Steevens quotes
Cogan, *Haven of Health*, 1595, 'This fish of nature
loueth flatterie, for being in the water, it will suffer it
selfe to be rubbed and clawed, and so be taken.'

S.D. F. 'Exit'/'Enter Maluolio'

31–2. *turkey-cock* Cf. *Hen. V*, 5. 1. 15 'swelling
like a turkey-cock.' The picture is continued in 'jets
under his advanced plumes.' v. G. 'jet,' 'advanced.'

34. *Peace, I say.* 38. *Peace, peace!* F. assigns
these speeches to 'To.' We give them to Fabian, following a conj. of Aldis Wright. Fabian's task is to keep
Sir Toby and Sir Andrew from spoiling the fun by
revealing their presence; he exclaims 'O, peace' at l. 31
and again at ll. 42, 51, 57. It is therefore only logical
to give him ll. 34 and 38. The F. error no doubt arose
from 'fab.' being taken for 'tob.'—an easy misreading
in the old English hand.

39–40. *the lady of the Strachy* Hitherto unsolved.
But Prof. Sisson tells me that he has found a reference
to one William Strachey of Saffron Walden, who was
a "sharer" in the Children of the Revels Company
in 1606 and went himself, or sent his wife, every week

to draw his takings at the theatre; and as the wardrobe man there was one David Yeoman, it looks as if Malvolio's allusion was an interpolated jest of some kind at the expense of the same company as the "little eyases" to which Hamlet refers [1949].

41. *Fie on him, Jezebel!* Jezebel is the stock type of shameless impudence: that Sir Andrew should apply the name to a man is simply an example of his 'scholarship.'   45. *state* i.e. the Count's chair, v. G.

52. *the humour of state* i.e. the whims of the great. The phrase might stand as a title to the first act of *King Lear*.

53. *travel of regard* i.e. a glance round the room.

60–1. *with my—some* (Collier) F. 'with my ſome' Brinsley Nicholson writes 'Malvolio…is about to say "play with my chain" but suddenly remembering that he would be no longer a steward…he stops short and then confusedly alters his phrase.'

62. *curtsies* So F. Most edd. read 'courtesies'

64–5. *drawn from us with cars* Cf. 3. 2. 58–9 'oxen and wainropes cannot hale them together' and *Two Gent*. 3. 1. 264–65 'a team of horse shall not pluck that from me.' The notion, I suspect, is derived from some torture of the period.

86, 87. *Now is* etc. *O, peace* etc. These speeches should probably be redistributed; cf. note ll. 34, 38 above.

90. *her very c's, her u's, and her t's* F. 'her very C's, her V's, her T's' The fact that Malvolio goes on to speak of 'her great P's' indicates that the other letters should be minuscules.

93. *Her c's…why that?* Readers and actors have been repeating Sir Andrew's question for 300 years without finding an answer, except that Shakespeare's 'regal indolence' did not trouble to make the letters correspond with anything in the superscription which Malvolio reads out (cf. Robert Bridges, *Collected Essays*, i. 27–8). But

if it is carelessness why does Sir Andrew underline it in this way? His question surely makes it certain that the letters possessed some point for Shakespeare's audience. Malvolio is unconsciously guilty of a bawdy jest, "cut" meaning the female pudendum; cf. Marston, *Malcontent* Ind. 25–32; Middleton, *Chaste Maid*, 2. 1. 137; and *Woodstock* (ed. A. P. Rossiter), 3. 1. 158. I owe this solution to Prof. G. B. Harrison.

96–7. *her Lucrece* We should expect Olivia to choose such a seal.

99. *liver and all* v. G. 'liver.'

100–3. *Jove knows...must know* F. prints as prose.

102. *Lips, do not* (Capell) F. 'Lips do not'

104–5. *the numbers altered* i.e. another stanza, but in different metre.

107. *brock* The epithet is perhaps suggested by Malvolio suddenly raising his voice in his excitement; Turbervile, *Booke of Hunting*, 1576, discussing 'the voyces and noyses' of beasts of chase, writes (p. 240) 'a Fox barketh: a Badgerd shriketh: an Otter whineth.'

108–11. *I may...my life* F. prints in two lines, with a colon after 'knife.'

111. *doth sway my life* Cf. *A.Y.L.* 3. 2. 4 'my full life doth sway.'

117–18. *with what...checks at it* i.e. how swiftly the staniel (an inferior kind of falcon) swerves aside to swoop upon it; v. G. 'stallion,' 'check.'

117. *stallion* Hanmer and all mod. edd. read 'staniel,' which gives the meaning required; but it is safer to retain the F. form, which N.E.D. suggests may have had dialectal currency; and, if so, then Sir Toby quibbles, since 'stallion'=lascivious fellow (v. G.).

121. *to any formal capacity* i.e. to anyone in his senses; v. G. 'formal.'

123. *alphabetical position* i.e. arrangement or disposition of letters, v. G. 'position.'

125. *O, ay* Sir Toby echoes two of the letters. For
'make up' v. G.

125–26. *he is now at a cold scent* i.e. that will baffle
him! Cf. below, l. 132.

127. *Sowter* The name of a hound (=bungler,
from 'souter' a cobbler).

128. *as rank as a fox* 'There were untrue hunters,
who would leave the sweet scent of a hare, and speak
to the rank scent of a fox' (J. W. Fortescue, *Sh. Eng.*
ii. 348). Cf. Madden, *Master William Silence*, p. 48n.

132. *excellent at faults* Cf. G. 'fault' and *Shrew*,
Ind. i. 18–19:

> Saw'st thou not, boy, how Silver made it good
> At the hedge corner, in the coldest fault?

133–34. *there is...probation* i.e. there is no consistency in what follows that permits of investigation.
All edd. since Rowe print a colon after 'sequel,' and
explain 'suffers' as 'fails.' But F. is right and 'suffers'
has the common Shakespearian meaning of 'allows.'

136. *O shall end* i.e. the hangman's noose (Johnson);
cf. 'hang thee, brock' l. 107 above.

143. *simulation* i.e. representation.

147. *If this fall...revolve* F. prints this in italics
(to denote something read aloud), but all that follows
in roman—a clear indication that the compositor had
nothing but the sense to guide him in distinguishing
the letter from Malvolio's own words.

148. *are born* (Rowe) F. 'are become' Cf. 3. 4. 43
and 5. 1. 370.   149. *achieve* (F2) F. 'atcheeues'

151–52. *them;...be*, F. 'them,...be:'

154. *arguments of state* Cf. 'cons state without book'
2. 3. 154–55 and v. G. 'argument,' 'tang.'

157–58. *yellow stockings...cross-gartered* Both probably old-fashioned at the time. Cf. Overbury, *Characters* (1616) 'If he goe to Court, it is in yellow
stockings' (of A Country Gentleman) and Ford, *The*

Lover's Melancholy (1629) 'As rare an old youth as ever
walked cross-gartered.' v. G. 'cross-gartered.' Cf. note
3. 2. 73–4.

160–64. *Fortune's...champian* F. 'Fortunes fingers
Farewell, Shee that would alter feruices with thee, tht
fortunate vnhappy daylight and champian' If the compositor was following 'copy' here, this passage throws
an interesting light on the condition of the manuscript;
cf. note l. 147 above. For 'champian' v. G.

165. *politic* (F2) F. 'pollticke'

168. *every reason* Capell conj. 'very reason'

175. *Jove* Cf. p. 97 and notes l. 181 below; 3. 4.
78; 4. 2. 12.

176. *Here...postscript* With this to guide him the
F. compositor sets up 'Thou canst...prithee' in italics;
cf. note l. 147 above.

180. *dear, O my sweet* (Daniel) F. 'deero my sweet'
All edd. read 'dear my sweet'

181. *Jove, I thank thee!* v. p. 97.

182. S.D. F. 'Exit.'

184. *pension...from the Sophy* An allusion to Sir
Anthony Shirley, who in 1599–1600 paid a visit to the
Persian court where he was received with much honour
and given the rank of Mirza or prince by the Sophy
or Shah; cf. pp. 95–6 and note 3. 4. 280.

189. S.D. F. 'Enter Maria.'

199. *aqua-vitæ* F. 'Aqua vite'
with a midwife Mrs Gamp has an ancient pedigree.

210. S.D. F. 'Exeunt.'/'Finis Actus fecundus.'
v. pp. 104–105.

3. 1.

S.D. F. 'Enter Viola and Clowne.' Collier added
'playing on his Tabor'; and if a tabor, then also a pipe,
since the two were inseparable and both traditional
properties of the stage-clown (cf. the well-known picture

of Tarlton, Sh. Eng. ii. 259) In short it seems that the
musical Feste was intended to give a performance, perhaps accompanied with dance (? a jig), between the acts.

3. *by the church* 'Live by' is of course a quibble
(= *a.* get one's living by, *b.* reside near); and there is
too a quibble on 'tabor'—'tabern,' the latter being a
common by-form of 'tabor' (v. N.E.D. 'taborn') and
also meaning 'tavern'; cf. *Dr Faustus* (1604), viii. 21
'I can make thee drunk with ippocras at any tabern in
Europe.' The same quibble recurs at l. 10.

8. *king lies* (F2) F. 'Kings lyes' Cf. note 3. 1. 68.
lies by a beggar i.e. has a beggar woman as his mistress; cf. N.E.D. 'lie' 20.

9. *stands by* i.e. depends upon, draws revenue from;
cf. Boorde, *Introd. Knowl.* (1547), iv. 137 'Muche of
theyr lyuing standeth by stelyng and robbyng' (N.E.D.
'stand' 70. e).

12. *cheveril glove* Cf. *R. & J.* 2. 4. 87 'Here's a
wit of cheveril, that stretches from an inch narrow to
an ell broad.' While Feste seems to compliment
Cesario on his quick wit (quick at turning the *wrong*
side outward!) he also rallies him upon the fact that he
can make a little of it go a long way; cf. G. 'cheveril.'

14–15. *they that dally...wanton* Viola turns the
tables on Feste: they that trifle idly with words may
soon be landed in equivocal meanings.

16–21. *I would...disgraced them* v. p. 172.

20. *want-one* F. 'wanton' Edd. have missed the
pun; 'one' and 'on' were pronounced and often spelt
alike at this period. Feste means that to dally with his
sister's good name would rob her of it and thus make
her a wanton indeed.

20–30. *But indeed words...make you invisible*
v. pp. 97–100.

33. *She will keep...married* A hit at Cesario, whose
long interviews with Olivia were the subject of domestic
gossip; cf. 2. 3. 138–40 and next note.

34. *pilchards* F. 'Pilchers'

41. *your wisdom* 'a sarcastic perversion of "your worship"' (Furness). Feste implies that Cesario is 'the fool' and hints that the young man is better with his master than hanging about Olivia.

42. *pass upon me* i.e. make a fool of me (cf. 5. 1. 352). The emphatic word is 'me.'

43. *expenses* i.e. the price of a drink.

44–5. *Now Jove...beard!* Beggars receiving alms asked God's blessing upon the donor; Feste follows suit in his own fashion. For 'Jove' v. p. 97.

45. *commodity of hair* Cf. 'commodity of brown paper and old ginger' *Meas.* 4. 3. 5. Feste hints that the miserly tip deserves a miser's 'commodity' (v. G.) in recompense.

51. *use* i.e. interest. v. *M.V.* 1. 3. 66–93 on the subject of the breeding of money.

56. *Cressida was a beggar* Alluding to Henryson's *Testament of Cresseid* which describes Cressida stricken with leprosy and condemned by Cupid to beg from door to door. Cf. *Hen. V*, 2. 1. 80. All this is of course a reflection upon the size of Cesario's coins.

57. *come;* F. 'come,'

57–8. *who you...would* etc. Another hint of his suspicions of Cesario.

59. *the word is over-worn* The word 'element' (v. G.) is constantly used by Horace (Ben Jonson) in Dekker's *Satiromastix* (1601), and Feste's remark is generally supposed to refer to this ridicule. 'You see,' he seems to say, 'we can hardly dispense with "element" without using "welkin," which is still more fantastic' (Luce). S.D. F. 'exit.'

60–68. *This fellow is wise enough* etc. There is a personal flavour about this passage which suggests that it was expressly written to compliment the actor who played Feste, i.e. Robert Armin (cf. pp. 94–5).

64. *like the haggard* The Fool is the haggard (wild

hawk) among tame men; he swoops upon every occasion for a jest and yet he must be tactful and wary at the same time; v. G. 'check.'

68. *wise men, folly-fall'n* (Capell) F. 'wife mens folly falne' Cf. l. 8 above. Compositors are prone to add (or to omit) an *s* for plur. subs. or 3rd pers. sing. in verbs.

S.D. F. 'Enter Sir Toby and Andrew.'

71. *vous garde* F. 'vou guard'

72. *Et vous... serviteur* F. 'Et vouz oufie voftre feruiture' The phonetic spelling is appropriate to a prompt-book.

73. *I hope, sir*, etc. Sir Andrew at once gets out of his depth.

74. *encounter the house* etc. This mock-ceremony is contemptuous. Viola gives as good as she gets; v. 'list' G.—a most pretentious word.

78. *Taste* i.e. make trial of; cf. 'taste their valour' 3. 4. 246.

82. *gate and entrance* With a quibble upon 'gait.' Sir Toby says 'go' and 'enter,' Viola replies with 'gate' and 'entrance.' 'Gate' = the right to a run or pasturage for cattle on a piece of land (N.E.D. 'gate²' 8).

83. S.D. F. 'Enter Oliuia and Gentlewoman.'

87. *well!* i.e. excellent!

91. *all ready* (Malone) F. 'already' i.e. 'ready for future use in conversation' (Furness).

93. S.D. F. gives no 'exeunt.'

99–100. *'Twas never merry world, Since* etc. Cf. *Meas.* 3. 2. 6; *2 Hen. VI*, 4. 2. 9 A proverbial expression.

105. *blanks* Olivia speaks, I think, not of empty sheets of paper, but of the metal discs at the mint, known as blanks, which when stamped with the royal face became coin.   107. *pray you;* F. 'pray you.'

111. *music from the spheres* Cf. note on *M.V.* 5. 1. 61–6 for Montaigne's account of this notion.

113. *you did here* (Warburton) F. 'you did heare' —a common sp. in Qq.

114. *you; so* F. 'you. So'

116. *Under your...sit* i.e. I must be very ill thought of by you.　　118. *yours: what* F. 'yours. What'

119–21. *Have you not...can think?* The metaphor gives a graphic picture of the bear or bull tied to the stake and baited by 'tyrannous' (= cruel) hounds; cf. note 2. 5. 9.

121–26. F. arranges 'That tyrannous...receiuing/ Enough...boſome,/Hides...ſpeake./I pittie...loue./ No not...proofe' For ll. 121–24 we follow a suggestion of Luce's and for the rest a private suggestion of Prof. Moore Smith.

122. *receiving* i.e. understanding.

123. *A cypress...heart* 'Cypress' (v. G.) was the black lawn Olivia wore; cf. *M.N.D.* 2. 2. 112–13

　　Transparent Helena! Nature shows an art,
　　That through thy bosom makes me see thy heart.

126. *vulgar proof* i.e. everyday experience.

131. S.D. F. 'Clocke ſtrikes.'

136. *due west* Cesario is the sun of her life—about to set.

westward-ho! The cry of watermen on the Thames about to put off to Westminster. Viola is returning to her king.

139. *Stay:* F. prints this with l. 140, and it is possible that it should be read with it, the 'I' being omitted.

142. *I think the same of you* Olivia is convinced that Cesario is a nobleman in disguise.

146. *now I am your fool* i.e. now you are treating me like a fool. But with the implied meaning of 'now I am fooling you.'

149–66. Note the rhyming couplets here, quite in Shakespeare's early manner.

155–58. *Do not extort...better* 'Fetter' carries on the metaphor of 'extort,' i.e. extract by torture.

157. *fetter,* F. 'fetter:'　　166. S.D. F. 'Exeunt.'

3. 2.

S.D. F. 'Enter Sir Toby, Sir Andrew, and Fabian.'

8. *thee the* (F3) F. 'the'

14–15. *upon the oaths of judgement and reason* Three
conditions were required, according to the theologians,
of every lawful oath, viz. truth, judgement and reason
or justice (v. pp. 98–9). Fabian purposely omits the
condition of 'truth.' Hitherto unexplained.

16. *grand-jurymen* i.e. those whose function it is to
determine whether the evidence ('argument' v. G.) is
sufficiently 'legitimate' to warrant a regular trial.

24–5. *the double gilt...wash off* Referring to gilt
plate twice washed with gold.

27. *like an icicle on a Dutchman's beard* Supposed
to be a reference to the voyage (1596–97) of the
Dutchman, William Barentz, round the north of Nova
Zembla. His name appears on the 'new map' (v. note
ll. 77–8 below) and was doubtless the talk of London.
A book by Gerrit de Veer of Amsterdam, describing
the voyage, was entered in Stat. Reg. June 13, 1598;
the earliest edition extant being dated 1609.

31. *Brownist...politician* v. G.

43. *with the license of ink* i.e. with the freedom that
pen and ink allows.

44. *'thou'st' him some thrice* Many think this refers
to the outburst of Sir Ed. Coke at the trial of Sir Walter
Raleigh: 'All that he did was by thy instigation, thou
viper; for I thou thee thou traitor.' If so it must be
a later insertion, since the trial took place in Nov.1603,
almost two years after the Middle Temple performance.
But surely so far from suggesting anything terrible, Sir
Toby is ironically recommending the mildest form of
abuse—if you venture *so far*, he implies, it will not be
amiss.

amiss; F. 'amiſſe,'

46. *the bed of Ware* v. G. 'Ware.'

47–8. *gall enough in thy ink* A quibble. Sh. Eng. ii. 140 quotes from a recipe for home-made ink of 1599: '2 oz of gum, 2 oz of copperas, and 4 oz of galls, costing 8d.'

48. *a goose-pen* Quill pens were made of goose-feathers, and 'goose' was a symbol of cowardice.

51. *at thy cubicle* F. 'at the Cubiculo' Hanmer read 'thy' for 'the'—a common misprint in Qq. (cf. *Lear*, 2. 4. 174; *R. & J.* 4. 1. 92; *T. & C.* 1. 3. 61), a small-sized *y* being very similar to the open English *e*. The F. 'Cubiculo' has hitherto been interpreted as 'either a humorous use of Latin, from the phrase "in cubiculo," or an affected use of It. "cubiculo"' (N.E.D.), but it is far more probably a simple misprint of the common *o* : *e* type (v. T.I. p. xlii) for 'cubicule,' a normal 16th cent. sp. of 'cubicle.' The term would no doubt make a special appeal to Inns of Court students.

S.D. F. 'Exit Sir Andrew.'

52. *manakin* i.e. puppet, v. G. Fabian refers not to the size of Aguecheek (as has hitherto been supposed) but to the skill with which Sir Toby manipulates him.

58–9. *oxen...together* Cf. note 2. 5. 64–5.

60. *find...blood in his liver* According to the old physiology the liver and not the heart was the source of the blood; cf. Sh. Eng. i. 426.

61. *anatomy* i.e. dissected corpse, v. G.

63. S.D. F. 'Enter Maria.'

64. *the youngest wren of nine* (Theobald) F. 'the youngeſt Wrenne of mine' Explained as the last hatched, and therefore the tiniest, of a brood of nine. It is clear that Shakespeare had a very diminutive boy in his company at this time; cf. notes 1. 5. 206; 2. 3. 183, 185; and *2 Hen. IV*, 1. 2. 14 'I do here walk before thee like a sow that hath overwhelmed all her litter but one.' Prov. 'least of nine' = least of all; v. *T.L.S.* corr. 15/6/46 [1949].

68. *renegado* (Rowe) F. 'Renegatho'

70. *passages* v. G.

73–4. *a pedant that keeps a school i'th' church*
Churches were occasionally used for school purposes
down to the beginning of the 19th cent. but the practice
was probably becoming obsolete in Shakespeare's day,
and such 'a pedant' would be regarded as an oddity;
cf. note 2. 5. 157–58.

77–8. *the new map...Indies* Note that 'augmentation' = 'increase in size,' and not 'addition' as some
have supposed. The 'Indies,' i.e. America, are to be
found in all maps of the world at this period, but in
'the new map,' the first English map drawn on the
principles of projection, and prepared in 1600 by Ed.
Wright, Ric. Hakluyt, and John Davis, the Indies take
a much larger place than in any before; v. Sh. Eng.
i. 174, which gives a reproduction of this map. The
'lines' Maria speaks of are the rhumb-lines which form
a very striking feature of the map—radiating out from
their centres exactly like wrinkles about eyes. Cf. *Hak.
Soc. Pub.* lix. 'Voyages of John Davis,' p. lxxxv.

82. S.D. F. 'Exeunt omnes.'

3. 3.

S.D. F. 'Enter Sebaſtian and Anthonio.'

5. *More...steel* F. encloses these words in brackets.
forth; F. 'forth,'

8. *travel* F. 'rrauell'

11. *unhospitable: my* F. 'vnhoſpitable. My'

15. *and ever thanks; and oft* (Theobald) F. 'and
euer oft' Many conjectures but the sense is plain, and
it seems likely that the compositor, confused by the
thrice repeated 'thanks' and 'and,' omitted the last
example of each.

16. *uncurrent pay* i.e. counterfeit or debased coin.

19. *relics* F. 'reliques' v. G.

21. *night:* F. 'night'

26. *the count his galleys* The old genitive form often

found in 16th and early 17th centuries. v. Abbott, *Shak. Grammar*, § 217.

35. *did: only* F. 'did. Onely'

36. *lapséd* v. G.

39. *In the south suburbs, at the Elephant* Shakespeare is as usual thinking of London, and probably refers to the inn now world-famous as the Elephant and Castle, which Aldis Wright traced back to the middle of the 17th century.

40. *diet* v. G.

42. *town;* F. 'Towne,'

45–6. *your store...markets* i.e. I fancy your own money will hardly run to more than bare necessities.

50. S.D. F. 'Exeunt.'

3. 4.

S.D. F. 'Enter Oliuia and Maria.'

4. *I speak too loud* F. prints this with l. 5.

14. S.D. F. 'Enter Maluolio.'

15. *merry* (F2) F. 'metry'

18–19. *Smil'st...occasion.* F. prints this as one line.

21. *blood,* F. 'blood:'

23. *Please...all* Halliwell saw here an allusion to 'A prettie newe Ballad, intytuled: The Crowe sits vpon the wall, Please one and please all' (ent. Stat. Reg. Jan. 18, 1592). The jest is that Malvolio should describe this as 'the very true sonnet.'

24–5. *Why, how dost thou* etc. F. heads this *Mal.* F2 assigned the speech to Olivia, and all edd. have since followed suit. The 'man' is perhaps more appropriate to Maria's mouth than Olivia's, but Maria nowhere else 'thou's' Malvolio.

28–9. *the sweet Roman hand* A reference to the Roman or Italian style of handwriting, which was at this period beginning to replace the English or secretary hand. It was the fashion in court circles; cf. *Ham.* 5. 2. 33–6.

30. *go to bed* i.e. go and lie down (cf. N.E.D. 'bed'
6.c). Olivia suggests that Malvolio is indisposed.

36. *At your request!* i.e. What! am I to answer
questions from such as you?

52. *Thy yellow stockings* 'In her amazement she
repeats his words; but she means *my*' (Verity). Olivia
has no idea that Malvolio is quoting, as is clear from
l. 57 'Am I made?' Part of the humour of this dialogue
(lost on a modern audience) consists in Malvolio
'thou-ing' his mistress so freely; cf. 3. 2. 44.

58. *let* (F2) F. 'ler'

59. S.D. F. 'Enter Seruant.'

68. *come near me* v. G.   73. *tang* (F2) F. 'langer'

77. *in the habit of some sir of note* Is this intended
to suggest that the yellow stockings and cross-gartering
had actually been made notorious by some foolish
gentleman at Elizabeth's court? One would like to
know how, for instance, Sir Posthumus Hoby dressed
(v. p. 95).

78. *it is Jove's doing* Luce suggests a reference to
Ps. cxviii. 23 'This is the Lord's doing; it is marvellous
in our eyes.' For 'Jove' cf. p. 97.

80. *fellow* 'originally meant "companion"...and
Malvolio takes it in the favourable sense' (Johnson).

82. *no dram of a scruple* A quibble, v. G. 'scruple.'

87. S.D. F. 'Enter Toby, Fabian, and Maria.'

88. *in the name of sanctity* Sir Toby invokes
'sanctity' before encountering the possessed Malvolio;
cf. *Ham.* 1. 4. 39 'Angels and ministers of grace defend us!' and note l. 122 below.

89. *in little* (v. G. 'little') i.e. 'contracted into a
small compass; the devils being supposed...to have the
power of altering their dimensions' (Aldis Wright).
Cf. *A.Y.L.* 3. 2. 139-40

> The quintessence of every sprite
> Heaven would in little show.

For 'Legion' cf. *Mark* v. 9.

92. *How is't with you, man?* F. prints this as part of Fabian's speech. I follow an anon. conj. (apud Clark and Wright) and assign it to Sir Toby. With its 'man' in place of the more respectful 'sir,' it certainly belongs to a different speaker from the first query. Once again (cf. note 2. 5. 34) it seems likely that confusion has arisen from the similarity between the *Tob.* and *Fab.* prefixes. Probably the compositor first duplicated the *Fab.* and then deleted the second prefix as superfluous. The two questions are printed in different lines in F.

95. *hollow* Hollow sounds and rumbling noises were commonly associated with evil spirits; cf. Lavater, *Of Ghostes and Spirites* (ed. J. Dover Wilson and M. Yardley), Introd. pp. xxv–xxvi. Malvolio doubtless had a deep voice.

100. *let me alone* i.e. I'll tackle him!

105. *bewitched* Not the same condition as 'possessed,' and needing different treatment.

106. *the wise woman* Cf. *M.W.W.* 4. 2. 163–73. Douce quotes Heywood, *Wise Woman of Hogsden*, 'You have heard of Mother Nottingham, who for her time was prettily well skilled in casting of Waters; and after her, Mother Bombie.'

114–15. *the fiend is rough* v. G. 'rough,' and cf. *Err.* 4. 2. 35 'A fiend, a fury, pitiless and rough.'

119. *Ay, Biddy, come with me.* Probably 'a scrap of some old song' (Ritson). Biddy = a child's name for 'chicken'; cf. the mod. 'chickabiddy.' 'Bawcock' and 'chuck' also suggest poultry.

120. *play at cherry-pit with* i.e. be on friendly terms with. Cf. G. 'cherry-pit'—a child's game. Sir Toby's cue is to treat Malvolio like a little child 'gently, gently.' The Devil, of course, had a 'cherry-pit' game of his own, with souls for cherry-stones.

121. *foul collier* The Devil was so called because (i) of his blackness, (ii) of his connexion with the Pit, and (iii) of his subterranean rumblings and working;

cf. *Ham.* 1. 5. 162–63 and Lavater, *Of Ghostes and
Spirites*, pp. xxv–xxvi.

122. *Get him to say his prayers* Cf. Lavater, *op. cit.*
p. 193 'It behoueth them that are vexed with spirites,
to pray especially, to giue themselues to fasting, so-
brietie, watching, and vpright and godly liuing.'

126. *godliness* Cf. 'godly liuing' referred to in
previous note.

128. *I am not of your element* i.e. I belong to a
different world. v. G. 'element.'

129. S.D. F. 'Exit.'

133. *genius* i.e. soul.

135–36. *take air and taint* i.e. become known and
therefore spoilt. A medical metaphor, fresh air being
considered very dangerous at this period. Cf. *Jul. Caes.*
2. 1. 261–67, and Boorde, *Dietary of Helth*, 1542,
'In the night let the windows of your house, specially
of your chamber, be closed.'

139–40. *in a dark room and bound* The customary
treatment for madmen.

143–44. *bring the device to the bar* Probably a reference to some custom at the Inns of Court, the 'bar'
being the barrier dividing the students from the benchers
in hall.

145. S.D. F. 'Enter Sir Andrew.'

146. *for a May morning* i.e. for a May-game or
pageant (cf. Chambers, *Med. Stage*, ch. viii). No
sooner does mad Malvolio go off than angry Aguecheek
comes on.

149. *saucy* v. G. A quibble, referring to 'vinegar
and pepper.'

150. *him* = Cesario.

157–58. *keeps...the law* Cf. l. 168 below 'keep
o'th' windy side of the law.' Fabian deliberately uses
expressions which suggest that Sir Andrew narrowly
escapes infringing the criminal code, while all the time
the 'law' he refers to is nothing more serious than the

law of the duello—a jest which would appeal to the
lawyers of the Middle Temple. Again, Sir Andrew's
challenge is so framed that while appearing fierce and
swaggering it avoids all phrases which might really
touch his opponent's honour, according to the carefully
worked out theory of the challenge in Segar's *Booke of
Honor and Armes* (1590) and similar treatises on the
duello. In other words, Sir Andrew wished to gain a
reputation as a duellist without incurring too much risk.
Thus, though he calls Cesario 'a scurvy fellow,' he is
careful to add that he 'will give him no reason for't.'
Again, he does not name him rogue and villain directly
but only says that 'if it be thy chance to kill me, thou
kill'st me like a rogue and a villain.' Lastly, though he
gives him 'the lie in his throat,' it is a lie of so remotely
'conditional' a character as to be entirely ineffective
according to the 'law' (cf. Touchstone on the 'degrees
of the Lie' *A.Y.L.* 5. 4. 67–100). Dr A. W. Pollard
(privately) suggests that Fabian may after all be merely
referring to the common law against provoking a breach
of the peace and quotes *R. & J.* 1. 1. 46–56.

162–63. *sense-less* F. 'fence-lesse'

168. *o'th' windy side of the law* Cf. note ll. 157–58
above, and G. 'windy side.'

175. *If this letter* etc. F. gives this a fresh speech-
heading *To.*

177. *You may* (F2) F. 'Yon may'

180–81. *scout...bum-baily* v. G. Bum-bailies were
petty officers who lay in wait to arrest for debt—a
reference which no doubt had point for young law-
students. Cf. too note l. 318 below.

183. *for it* (F2) F. 'for t' The 'i' has dropped
from the forme at the beginning of a line.

187. S.D. F. 'Exit.'

191. *no less;* F. 'no lesse.'

195. *valour;* F. 'valor,'

199. *kill...like cockatrices* Tilley (p. 358) quotes

Pettie's *Petite Pallace* 'the cocatrice by sight only slayeth.' v. G. 'cockatrice.'

S.D. F. 'Enter Oliuia and Viola.'

205. *unchary out* (Theobald) F. 'vnchary on't' v. G. 'lay out.' 'Laid on't' would mean 'wagered or staked on it.' As Aldis Wright notes 'The change is at once justified and rendered necessary by the meaning of "unchary"' (= unchary, thriftlessly).

210. *Goes...grief* (Rowe) F. 'Goes...greefes'

211. *jewel...picture* Cf. the 'lady walled about with diamonds' *L.L.L.* 5. 2. 4 and Sh. Eng. ii. 114–15.

220. S.D. F. gives no 'exit' for Olivia.

F. 'Enter Toby and Fabian.'

223. *thee to't* F. 'the too't'

225–26. *bloody as the hunter* i.e. bloodthirsty as the sleuth-hound.

226–27. *dismount thy tuck* i.e. draw thy sword. No other recorded instance of 'dismount' (v. G.) in this sense; but taken in connexion with Osric's affected use of 'carriages' for sword-hangers (*Ham.* 5. 2. 158–67) it is clearly intended as a parody of the ludicrous terms employed by contemporary duellists; cf. note ll. 157–58 above.

238. *on carpet consideration* i.e. 'on some peaceable occasion, when knights receive their dignity kneeling not on the ground as in war, but on a carpet...the origin of the contemptuous term "a carpet knight"' (Johnson). Cf. *Ado*, 5. 2. 32 'these quondam carpet-mongers.'   239. *brawl* (F3) F. 'brall'

248. *competent* F. 'computent' A legal term (for the Middle Temple). Sir Toby is of course referring to the law of the duello; cf. note ll. 157–58 above.

250. *undertake that with me* etc. i.e. fight a duel with me.

252. *meddle* v. G.

259. S.D. F. 'Exit Toby.'

273. *sir priest* 'Sir' (= dominus) was used to desig-

nate a Bachelor of Arts and is commonly found as a
title for clergymen at this period. Cf. Sir Topas (below,
4. 2.) and in *M.W.W.* Sir Hugh Evans.

274. S.D. F. 'Exeunt.'/'Enter Toby and Andrew.'
As the stage is left bare here with the 'exeunt' of Fabian
and Viola, the entry of Sir Toby and Sir Andrew should
rightly begin a new 'scene' (cf. *Two Gent.* pp. 77–8),
though the omission in F. is of no theatrical significance.
On the other hand, there is no doubt that Shakespeare intended his audience to imagine a change of place here; he
leads up to it in 'attends thee at the orchard-end' (l. 226
above), and 'Will you walk towards him?' (ll. 269–70),
while it would be absurd for Antonio and the officers
to be wandering about Olivia's garden; indeed we are
definitely told that Antonio was arrested 'in the streets'
(5. 1. 63). Yet no editor except Dyce has had the pluck
to mark a change of scene.

276. *firago* i.e. virago. Sir Toby knows that the
'scholarly' Sir Andrew will not recognise the word,
and gives it a pronunciation suggesting 'fire-drake'
(= fire-eater), while hinting (to the audience) his belief
that Cesario is a drake that will not fight by using a word
appropriate to a woman.

277–79. *with such...pays you* i.e. with such a
deadly pass that it could not be escaped, and on the
return hit he runs you through.

279. *hit* (Rowe) F. 'hits'

280. *fencer to the Sophy* The Sophy of Persia was
much in men's minds in 1600–1; cf. pp. 95–6 and
note 2. 5. 184.

283. *yonder* Some have supposed from this that
Fabian and Viola are visible in the distance; but F.
gives them an entry at l. 290. All Sir Toby does is to
point over the wall, i.e. (on the Elizabethan stage) at
the door through which he and Sir Andrew have just
come.   287. *Capilet* v. G.

290. S.D. F. 'Enter Fabian and Viola.'

291. *take up* v. G.

305. *by the duello* i.e. by the law of the duel; cf. note ll. 157–58 above.

309. S.D. F. 'Enter Antonio.' The name is spelt 'Anthonio,' as usual in Shakespeare, for the rest of the play.

316. *undertaker* i.e. one who takes up a challenge for another. But the word also meant a 'contractor,' and I think that Sir Toby may be quibbling upon this meaning. A contractor who had bought up his debts for the purpose of making him pay them would be the worst enemy he could meet. Cf. note l. 318 below.

S.D. F. 'Enter Officers.'

318. *I'll be with you anon* Fabian's warning, this abrupt speech, and Sir Toby's complete silence until after the departure of the officers make it clear, I think, that the knight, heavily in debt, found it best to avoid contact with the law. The point would not be lost upon the students of the Middle Temple.

323. *He will...reins well* Aguecheek refers to his horse Capilet: cf. ll. 286–7 [1949]. The 'you' is an ethic dative.

332. *do, now* (Dyce and Staunton) F. 'do: now'

348. *unsound* In the theological sense; Viola's conduct is shaking Antonio's faith (in friendship); cf. Hooker, *Ecc. Pol.* v. lii. § 4 'So Eutychus, of sound beliefe...became vnsound by denying the difference.'

353. *lying vainness, babbling drunkenness,* (Rowe) F. 'lying, vainneſſe, babling drunkenneſſe'

356–57. *Let me...see here* F. prints as one line. We follow S. Walker, who however also tampers with the text. The broken half-line perhaps denotes excision.

366. *unkind:* F. 'vnkinde' v. G.

368. *trunks o'erflourished* A quibbling reference to the great chests, for linen etc., which were a feature of the Elizabethan household and were often covered with painting or carving.

371. S.D. F. 'Exit.'

373. *so do not I?* F. 'ſo do not I:'—where the colon, as often, probably stands for a query. To read 'so do not I' as a statement of fact, which all edd. do, is to spoil the effect. The query marks Viola's dawn of hope, inspired by Antonio's passion.

374. *O prove true* F. 'Oh proue ttue'

377–78. *whisper...sage saws* Sir Toby mocks at Viola's couplets, and perhaps Shakespeare (in revising) is himself mocking at verse which he originally took seriously. Cf. note 5. 1. 176 and Jaques's jibe at 'blank verse' *A.Y.L.* 4. 1. 29.

379–80. *I my brother...glass* i.e. I am the living image of my brother.

384. S.D. F. gives no 'exit.'

394. S.D. F. gives no 'exit.'

396. S.D. F. 'Exit.'

4. 1.

S.D. F. 'Enter Sebaſtian and Clowne.'

7. *speak with her,* F. 'ſpeake with her:'

9–10. *I prithee, vent...not me* F. prints as prose.

11–12. *Vent...some great man* Possibly a topical allusion. Some doubt whether Feste ridicules 'vent' as an affected expression; but if not, why does he fear that 'the world will prove a cockney' (= an affected fop)?

13–14. *lubber...cockney* v. G. Both terms might be applied to a schoolboy; the world was still young.

14. *ungird thy strangeness* i.e. put off this pretence of not knowing me.

17–19. *I prithee...payment* F. prints as prose.

17. *foolish Greek* v. G. 'Greek.' The word hardly implies 'pandar' as Warburton and others interpret.

22. *report—after...purchase.* F. 'report, after... purchaſe.' The F. comma points the jest. A legal quibble again for the benefit of the Middle Temple. 'Report' = the official record of a decision in a case,

i.e. the end of a case; and 'after fourteen years' purchase' = at a high price (the current price of land at this period being 12 years' purchase)—probably Feste also hints that the tip must be repeated at least fourteen times to be effective.

S.D.　F. 'Enter Andrew, Toby, and Fabian.'

23–4. *there's for you* To encounter 'a most devout coward' and take him at a disadvantage is the opportunity of Sir Andrew's life.

30.　S.D.　F. gives no 'exit.'

31. *Come on, sir! hold!* i.e. Come along! stop that! (as Sebastian struggles to free himself).

33–4. *action of battery* Yet another legal jest. Sir Andrew having struck the first blow has, of course, no right of action at all.

38–9. *Come, my young soldier...fleshed* Badham, Furness and Luce agree in supposing these words addressed to Sir Andrew; they are certainly right. He has just shown himself a 'young soldier' indeed, and is the only one present with a naked weapon.

39. *you are well fleshed* In reference to the expression 'flesh one's virgin sword' (of a young knight in his first battle). Sir Toby speaks ironically as Sir Andrew picks himself up from the ground, leaving his 'iron' sprawling some yards off, where it fell when Sebastian knocked him down. Note also that Sir Toby's attention being transferred to Sir Andrew, Sebastian gets his chance of escape.

44.　S.D.　F. 'Enter Oliuia.'

51.　S.D.　F. gives no 'exeunt.'

59. *He started...heart* Most edd. agree that Olivia is quibbling upon 'hart'; cf. 1. 1. 16–17.

60. *What relish is in this?* i.e. what is the meaning of all this? With Shakespeare 'relish' often means 'hint'; cf. *Ham.* 3. 3. 92 'no relish of salvation in't,' 2 *Hen. IV*, 1. 2. 111 'some smack of age...some relish of the saltness of time.'

61–3. *Or I am mad* etc. 'This speech recalls that of Antipholus of Syracuse, under similar circumstances of bewilderment, *Err.* 2. 2. 212–13' (Staunton).

62. *fancy* i.e. love.

65. S.D. F. 'Exeunt.'

4. 2.

S.D. F. 'Enter Maria and Clowne.'

2. *Sir Topas* Shakespeare may of course have borrowed this name from Chaucer's *Rime of Sir Thopas*, but Furness ingeniously suggests that he perhaps owed it to Scot's *Discoverie of Witchcraft*, a book well-known to him, where he would find that 'a topase healeth the lunaticke person of his passion of lunacie' (ch. vi. p. 294, ed. 1584). For 'sir' v. note 3. 4. 273.

3. S.D. F. gives no 'exit.'

4. *dissemble myself* i.e. disguise myself.

8. *student* F. 'Studient'—probably a Shakespearian spelling; cf. *Ham.* 1. 2. 177, *M.W.W.* 3. 1. 37.

10. *competitors* v. G.

11. S.D. F. 'Enter Toby' Maria has no 'exit' at l. 3 and no entry here; she is not theatrically 'off' at all.

12. *Jove bless thee, Master Parson!* v. p. 97.

14. *the old hermit* The old hermit of Prague and the niece of King Gorboduc (v. G.) belong to the same Rabelaisian corner of Feste's brain as Quinapalus and Pigrogromitus.

15. *Gorboduc* F. 'Gorbodacke'

22. S.D. F. 'Maluolio within.'

27. *hyperbolical* i.e. vehement. Sir Topas speaks learnedly and employs a term of rhetoric.

36. *that house is dark* A 'dark house' was the technical term for a place of confinement for madmen; cf. *All's Well*, 2. 3. 296, *A.Y.L.* 3. 2. 391.

39. *clerestories* (Blakeway) F. 'cleere stores' The jest is that the dark hole into which Malvolio had been

thrown bound being technically a 'house' (cf. previous note) Feste describes it as if it were a large mansion or hall in the Elizabethan style with the latest devices for letting in the maximum of daylight. v. G. 'clerestory.'

53. *haply* (Capell) F. 'happily' The two forms were interchangeable.

64. *for all waters* i.e. ready for anything. The origin of the phrase has not been traced.

68–73. *I would we were rid...chamber* It seems clear that these words were spoken to Maria alone, and the last sentence suggests that the couple are already married (cf. 5. 1. 364 note). Feste no doubt, after removing his disguise, has turned back, as Sir Toby bids, to the closet.

72. *to the upshot* (Rowe) F. 'the vppeſhot' v. G. 'upshot'—a term of archery.

73. S.D. F. 'Exit.'

74. *Hey Robin, jolly Robin* etc. Feste sings snatches from the first two stanzas of a popular ballad, which are thus given in Percy's *Reliques*, ii. 4:

> A Robyn, Jolly Robyn,
> Tell me how thy leman doeth,
> And thou shalt knowe of myn.
>
> 'My Lady is unkynde, perde,'
> Alack! why is she so?
> 'She loveth another better than me;
> And yet she will say no.'

87. *besides your five wits* Cf. *Ado*, 5. 1. 127.

92. *propertied me* i.e. stowed me away like a theatrical property. This follows a suggestion of Collier's endorsed by Furness and Luce. Others explain 'made a tool of me' and quote *John*, 5. 2. 78. Probably both meanings are intended. For a third possibility v. G. 'property.'

101. *God buy you* v. G.

117–18. *I'll ne'er believe...brains* Quibbling on

the proverbial expression, 'You'll not believe he's bald
till you see his brains' (Tilley, 29).

121–30. *I am gone, sir*, etc. This song enables
Feste 'to withdraw gradually and with mock ceremony
and to disappear on the final insult "devil"' (Richmond
Noble, *Shakespeare's Use of Song*, p. 85).

123. *the old Vice* i.e. the Fool of the old interludes,
clad (like Feste) in the long coat of the domestic fool
(cf. note 2. 3. 28–30 and v. Chambers, *Med. Stage*,
ii. 204–5). He also generally carried—like the fool once
more—a sword or dagger of lath, and Feste's reference
to this (l. 125) suggests that he too wore such a dagger
and made play with it as he sang this song. The old
Vice belaboured the Devil with his sham sword and
often attempted to cut his talons with it. It is of course
obvious that in Feste's little interlude Malvolio, the
possessed, plays the devil. Cf. *Hen. V*, 4. 4. 75–7
'ten times more valour than this roaring devil i'th'old
play, that every one may pare his nails with a wooden
dagger.'

130. *goodman* (Rowe) F. 'good man'
S.D. F. 'Exit.'

4. 3.

S.D. F. 'Enter Sebaſtian.'
18. *Take and give...dispatch* Aldis Wright quotes
Wint. 3. 2. 164–65 and *Macb.* 1. 3. 60 'who neither
beg nor fear/Your favours nor your hate,' and adds
'In the present passage "take" goes with "affairs" and
"give back" with "their dispatch." The phrase is thus
equivalent to "take a business in hand and discharge it."'
21. S.D. F. 'Enter Oliuia, and Prieſt.'
24. *chantry* v. G. Olivia's chantry is as much in
character as her Lucrece seal. It is a subtle touch that
she should plight her troth there, after vowing to mourn
for seven years.

27. *jealous* F. 'iealious'

29. *Whiles* = until.

35. *fairly note* i.e. regard with favour.

S.D. F. 'Exeunt.'/'Finis Actus Quartus'—cf. pp. 104–105.

5. 1.

S.D. F. 'Enter Clowne and Fabian.'

2. *Master Fabian* F. 'M. Fabian'

6–7. *give a dog...dog again* B. Nicholson quotes from Manningham's *Diary* (March 26, 1603) 'Mr Francis Curle told me howe one Dr Bullein, the Queenes kinsman, had a dog which he doted on, soe much that the Queene vnderstanding of it requested he would graunt hir one desyre, and he should haue what soeuer he would aske. Shee demaunded his dogge; he gaue it, and "Nowe Madame" quoth he, "you promised to giue me my desyre." "I will," quoth she. "Then I pray you giue me my dog againe."'

7. S.D. F. 'Enter Duke, Viola, Curio, and Lords.' Most mod. edd. give Curio an entry, but he has nothing to say and his presence here may be a relic of some earlier stage of the text; cf. p. 104.

18. *me; now* F. 'me, now'

20–23. *so that, conclusions...my foes* No one seems yet to have fathomed this simple jest, the basis of which is that a kiss is made by four lips (contraries or negatives) brought together by two ardent mouths (affirmatives). If conclusions are like this, says Feste, then the conclusion that I am not an ass is only half the value of the conclusion that I am one. For the construction of 'conclusions to be as kisses,' i.e. the infinitive absolute, cf. Abbott, *Shak. Gram.* § 356.

32. *your grace* A triple quibble = (*a*) 'your Grace,' i.e. he is speaking to the Duke; (*b*) 'your virtue,' i.e. yield for this once to temptation; (*c*) 'your generous impulse,' i.e. let your generosity carry your hand to your pocket.

36. *Primo, secundo, tertio* A schoolboy game; cf.
Scot, *Discoverie of Witchcraft* (XI. X. I 59) 'Lotterie...
is a childish and ridiculous toie, and like vnto children's
plaie at Primus secundus, or the game called The
Philosophers table.'

38. *the bells of St Bennet* 'The allusion is, perhaps,
to some old rhyme which has been lost; or it may be
to the real bells of St Bennet Hithe, Paul's Wharf, just
opposite the Globe Theatre' (Aldis Wright).

40–1. *at this throw* A quibble = (*a*) at this throw
of the dice—implying that Feste is a cheat (cf. 'foolish
Greek' 4. I. 17), and (*b*) at this time; v. G. 'throw.'

48. S.D. F. 'Exit.'/'Enter Anthonio and Officers.'

53–8. *A baubling vessel...honour on him* The
description reminds one of the last fight of the Revenge
in 1591, which Shakespeare may have had in mind.
v. G. 'baubling.'

60. *Candy* i.e. Candia or Crete. The form still
persists in names like 'candytuft.'

63. *desperate of shame and state* i.e. with no regard
for personal shame (for his crimes) or for civil order; cf.
R. II, 4. I. 225 'Against the state and profit of this land.'

65. *drew* i.e. drew his sword.

67. *I know not...distraction* i.e. I cannot explain
it unless some madness seized him.

68. *salt-water thief* Cf. *M. of V.* I. 3. 23 'water-
thieves—I mean pirates.'

70. *dear* i.e. grievous, v. G.

71. *Orsino,* F. 'Orsino:'   78. *wrack* v. G.

93. *for three months before* Daniel writes (*Time-
Analysis,* p. 176) 'Viola and Sebastian both suffered
the same shipwreck, and when they arrive in Illyria it
is evident that but a very few days can have elapsed
since their escape.' It is only so evident to the careful
reader; the spectator would notice nothing wrong.

94. *interim* F. 'intrim' The same sp. found in
Son. 56. 9.

95. S.D. F. 'Enter Oliuia and attendants.'

98. *Three months . . . hath tended* Cf. note l. 93 above. 'This is in absolute contradiction to Valentine's speech on the second day of the action (1. 4. 3), where he says that the Duke "hath known you [Viola] but three days"' (Daniel, *op. cit.*). No audience would perceive the contradiction. Shakespeare wishes to remind us that Viola's service with Orsino and Sebastian's friendship with Antonio were of the same duration, and 'three months' was as good a period as any other for the purpose.

105. *Good my lord,—* 'Probably accompanied by a gesture to the Duke to keep silent and let Cesario speak' (Furness).

108. *fat and fulsome* i.e. gross and distasteful.

113. *hath* (Capell) F. 'haue'

117. *the Egyptian thief* i.e. Thyamis in the story of *Theagenes and Chariclea* from the *Ethiopica* of Heliodorus, englished by T. Underdowne in 1569, a popular book running into several editions. Thyamis, a bandit-chief, beset by his enemies and despairing of life, intends to kill Chariclea whom he loves, though as a matter of fact in the darkness of his cave he slays another by mistake. Shakespeare's words read like an echo of Heliodorus's comment on the incident: 'If the barbarous people be once in despair of their own safety, they have a custom to kill all those by whom they set much, and whose company they desire after death.'

122. *favour,* F. 'fauour:' 123. *still;* F. 'ſtill.' Probably a case of transposed pointing.

130. *a raven's heart within a dove* Cf. 'O tiger's heart wrapt in a woman's hide!' (3 *Hen. VI*, 1. 4. 137).

138. *detested* i.e. renounced with an oath. Cesario has just called heaven to witness that he loves Orsino and not Olivia.

146. *strangle thy propriety* i.e. 'deny your identity' (Halliwell)

149. S.D. F. 'Enter Prieſt.'

153. *ripe*— F. 'ripe:'

164. *When time...case* i.e. when your hair begins to turn grey; v. G. 'grizzle,' 'case.' Orsino calls Cesario a fox-cub.

166. *trip...overthrow* A metaphor from wrestling with a quibble on 'trap.' v. G. 'trip.' Cf. *Ps.* lvii. 6 'They have prepared a net for my steps...they have digged a pit before me, into the midst whereof they are fallen themselves.'

170. S.D. F. 'Enter Sir Andrew.' Rowe read 'Enter Sir Andrew Aguecheek with his head broke.' Mr Richmond Noble draws my attention (privately) to a point which I do not think has hitherto been noticed, viz. that this *second* affray between Sebastian and the knight is not led up to in any way and is spoken of in the dialogue as if it were a first encounter. Apart from this, after his experience of Sebastian's unexpected vigour at 4. 1. 23–44, Sir Andrew is most unlikely to have returned to the charge, while Sir Toby himself would hardly have risked the further displeasure of Olivia after her stern words at 4. 1. 45–51. In a word, Shakespeare himself has not troubled to relate the two incidents or noticed that they needed relating—a pretty sure indication of revision or adaptation. The point is of merely historical interest: that dramatically it has no importance is proved by the fact that it has passed unobserved until 1929.

176. *I had rather than forty pound* Cf. note 2. 3. 22. Aldis Wright notes that 'Sir Andrew was willing to spend twenty times as much upon his safety as upon his accomplishments.'

I were at home Cf. Rosalind's famous 'I would I were at home' (*A.Y.L.* 4. 3. 160). If this made as big a hit at the Globe as it has often done on the modern stage, it would I think be like Shakespeare to fling a jest at it in his next comedy, as (for instance) he laughs

at *Romeo and Juliet* in the Pyramus and Thisbe play
of *M.N.D.*; cf. note 3. 4. 377–78.

179–80. *incardinate* F. 'incardinatc'

182. *'Od's lifelings* Cf. *M.W.W.* 3. 4. 57 'Od's
heartlings.' Slender and Sir Andrew even swear alike.
Cf. note 1. 3. 20.

189. *set nothing by* i.e. think nothing of.

S.D. F. 'Enter Toby and Clowne'—at l. 187.

198. *set* i.e. closed (gone out like stars in the morning), cf. *Temp.* 3. 2. 10 'thy eyes are almost set in thy
head.'

199–200. *a passy-measures pavin* (Clark and Wright)
F. 'a paſſy meaſures panyn.' Steevens reads 'a passy-
measure pavin.' Naylor (*Shakespeare and Music*, 1896,
p. 114) first explained the point of the expression. The
pavin or pavane was a slow stately dance, a variety of
it being the Passamezzo or (in the English form) 'passy-
measures.' Naylor points out that the 'strains' of this
dance consist of eight bars each, and Sir Toby in his
half-sober condition associates Feste's remark about the
surgeon's eyes with the dance; both were 'set at eight.'
To Naylor's explanation one further point may be
added: Sir Toby's wounds smart, the doctor is *slow* in
coming, and the pavin was a slow dance, the kind of
dance Sir Toby detested; what he liked were lively
dances such as the galliard and the coranto; cf. 1. 3.
122–42.

205. *Will you help? an ass-head* (Malone) F. 'Will
you helpe an Aſſe-head'

206. *a thin-faced knave* Another link between Sir
Andrew and Slender in *M.W.W.* who had 'a little
wee face.' Cf. note 1. 3. 20.

207. S.D. F. 'Enter Sebaſtian.' No 'exeunt' is
given for Clown, etc.

210. S.D. We take this from Theobald.

211. *You throw...that* Pope rid the line of its
extra foot by reading 'on me, by which,' S. Walker

by printing 'You throw' as a separate line. Possibly the 'and' has been caught from the previous line; omit it and all seems well.

216. *A natural perspective* etc. i.e. the brother and sister, exactly alike in features and dress, are like the pictures in a stereoscope which give the illusion of a single living man but yet are only pictures; *v.* G. 'perspective' and cf. 'the glass' (l. 264 below).

226–27. *that deity . . . Of here and every where* i.e. 'the divine attribute of ubiquity' (Abbott). Cf. Hamlet's ejaculation in the cellarage scene 'Hic et ubique!'

234–35. *If spirits . . . fright us.* One of the moot questions of Shakespeare's day was whether the souls of the departed could 'assume' their mortal forms, or whether ghosts were not rather devils masquerading as the dead; cf. note 2. 2. 27–8, Lavater, *op. cit.* (note 3. 4. 95) and *Ham.* 1. 2. 244 'If it assume my noble father's person,' 3. 4. 135 'My father, in his habit as he lived!'

243. *died* F. 'dide'

249. *attire,* F. 'attyre:'

259. *nature to her bias . . . that* i.e. nature was true to her bent in that. Cf. *L.L.L.* 4. 2. 116 'Study his bias leaves.' Furness writes, 'Sebastian is happy in the thought that nature prompted Olivia to fall in love with a reflexion of himself, as she saw it in his twin sister, Viola.'

264. *the glass* i.e. the 'perspective' he spoke of in l. 216.

270. *that orbèd continent* i.e. the firmament of heaven, or the sphere in which (according to the Ptolemaic cosmology) the sun was fixed.

274–75. *upon some action . . . at Malvolio's suit* We have heard nothing before of this lawsuit; it is Shakespeare's device for bringing Malvolio back upon the scene.

279. S.D. F. 'Enter Clowne with a Letter, and Fabian.'

280. *extracting* Not satisfactorily explained hitherto. The term is probably alchemical or medical, meaning extracting the quintessence. Olivia has been in the crucible of Love and among other things purged from her was the memory of Malvolio's madness, v. G. 'extract.'

282. *sirrah* F. 'firah'

283-84. *at the stave's end* i.e. at a distance. Proverbial; N.E.D. quotes Dent, *Pathway to Heaven* (1601) 'So that wee both keepe Satan at the staues end, and also much sinne out of our soules.'

286-87. *but as...epistles are no gospels...delivered.* This looks like a reference to some ecclesiastical matter of topical interest. *morning:* F. 'morning.'

290. S.D. It is clear from ll. 293-95 that Feste begins to read in a frantic tone of voice.

294-95. *you must allow Vox* 'The Clown had enter'd upon his reading in a very extravagant manner, and tells his lady who checks him for't, that *voice* and tone must be granted him if she'd have it read right' (Capell). In other words 'you must allow for an actor's rendering.' Cf. *The Art of Pronuntiation...Vox audienda & Vox videnda*...by Robert Robinson, 1617 (discussed by H. G. Fielder, Bulletin 15, Mod. Hum. Research Assoc.) [1949].

315. S.D. F. gives no 'exit.'

324. *so long,* F. 'fo long:'

325. *hand—* F. 'hand,'

326. *A sister! you are she.* Possibly we should read 'Ah sister!' Cf. note 1.4.41. But 'you are she' is not very intelligible as it stands. It is of course clear that both Olivia and Orsino are content to find a sister in the original object of their passion. Perhaps a line has been omitted.

S.D. F. 'Enter Maluolio.'

327-28. *Ay, my lord...Malvolio?* F. prints this as one line.

332. *Write from it* i.e. write differently from it; cf. 1. 5. 190 'from my commission.'

333. *invention* i.e. composition.

336. *given...clear lights* Perhaps a nautical metaphor.

349. *then cam'st* 'The inflexion of the second person singular allows the nominative to be readily understood, and therefore justifies its omission' (Abbott).

352. *passed upon thee* v. G. 'pass upon.'

362. *conceived in him* (Tyrwhitt) F. 'conceiu'd against him' Dyce follows Tyrwhitt, and Luce approves, adding 'the word "in" suits the metre, and "against" in this line is probably a compositor's error, due to the near presence of the other "against" (l. 360).' *him:* F. 'him.'

364. *married her* Critics have been severe upon Shakespeare for this abrupt announcement. But there has been ample warning. Feste knows it is coming (v. notes 1. 5. 19, 27–8); Sir Toby himself hints at it as a fit 'recompense' for the device of the letter (2. 5. 185–94), and his confidential speech to Maria at 4. 2. 68–73 suggests that she may have taken him at his word while he was in the mood, after the discomfiture of Malvolio. Secret marriages were common in Shakespeare's day. But what matters is that the audience would not have gone home happy unless Maria had become Lady Belch.

369. *poor fool!* An expression partly of pity and partly of endearment; cf. Sidney, *Astrophel and Stella,* 73 'O heauenly foole, thy most kiss-worthy face.' But 'fool' also means 'dupe,' and it is Olivia's use of the word that brings Feste into the dialogue.

371. *thrown* So F. Theobald read 'thrust'

373. *By the Lord* F. 'By the Lotd'

374–75. '*Madam...he's gagged*' Cf. 1. 5. 81–7.

377. S.D. F. gives no 'exit.'

387. S.D. F. 'Exeunt.'/'Clowne sings.'

388–407. *When that I was* etc. Cf. pp. 93, 96–7 and *Lear*, 3. 2. 74–7:

> He that has and a little tiny wit,—
> With hey, ho, the wind and the rain,—
> Must make content with his fortunes fit,
> For the rain it raineth every day.

Feste's song seems a mere development, and a clumsy one, of this quatrain, which contains all the 'philosophy' which Knight, one of the very few champions of the song among the older critics, professed to find in it. I suggest that it is Armin's composition—his *Nest of Ninnies* is full of doggerel and he had already in 1592 become known as a ballad-maker (v. Nashe, *Works*, i. 280)—inspired by the verse given him to sing in *Lear* and tacked on to the playhouse version of *Twelfth Night* about 1606. 'The Song,' writes Aldis Wright, '...is an old one scarcely worth correction. It was probably introduced by the actor of the Clown's part.' And Wright merely echoes the opinion of critics like Farmer, Steevens, Warburton, Capell and Staunton. Two modern writers have taken the other line. Mr Richmond Noble (*Shakespeare's Use of Song*, p. 85) reminds us 'that Shakespeare was not of a dry anti-quarian cast of mind like some of his commentators; he was an actor and a practical man of affairs, out to entertain all those willing to pay for their amusement, and he well knew, none better, the value of nonsense in attaining that end.' Dr A. C. Bradley (*A Book of Homage*, ed. I. Gollancz, p. 169) arguing in similar fashion, points out 'how appropriate the song is to the singer, and how in the line "But that's all one, our play is done" he repeats an expression used a minute before in his last speech.' Shakespeare may have countenanced the song, he may even, as Dr Bradley contends, have contributed himself the last stanza (though the phrase 'that's all one' seems to have been a favourite of Armin's and occurs in the preface of *A Nest of*

Ninnies), but he could not have written the fourth stanza.

388. *and a* This use of 'and a' occurs again in *Lear* 3. 2. 74 (v. previous note) and *Oth*. 2. 3. 92 (F., not Q.) 'King Stephen was and a worthy peer,' but apparently nowhere else. Abbott (*Shak. Gram.* §96) explains it as 'emphatically used for "also," "even," "and that too," and Furness as 'a meaningless redundant expression, not uncommon in old ballads, where some syllables are needed to complete the measure.' But Furness quotes no examples from the old ballads he speaks of. It is to be noted that the 'and' is found in the Q. neither of *Lear* nor of *Oth*. It is possibly therefore an insertion of the playhouse musician entrusted with the arrangement of the songs.

tiny boy (Rowe) F. 'tine boy' The sp. recurs in *Lear* (Q., F. 'tyne').

390. *A foolish thing was but a toy* i.e. my mischievous pranks were not taken seriously.

392–94. *But when...their gate* i.e. but when I grew up I found men's doors shut against me as a knave and a thief.

400–403. *But when I came unto my beds* etc. The exceeding clumsiness of this stanza is, to my mind, conclusive proof that Shakespeare did not write it. The meaning, which seems to have escaped previous commentators, is apparently 'My wife and I always went drunk to bed together.' But the phrasing is very awkward. Perhaps, Dr Pollard suggests, 'With' (l. 402) has been substituted (from l. 401) for 'We.'

405. *With hey, ho,* (F2) F. 'hey ho,'

407. F. gives no exit. This fact, combined with the 'Exeunt' at l. 387, is not without its bearing upon the question discussed in note ll. 388–407.

ADDENDA TO NOTES

1. 3. 43. *Castiliano vulgo* It is possible that 'Castiliano' is a reference (? misp. for 'Castilione') to Baldassare Castiglione, author of *The Courtier*, the most famous courtesy book of the age.

3. 1. 16–21. *I would . . . disgraced them* In this talk of 'names' and 'bonds' there seems to be some reference to the obscure jest about 'names' (= *nomina* or signatures to a bond) which occurs in *L.L.L.* 2. 1. 197–98, and *A.Y.L.* 2. 5. 20–1.

Addenda [1949]

1. 3. 43. *Castiliano vulgo* Sir Henry Thomas (*T.L.S.* corr. 4/6/33) conj. 'Castiglione voglio' i.e. Lacrima Christi, a costly wine.

2. 3. 131. The parallel in *Jul. Caes.* 4. 1. 26 suggests a wish that Mal. should be turned adrift like an old ass to shift for himself.

THE STAGE-HISTORY OF
TWELFTH NIGHT

The first recorded mention of a performance of
Twelfth Night is the entry in the *Diary* of John Manningham, February 2, 1602, which is quoted in the
Introduction to this volume, and in the note on 'The
Copy' reasons are given for believing that the play
may have been revived and in part revised for a performance some time in 1606. On Easter Monday,
April 6, 1618, '*Twelfte night* the play soe called' was
acted before the King by the King's Company; and
on Candlemas, February 2, 1622, *Malvolio* was acted
at the Court of Whitehall by the King's Servants.
Malvolio seems to have been the most prominent
character in the opinion of that day, for his is the
name chosen for mention by Leonard Digges (author of
some lines to the memory of Shakespeare prefixed to
the First Folio) in his commendatory poem printed in
Poems: written by Wil. Shake-speare. Gent. London,
1640, which, rather confusedly, tells how

> let but *Beatrice*
> And *Benedicke* be seene, loe in a trice
> The Cockpit, Galleries, Boxes, all are full
> To hear *Maluoglio* that crosse garter'd Gull.

At the Restoration, this was one of the plays allotted
to D'Avenant for the Duke's Company by a regulation
of December 12, 1660; and he lost little time in pro-
ducing it, since Pepys saw a play of that name (though
whether it was as Shakespeare left it or as D'Avenant had
'reformed and made it fit for the Company of Actors'
there is no telling) at the Opera in Lincoln's Inn Fields
in the King's presence on September 11, 1661. Seeing
it 'against my own mind and resolution,' he 'took no
pleasure in it at all.' He saw it again at the same theatre

on Epiphany ('Twelfth Day'), 1663; and though this time he went on purpose and had no remorse for broken vows to spoil it for him, he thought it 'but a silly play, and not related at all to the name or day.' It was 'acted well' however; and Downes in *Roscius Anglicanus* records that it 'had mighty Success by its well Performance,' with Betterton as Sir Toby, Harris as Sir Andrew, Underhill as the Clown, Lovel as Malvolio, and Mrs Gibbs as Olivia. Who played Viola he forgets to say: it was probably Mrs Betterton—lately Mrs Sanderson; but he seems to answer one such criticism as Pepys had made by noting particularly that 'It was got up on purpose to be Acted on Twelfth Night.' When Pepys, poor man, saw the play a third time, on January 20, 1669, he thought it 'one of the weakest plays that ever I saw on the stage.' Shakespeare's comedies were out of favour by then; and when next we hear of *Twelfth Night*, it is in the sentimental form of *Love Betray'd; or, the Agreable Disapointment* by Charles Burnaby, author of one or two modish comedies of the day. 'Part of the Tale of the Play, I took from Shakespear, and about Fifty of the Lines' (the precise number is 58, and among them are: 'If music be the food of love, play on' and Viola's speech from ' My father had a daughter' down to 'smiling at grief'). Those who care to may learn from the quarto edition, published in 1703, how Cesario (Viola) ran away and came to be Duke Moreno's page merely because she loved him, how Taquilet (Malvolio), steward to Villaretta (Olivia), is egged on by Drances (Sir Toby) to fight the Duke's messenger whom he believes to be his rival for Villaretta's love, and how Cesario visits Villaretta in the disguise of a physician. It is more interesting to learn from the book that at the first performance (date unknown) at Lincoln's Inn Fields Moreno was played by Verbruggen, Drances by Powell, Taquilet by Doggett, Villaretta by Mrs Bracegirdle, Cesario by Mrs Prince and lesser parts by Barton Booth and Mrs Leigh. The play had at least one revival, at the same theatre in the spring of 1705.

Then comes a gap of thirty-six years, and after it a long era of popularity, which for this, as for others of Shakespeare's comedies, may have been started, as Professor Odell suggests, by Macklin and by the growing influence of women on the theatre. Macklin, at any rate, was the Malvolio of the performances at Drury Lane in January, 1741; and this part remained his undisputed for several years. Between those performances and the year 1814 *Twelfth Night* was only twice out of the bill at Drury Lane for as much as eight years at a time; and Covent Garden, taking it up in 1772, performed it pretty frequently till 1819. A good many of the performances at both theatres were given on or about January 6. After Macklin, the chief players of Malvolio (Garrick staged the play several times but never acted in it) were Yates from 1748 to 1776; Bensley from 1776 to 1792; Dowton from 1798 to 1814; and Liston, who seems to have done his best with 'a part out of his line,' from 1811 to 1819. In 1782 Henderson played the part for the first time; in 1789 John Philip Kemble himself played it, apparently not more than once; and Munden made faces in it in 1801. There were several others. In Sir Toby Belch, Macklin's fellow, Berry, was the first of note, but the greatest was Palmer, who acted it between 1773 and 1814, while Emery took it up in 1801 to carry it beyond the period now under notice. Of Sir Andrews the most eminent was Woodward, who acted the part from Macklin's first revival till 1772, and was followed by Dodd, Suett, William Blanchard, and in 1819 by William Farren. Dukes and Sebastians are too many to be noted here; but the Clowns are an interesting list. Yates was the first, under Macklin; and among the others were Thomas Blanchard, Shuter, Lee Lewes, Parsons, Suett, Dowton, Russell, Wathen, William Blanchard, Fawcett and Knight. In and after

1799 all the Drury Lane play-bills take care to state that
the Clown's part is 'with the original epilogue song,'
which raises one out of several little puzzles about the
singing parts in the history of this play. And now for the
Violas and the Olivias. The first great pair were Mrs
Pritchard as Viola and Mrs Clive as Olivia, and they
held the field till 1752. Mrs Woffington's first appearance as Viola was in 1746. The other great pair were
Mrs Jordan (with song, as the play-bill states) as Viola
and Mrs Crouch as Olivia. In 1789 Mrs Jordan had
her brother, Bland, for Sebastian (a similar test of the
value of family likeness was made at Edinburgh in 1815,
when Mrs Henry Siddons as Viola had her brother,
W. Murray, for Sebastian), but the experiment was not
repeated: Bland was a poor actor. Mrs Jordan played
a scene as Viola with the elder Mathews as Sir Andrew
so late as 1808. Miss Younge, Mrs (Perdita) Robinson,
Miss Sally Booth and Miss Brunton are among many
Violas, and Mrs Abington (with song), Mrs Mattocks,
Mrs Powell, Miss De Camp, Mrs Charles Kemble,
Mrs Glover and Mrs Faucit all played Olivia. Of many
Marias two constant lights call for mention: Miss Harriet
Mellon and Mrs Gibbs.

The play which these players acted was probably very
much what Shakespeare wrote. John Philip Kemble's
acting edition, published in 1810, adds a few odd
names, Paolo, Cosmo and so forth, to Shakespeare's, and
transposes certain scenes, among which are the first two.
The singing of Mrs Abington and others as Olivia suggests some alterations; and at Covent Garden in 1818
and 1819 Mr Duruset is cast for Sebastian 'with a song
composed by Mr Bishop.' But not till the next year did
Mr Bishop and with him Mr Frederic Reynolds really
get to work to fit *Twelfth Night* to the taste of the post-
Waterloo town. At Covent Garden on November 8,
1820, their *Twelfth Night* was produced, 'the Musick
(with a few exceptions) composed by Mr Bishop,' and

a note on the play-bill to say that 'in the course of the comedy' (not, be it noted, the opera) 'will be introduced Songs, Glees, and Choruses, the Poetry selected *entirely* from the Plays, Poems, and Sonnets of Shakspeare.' The libretto of this entertainment was not printed, and there is no telling what happened to Shakespeare's text, nor what function Solanio may have performed in the piece. The cast, at least, was first-rate. William Farren played Malvolio; Emery, Sir Toby; Liston, Sir Andrew; Fawcett, the Clown; Abbott, the Duke; Duruset, Fabian; Miss Greene, Olivia; Mrs Gibbs, Maria; and Maria Tree, Viola. The play was given at least eleven times in that season. With a few changes in the cast it came on again in the season of 1822–23, at the end of which Ellen Tree appeared for the first time as Olivia to the Viola of her sister Maria; and in 1825 this Reynolds-Bishop entertainment was still in the repertory of Covent Garden.

When Shakespeare's comedy came back to the London stage twenty-one years later, it was with the help of the American theatre. *Twelfth Night* had been introduced to New York by the Hallams in 1804; and while Reynolds and Bishop held the Covent Garden stage, Henry Wallack had been playing Malvolio to the Sir Toby of Kilner. The Viola of Clara Fisher had been acclaimed as one of the most enchanting of her many beautiful performances; but there is apparently no record of the Cushman sisters, Charlotte and Susan, having acted in *Twelfth Night* in their own country. Yet it was they for whom it was staged at the Haymarket by Benjamin Webster in 1846. They had just finished their famous series of performances of *Romeo and Juliet*, with Charlotte as Romeo and Susan as Juliet; and in the revival of the comedy 'from the text of Shakespeare' Charlotte was Viola, and Susan Olivia, with Buckstone as Sir Andrew and Webster as the Clown. Perhaps in imitation of this idea, Fanny Vining (later Mrs E. J.

Davenport) and Mrs Mowatt acted Viola and Olivia at the Theatre Royal, Marylebone, in 1849. Meanwhile at Sadler's Wells in January, 1848, Samuel Phelps had given the comedy one of his sound and beautiful productions, playing Malvolio himself excellently well, with Laura Addison as Viola and Scharf as the Clown; he repeated it nine years later with a slightly different cast. In September, 1850, Charles Kean and Robert Keeley chose *Twelfth Night* for the opening bill of their new Princess's Theatre. This was not a typical, archaeological and magnificent Charles Kean production; but it must have been lively with Mrs Keeley as Maria, Miss Philips playing Olivia 'in a lady-like manner,' Meadows as Malvolio, Addison as Sir Toby, Keeley as Sir Andrew, Harley as the Clown, and Mrs Charles Kean as Viola. The last name becomes more exciting when it is realised that Mrs Charles Kean was none other than Ellen Tree, who had succeeded, as it were, to her sister's part, and in it had been delighting New York a decade or more before this. At the Olympic Theatre in June, 1865, Kate Terry improved upon the Jordan-Bland, Siddons-Murray experiments by playing both Viola and Sebastian herself; and the Clown in this production was played by Ellen Farren. At the Haymarket under Buckstone the piece was a favourite, with the manager as Sir Andrew and 'Old Howe' as Malvolio. In 1878 Adelaide Neilson, who had been playing Viola with great success at Daly's Theatre in New York, charmed London in the part at the Haymarket. In 1881 the company from the Royal Theatre of Saxe-Meiningen brought this comedy, among others, to London in that series of performances at Drury Lane which impressed on players and critics of the day the possibilities of well-organized crowds and carefully planned *ensemble*. Henry Irving's production of *Twelfth Night* at the Lyceum in July, 1884, was overweighted, perhaps, by care for the *ensemble* at the expense of the characters. It lacked grace and lightness, although the

Viola was Ellen Terry and the Malvolio Irving himself. Ten years later came Augustin Daly's perversion of the comedy, with the Viola of Ada Rehan to redeem all its distortions of the text; and perhaps as a protest against Daly's methods, in 1895 the Elizabethan Stage Society gave the first of its several revivals of the play in the Elizabethan manner. In the present century the play has been often staged. Beerbohm Tree first put on his version of it at His Majesty's Theatre in 1901. In 1907 E. H. Sothern and Julia Marlowe came from New York with this and other plays to London and disappeared again before London had had time to learn how good their work was. The most notable production of the play in modern times was that by Granville-Barker at the Savoy Theatre in November, 1912. This, the second of his Shakespearian ventures, was hotly criticized; but, could it only be revived to-day, there would be nothing but admiration for the clean and purposeful *ensemble* combining tradition and the modern spirit, and for certain unforgettable performances: the Malvolio of Henry Ainley, the Toby Belch of Arthur Whitby and the Feste of Hayden Coffin. Arthur Whitby was seen again as Sir Toby, with Herbert Waring as Malvolio, in James Bernard Fagan's production of the play at the Court Theatre in November, 1918. Among innumerable other performances—at the Gaiety Theatre, Manchester, at the 'Old Vic.,' by the Benson Company, by the Ben Greet companies indoors and outdoors—those at the Birmingham Repertory Theatre perhaps call most for mention. Like Kean and Keeley, the management chose *Twelfth Night* for the first bill of the newly-built playhouse and presented it before hangings on an 'apron-stage' on February 17, 1913. Three years later the production was revived on the same stage and with the text given whole.

HAROLD CHILD.

GLOSSARY

Note. Where a pun or quibble is intended, the meanings
are distinguished as (*a*) and (*b*)

ABATEMENT, depreciation, reduction (commercial term; cf.
Bacon, *Essayes*, viii. 'a great
charge of children; as if it were
an abatement to his riches');
1. 1. 13

ACCOST. A nautical term (lit. = to
coast) coming into fashion as
signifying 'to greet politely' (cf.
Sir Giles Goosecap, 1606, 4. 2.
37–9 'In the three quarter leg
and settled look,/The quick kiss
of the top of the forefinger,/
And other such exploits of good
accost'); 1. 3. 50

ADHERE, cohere; 3. 4. 81

ADVANCED, raised (cf. *Temp.* 1.
2. 413 'The fringed curtains
of thine eye advance'); 2. 5.
32

ADVISE, take care, consider; 4. 2.
95

AFFECTIONED, affected (cf. *L.L.L.*
5. 1. 4 'witty without affection'); 2. 3. 154

ALLOW, prove, approve (cf. *Lear*,
2. 4. 193–94 'if your sweet
sway/Allow obedience'); 1. 2.
58; 4. 2. 60

ALLOWED, licensed, permitted by
authority; 1. 5. 92

ALONE, beyond compare, peerless
(cf. *Two Gent.* 2. 4. 165 'she is
alone'); 1. 1. 15

AMPLE, full (cf. *Troil.* 3. 3. 89 'at
ample point'); 1. 1. 26

ANATOMY, a corpse for dissection
by surgeons (v. *N.E.D.* 'anatomy' 2. b); 3. 2. 61

ANSWER (sb.), the return hit in
fencing; 3. 4. 278

ANSWER (vb.), atone for, make
amends; 3. 3. 28, 33; 3. 4. 331

ANTIC, quaint; 2. 4. 3

APPROBATION, credit; 3. 4. 185

AQUA-VITÆ, spirit (for drinking);
2. 5. 199

ARGUMENT, (i) matter, theme;
2. 5. 154; 3. 4. 74; (ii) evidence,
proof; 3. 2. 11; (iii) subject of
contention; 3. 3. 32

ARION. The Greek musician who,
being threatened with assassination on board ship, threw himself
into the sea and was carried to
land by a dolphin which had heard
him playing upon his lute (cf.
M.N.D. 2. 1. 150–52); 1. 2. 15

BACK-TRICK. Meaning uncertain:
'a caper backwards in dancing'
(Schmidt), 'the reverse in the
galliard, where all five steps are
reversed or taken backwards'
(Furness); 1. 3. 125

BAFFLE, (i) subject to public disgrace; 2. 5. 165; (ii) dupe, hoodwink; 5. 1. 369

BALK, omit, neglect; 3. 2. 24

BARFUL, full of difficulties (*N.E.D.*
quotes no other example of the
word); 1. 4. 41

BARREN, dull-witted (cf. *Ham.* 3. 2.
46 'barren spectators'); 1. 3. 81;
1. 5. 82

BAUBLING, trifling, toy-like (cf.
Troil. 1. 3. 35 'shallow bauble
boats'); 5. 1. 53

BAWCOCK, fine fellow (Fr. 'beau coq'). A colloquial term of endearment; 3. 4. 116

BEAGLE, a small type of hound (v. note); 2. 3. 185

BED OF WARE, v. *Ware* (*bed of*); 3. 2. 46

BENT, lit. the extent to which a bow may be bent, hence—limit of capacity or endurance (*N.E.D.* 'bent' 9; cf. *Ham.* 3. 2. 401 'fool me to the top of my bent'); 2. 4. 37

BIBBLE BABBLE, idle prating (intensive of 'babble'); 4. 2. 98

BIDDY, fowl, chicken; 3. 4. 119

BIRDBOLT, a blunt wooden-headed heavy arrow, used for shooting small birds from a short distance; 1. 5. 91

BLAZON, armorial bearings, coat of arms; 1. 5. 297

BLENT, blended, mingled; 1. 5. 243

BLOODY, blood-thirsty (cf. *Ps.* v. 6); 3. 4. 225

BLOW, blow out, puff out; 2. 5. 43

BOARD, accost, make advances to (orig. a nautical term); 1. 3. 58

BOOK (without), from memory, by heart (cf. *R. & J.* 1. 4. 7 'no without-book prologue faintly spoke'); 2. 3. 155

BOTCHER, a repairing tailor, a bungling workman; 1. 5. 45

BOTCH UP, put together or stitch together clumsily; 4. 1. 56

BRABBLE, brawl; 5. 1. 64

BRANCHED, figured; 2. 5. 48

BREACH (of the sea), lit. break, hence—where the waves break, the surf; 2. 1. 21

BREAST, voice for singing; 2. 3. 22

BROCK, badger, stinker; 2. 5. 107

BROWNIST, lit. a follower of Robert Browne (one of the founders of Independency), hence—any extreme type of puritan; 3. 2. 31

BUM-BAILY, petty sheriff's officer who arrested for debt; 3. 4. 181

BUTTERY-BAR, ledge at the door of the buttery-hatch on which to rest tankards, etc.; 1. 3. 72

CANARY, a sweet wine from the Canaries; 1. 3. 82, 85

CANTON, a variant form of 'canzon' =a song; 1. 5. 274

CAPACITY, (i) power to receive or contain; 1. 1. 10; (ii) intelligence; 2. 5. 121; 3. 4. 190

CAPER, lit. a goat's leap. 'As a dancing movement it consisted in beating the feet together in the air; it was introduced into some galliards' (*Sh. Eng.* ii. 447); 1. 3. 123, 142

CAPILET, a name for a horse, from 'caple' or 'capul' (=horse), v. *N.E.D.*; 3. 4. 287

CASE, tech. term for the skin of a fox and other vermin (cf. *All's Well*, G. and *Wint.* 4. 4. 843–44 'though my case be a pitiful one I hope I shall not be flayed out of it'); 5. 1. 164

CAST, put into a state or category of (cf. *O.E.D.* 33, and 'cast into prison, into a deep sleep'); 5. 1. 120

CATAIAN, a cheat, lit. an inhabitant of Cathay. The Elizabethans had news of the wiles of 'the heathen Chinee' before Bret Harte (cf. *M.W.W.* 2. 1. 130); 2. 3. 78

CATCH. 'Originally, a short composition for three or more voices which sing the same melody, the second singer beginning the first line as the first goes on to the second line, and so with each successive singer...Subsequently applied to rounds in which the words are so arranged as to produce ludicrous effects, one singer catching at the words of another' (*N.E.D.*); 2. 3. 20, 61, 64, 66, 95

CHAMPIAN, a variant of 'champaign' ('during the 17th cent. it was much more frequent' *N.E.D.*); 2. 5. 164

CHANCE, opportunity, possibility of good or bad fortune (cf. *M.V.* 2. 1. 43 'bring me unto my chance'); 1. 2. 8

CHANTRY, a private chapel, endowed for the maintenance of one or more priests to sing daily mass for the souls of the departed; 4. 3. 24

CHECK. A hawking term. *N.E.D.* quotes Latham, *Falconry* (1615) 'Checke, or to kill Checke, is when Crows, Rooks, Pies, or other birds comming in the view of the Hawke, she forsaketh her naturall flight to flie at them'; 2. 5. 117; 3. 1. 64

CHERRY-PIT, 'a children's game which consists in throwing cherry-stones into a small pit or hole' (*N.E.D.*); 3. 4. 120

CHEVERIL, lit. of kid leather (and therefore easily stretched), hence —pliable, elastic. Aldis Wright quotes Florio's *Montaigne* 'some cheverell judge or other,' and *N.E.D.* quotes Stubbes, *Anat. Abuses*, ii. 12 'the Lawiers haue such chauerell consciences'; 3. 1. 12

CHUCK, (*a*) a term of endearment (e.g. for a child), (*b*) chicken, fowl; 3. 4. 117

CHURCHMAN, clergyman; 3. 1. 4

CIVIL, becoming, seemly, decent; 1. 4. 21; 3. 4. 5

CLERESTORY, orig. the upper part of the nave, etc. in a church, containing windows clear of the roofs of the aisles, hence—any kind of large window high up in the wall of a hall or great chamber; 4. 2. 39

CLODPOLE, numskull, clodpate, thick-head; 3. 4. 193

CLOSE (adv.), i.e. still! 2. 5. 20

COCKATRICE, a fabulous reptile, also called basilisk, half cock and half serpent, supposed to be able to kill by its breath or look; 3. 4. 199

COCKNEY, spoilt child, effeminate creature, pampered darling; 4. 1. 14

CODLING, orig. a hard kind of apple unsuitable for eating raw, later —any immature or half-grown apple (*N.E.D.*); 1. 5. 158

COFFER, lit. strong-box, so—a person's whole wealth; 3. 4. 345

COLD SCENT, weak or faint scent in hunting; 2. 5. 125–26

COLOURS (fear no), fear no foe, have no fear (of any kind). The saying, as Maria remarks, was 'born in the wars' and perhaps orig. meant 'fear no foeman's flag'; 1. 5. 6

COME AWAY, come here, come along (cf. *Temp.* 1. 2. 187 'Come away, servant'); 2. 4. 51

COME NEAR (one), begin to understand; 3. 4. 68

COMEDIAN, stage-player; 1. 5. 183

COMMODITY, a parcel of worthless rubbish (e.g. brown paper, hair-clippings from a barber's shop, etc.) which a usurer included at his own valuation in a loan in order to evade the Act of 1571 restricting the rate of interest chargeable on loans (cf. *Meas. G.*); 3. 1. 45

COMPETENT, legally admissible; 3. 4. 248

COMPETITOR, confederate, partner (the usual Shn. use); 4. 2. 10

COMPLEXION. A word of much wider implication than now; perhaps 'appearance' comes nearest to it in 2. 4. 26

COMPTIBLE, lit. countable, liable to give account, and so here—liable to answer to, sensitive to (*N.E.D.* quotes no other instance of this meaning); 1. 5. 176

CON, learn one's part as an actor; 1. 5. 175; 2. 3. 154

CONCEIT (vb.), form notions, entertain ideas; 3. 4. 293

CONDUCT (sb.), escort, safe-conduct; 3. 4. 244

CONSONANCY, consistency; 2. 5. 133

CONSTANT, 'constant question' = 'formally conducted discussion' (Aldis Wright); 4. 2. 50

CONSTELLATION, the configuration or position of 'stars' (i.e. planets) in regard to one another, as supposed to have influence upon men, esp. at birth; hence—disposition or character, as determined by one's 'stars' (*N.E.D.*); 1. 4. 35

CONSTER, old form of 'construe' = unfold, explain; 3. 1. 57

CONTAGIOUS, (*a*) catchy, (*b*) catching—like a disease; 2. 3. 57, 58

CONVENT, meaning doubtful; either 'to be convenient' or 'to summon, call together'; 5. 1. 381

CORANTO, a light gliding dance in 2/4 time (cf. *Sh. Eng.* ii. 449); 1. 3. 131

COYSTRILL, lit. groom, hence—knave, base fellow (*N.E.D.*). The word is sometimes found as a variant of 'kestrel'; 1. 3. 40

COZIER, cobbler; 2. 3. 94

CREDIT, report (*N.E.D.* gives no other instance); 4. 3. 6

CROSS-GARTERED, 'wearing the garters both above and below the knee, so as to be crossed at the back of the leg' (Aldis Wright); 2. 5. 157–58, 170–71; 3. 2. 72; 3. 4. 21, 53

CROWNER, coroner; 1. 5. 134

CUCULLUS NON FACIT MONACHUM, i.e. The hood does not make the monk; 1. 5. 54

CURST, savage, vicious; 3. 2. 41

CUT, lit. cart-horse, 'common or labouring horse' (doubtful whether the sense is 'cut-tail' or 'gelding'), hence—a term of abuse (cf. 1 *Hen. IV*, 2. 4. 215 'call me horse'); 2. 3. 193

CYPRESS, (i) the cypress-tree; 2. 4. 52; (ii) a piece of black lawn (or 'cypress') used as a kerchief for the neck in sign of mourning; 3. 1. 123

DALLY WITH, 'linger lovingly over' (Luce); 2. 4. 47

DAY-BED, sofa—'probably introduced towards the end of the 16th cent.' (*Sh. Eng.* ii. 125) and then regarded by old-fashioned persons as luxurious or even wicked (cf. *R. III*, 3. 7. 72 'lolling on a lewd day-bed'); 2. 5. 48

DEADLY, death-like; 1. 5. 269

DEAR, sore, grievous, dire; 5. 1. 70

DECEIVABLE, deceptive; 4. 3. 21

DELIVER, declare, make known, discover; 1. 2. 41

DENAY, variant of 'deny'; 2. 4. 124

DETERMINATE, intended, determined upon; 2. 1. 10

DETESTED, abjured, renounced by oath; 5. 1. 138

DEXTERIOUSLY, a 17th cent. variant of 'dexterously' (*N.E.D.* also gives 'dexterious'); 1. 5. 58

DIET, board and lodging (cf. *All's Well*, G. and 1 *Hen. IV*, 3. 3. 84 'You owe money here besides, Sir John, for your diet'); 3. 3. 40

DILUCULO SURGERE. In full 'Diluculo surgere saluberrimum est,' i.e. To get up at dawn is most healthy; 2. 3. 3

DIMENSION, bodily frame, proportions; 1. 5. 265; 5. 1. 236

DISCARD, dismiss, discharge; 3. 4. 93

DISCOURSE, reason, thought (cf. *Ham.* 1. 2. 150 'discourse of reason,' and *ibid.* 4. 4. 36–7 'with such large discourse, Looking before and after'); 4. 3. 12

DISMOUNT, remove something from that on which it has been mounted, e.g. a cannon from its carriage, or a gem from its setting; 3. 4. 226

DISTEMPER (vb.), render unhealthy (from the notion that diseases proceeded from a disturbance of the due proportion or 'temper' of the four humours); 2. 1. 4–5

DIVULGED, v. *well divulged*; 1. 5. 264

DOG AT (to be a), to be clever at (cf. *Two Gent.* 4. 4. 12 'to be... a dog at all things'); 2. 3. 63

DRIVE, drift (cf. *Per.* 3, Gow. 50 'the poor ship drives'); 1. 2. 11

DRY, (i) 1. 3. 75, signifies (*a*) thirst, (*b*) meanness, (*c*) lack of amorousness; (ii) 1. 3. 78=(*a*) stupid, (*b*) ironical; (iii) 1. 5. 42 stupid

DUCAT, a gold coin, valued under Philip and Mary at 6/8 (v. *Sh. Eng.* i. 342); 1. 3. 22

DUELLO, the established code of duellists (cf. *L.L.L.* 1. 2. 172

'the duello he regards not'); 3. 4. 305

ELEMENT, (i) sky, firmament of heaven; 1. 1. 25; (ii) 'out of my ... element' = beyond the sphere of my comprehension; 3. 1. 58–9; (iii) 'of your element' = belonging to your sphere of life; 3. 4. 128

ELEMENTS (the four), i.e. earth, water, air and fire, out of which everything, according to the old 'philosophy,' was composed, including man himself (cf. *Hen. V*, 3.7. 22–4 'he is pure air and fire, and the dull elements of earth and water never appear in him'); 2. 3. 11

EMPLOYMENT, business; 2. 5. 84

EQUINOCTIAL, probably = the celestial equator; 2. 3. 26

EVEN (to go), tally, balance; 5. 1. 238

EXPRESSURE, expression; 2. 3. 163

EXTENT, lit. seizure of property under writ, sequestration, hence —predatory attack, assault (*N.E.D.* quotes *Selimus*, 1594, 'On all the world we make extent'); 4. 1. 53

EXTRACT, distil, extract the quintessence (cf. Cotgrave, 1611, 'an Alchemist or extractor of quintessences' *N.E.D.* 'extractor'); 5. 1. 280

FADGE, turn out, succeed; 2. 2. 33

FALL, cadence; 1. 1. 4

FANCY (vb.), fall in love; 2. 5. 26

FANCY (sb.), love; 1. 1. 14; 2. 4. 33; 4. 1. 62; 5. 1. 387

FANTASTICAL, imaginative; 1. 1. 15

FAT, gross, nauseating; 5. 1. 108

FAULT, hunting term = a break in the scent; 2. 5. 132

FAVOUR, look, appearance; 2. 4. 24; 3. 4. 327, 381

FEATURE, shape, proportions, comeliness of body; 3. 4. 351, 364

FEELINGLY, with just perception, exactly; 2. 3. 165

FIRE-NEW, just coined; 3. 2. 22

FIT, apt, to the point; 3. 1. 67

FLESH, i.e. 'flesh one's maiden sword' = fight one's first battle (v. *N.E.D.* 'flesh' 3); 4. 1. 39

FORMAL, sane, normal in mind (cf. *Err.* 5. 1. 105 'make of him a formal man again'); 2. 5. 121

FRAUGHT, cargo; 5. 1. 60

FREE, free from care, easy in mind; 2. 4. 45

FRESH, hungry or thirsty (often in the phrase 'fresh and fasting' *N.E.D.* 'fresh' 11. b); 1. 1. 9

FUSTIAN, lit. coarse cloth, hence—worthless, rubbishy; 2. 5. 112

GALLIARD, 'a quick lively dance in triple time' (*N.E.D.*); 1. 3. 122, 130, 135

GASKINS, short for galligaskins, wide hose; 1. 5. 25

GIDDILY, lightly, carelessly; 2. 4. 84

GOD BUY YOU, an intermediate form of 'good-bye' (orig. 'God be with you'); 4. 2. 101

GORBODUC, a mythical king of Britain, hero of the tragedy by Sackville and Norton, *Gorboduc*; 4. 2. 15

GRAIN (in), for 'dyed in grain' = fast-dyed, indelible (cf. *Err.* 3. 2. 106 '*Ant.* That's a fault that water will mend. *Drom.* No, sir, 'tis in grain—Noah's flood could not do it'); 1. 5. 241

GRATILLITY, Feste's contemptuous diminutive of 'gratuity'; 2. 3. 28

GREEK, (*a*) 'a cunning or wily person, a cheat, sharper'(*N.E.D.* sb. 4); (*b*) merry-greek, buffoon; 4. 1. 17

GRISE, step; 3. 1. 125

GRIZZLE, a sprinkling of grey hairs (cf. *Ham.* 1. 2. 240 'His beard was grizzled'); 5. 1. 164

GROUND, foundation; 2. 3. 157

GUARD (out of his), disarmed; 1. 5 84

HAVING, property, possessions; 3. 4. 343

HOB, NOB, a variant of 'hab, nab' = have it, have it not, i.e. come what may (the motto of a desperado); 3. 4. 242

HOLD OUT, keep up, persist; 4. 1. 5

HULL (vb.), to drift with sails furled; 1. 5. 205

HUMOUR, caprice; 1. 4. 5; 2. 5. 52, 87

HUNTER, dog for hunting; 3. 4. 226

IMPETTICOAT (vb.), pocket, in reference to the fool's long coat; 2. 3. 28

IMPORTANCE, importunity; 5. 1. 363

INDIFFERENT (adv.), tolerably, fairly, pretty; 1. 3. 136; 1. 5. 251

INTENT, destination; 2. 4. 77

JADE (vb.), fool, play tricks with; 2. 5. 168

JEALOUSY, suspicion, anxiety (cf. *Ado*, 2. 2. 45 'jealousy shall be called assurance'); 3. 3. 8

JET, strut (like a turkey, v. *N.E.D.* 'jet' 1. a); 2. 5. 32

JEWEL, precious ornament, piece of jewelry; 3. 4. 211

JIG, lively rapid dance; 1. 3. 131

JUMP, coincide, tally; 5. 1. 251

KICKSHAW (Fr. quelque chose), orig. a fancy dish in cookery, a 'something French' not one of the known 'substantial English' dishes, hence—trifle, gewgaw (*N.E.D.*); 1. 3. 118

LABEL, lit. to add to a document a 'label' or strip of parchment containing supplementary matter, hence—to add a codicil; 1. 5. 250

LAPSED, apprehended, arrested. *N.E.D.* suggests association with 'lap' and quotes Strype (1558) 'fallen into the lapse of the Law'; 3. 3. 36

LAY OUT, expend; 3. 4. 205

LEASING, lying; 1. 5. 95

LENTEN, meagre, feeble (cf. *Ham.* 2. 2. 329 'lenten entertainment'); 1. 5. 9

LET ME ALONE (to, for, with, etc.), rely on me to (do so and so); 2. 3. 140–41; 3. 4. 187

LIE BY, (a) dwell near, (b) take a mistress; 3. 1. 8

LIME, lit. catch with bird-lime, hence—entangle, snare; 3. 4. 78

LIST, lit. selvage of cloth, hence—limit, bound, farthest point; 3. 1. 77

LITTLE (in), lit. in miniature, hence—on a small scale, within a small compass; 3. 4. 89

LIVE (of a vessel in a storm), escape destruction, remain afloat; 1. 2. 14

LIVE BY, (a) get one's living by, (b) dwell near; 3. 1. 1–5

LIVER. According to the old physiology, the seat both of love and of courage; 1. 1. 36; 2. 4. 98; 2. 5. 99; 3. 2. 21, 60

LUBBER, overgrown loutish fellow; 4. 1. 13

MADONNA, mistress, my lady; 1. 5. 41, 55, 58, 60, etc.; 5. 1. 297

MAKE UP, piece together, make good; 2. 5. 125

MALIGNANCY, baleful or virulent character. The term is both medical (= extreme virulence, or exceptional contagion) and astrological (= highly evil 'influence'); 2. 1. 4

MANAKIN or manikin, an artist's lay-figure (*N.E.D.* quotes Dee, 1570, 'a Manneken as the Dutch painters terme it'); 3. 2. 52

MASTERLY, like a skilled craftsman or one deeply learned; 2. 4. 22

MAUGRE, in spite of; 3. 1. 153

MEDDLE, engage in conflict; 3. 4. 252, 281

MEND, (a) make amends, (b) improve, grow more perfect; 1. 5. 72

MISCARRY, come to harm; 3. 4. 66

MISPRISION, mistake of identity (v. note); 1. 5. 53

MODEST, moderate; 1. 3. 9; 1 5. 181; 4. 2. 34

MOTION, (i) impulse, desire (cf. *Meas.* 1. 4. 59 'The wanton stings and motions of the sense'); 2. 4. 18, 98; (ii) 'a practised and regulated movement of the body ...acquired by drill and training' (*N.E.D.* 3. c, cf. *Ham.* 4. 7. 102); 3. 4. 278; (iii) proposal; 3. 4. 288

NATURAL, like a 'natural fool' or 'idiot'; 1. 3. 29

NAYWORD, byword, proverb; 2. 3. 141

NICELY, ingeniously; 3. 1. 14

NOTORIOUS, disgraceful, shameful (*N.E.D.* quotes no instance of this meaning before 1666); 5. 1. 329, 343

NOTORIOUSLY (cf. *notorious*), in-
famously, shamefully; 4. 2. 88;
5. 1. 378

NUMBERS, lit. metrical feet, hence
—lines, verses, metre; 2. 5. 104

OBSTRUCTION, stoppage, anything
causing stoppage (of light, blood,
etc.); 2. 5. 122; 3. 4. 21; 4. 2. 41

'OD'S LIFELINGS, a perversion of
the oath 'God's life'; 5. 1. 182

OLD, (i) 'of long practice and experience in some matter or
respect...also in slang use,
clever, knowing' (*N.E.D.* 5, cf.
L.L.L. 2. 1. 252 'an old love-
monger'); 1. 3. 121; (ii) stale,
worn-out; 1. 5. 108

OPPOSITE (sb.), opponent (cf. *Ham.*
5. 2. 62 'mighty opposites');
3. 2. 62; 3. 4. 234, 268

OPPOSITE (adj.), contradictory, ob-
structive, hostile; 2. 5. 153;
3. 4. 72

ORCHARD, garden; 3. 2. 7; 3. 4. 226

ORDINARY. Either 'commonplace,
vulgar' or 'belonging to an
ordinary' (= eating-house); 1. 5.
83

OTHERGATES, in another fashion;
5. 1. 192

OUT, out of pocket (*N.E.D.* quotes
Massinger, *City Madam*, 'I am
out now six-hundred in the
cash'); 2. 3. 191

OVERTURE, declaration; 1. 5. 213

OWE, own; 1. 5. 314

PART (adv.), partly; 3. 4. 341

PART (sb.), (i) allotted portion, lot
in life (*N.E.D.* 7. b); 2. 4. 57;
(ii) wealth, rank; 2. 4. 83

PARTICIPATE, share in common
with others (*N.E.D.*). Furness
interprets 'acquire as part of
what constitutes one'; 5. 1. 237

PASS UPON, impose upon, make a
fool of; 3. 1. 42; 5. 1. 352

PASSAGE, act, incident, proceeding;
3. 2. 70

PASSION, suffering; 2. 4. 4

PAY, punish, give an opponent his
'deserts' (cf. 1 *Hen. IV*, 2. 4.
242 'seven of the eleven I paid');
3. 4. 279

PEDANT, schoolmaster (without
any necessary implication of
contempt); 3. 2. 73

PEEVISH, silly; 1. 5. 304

PERDY, verily, indeed (lit. 'by
God,' *par dieu*); 4. 2. 77

PERPEND, consider, attend to; 5. 1.
298

PERSPECTIVE, some kind of stereoscope (cf. Bacon, *Essayes*, xxvi.
'Prospectives to make superficies
to seeme Body that hath Depth
and Bulke'); 5. 1. 216

PIA MATER, brain (lit. a membrane
enclosing the brain); 1. 5. 113

PITCH, lit. height, hence—excellence of any kind (cf. *Ham.* 3. 1.
86); 1. 1. 12

POINT-DEVISE, extremely precise,
perfectly correct; 2. 5. 167

POINTS, (*a*) matters in discussion,
(*b*) tagged laces for fastening the
gaskins or hose to the doublet,
etc. (the 16th cent. equivalent
of buttons); 1. 5. 23

POLITICIAN, schemer, intriguer;
2. 3. 78; 3. 2. 31

POSITION, arrangement, disposition
(v. *N.E.D.* 4); 2. 5. 123

POSSESS, inform (cf. *Ado*, 5. 1.
274); 2. 3. 144

PRANK, adorn (not in any dis-
paraging sense; cf. *Wint.* 4. 4. 10
'most goddess-like pranked up');
2. 4. 86

PREGNANT, resourceful, teeming
with devices; 2. 2. 28

PRIVATE (sb.), privacy (*N.E.D.* B. 6); 3. 4. 94

PROOF, (i) experience; 3. 1. 126; (ii) trial; 3. 4. 185, 266

PROPER, (i) goodly, handsome, comely; 2. 2. 29; 3. 1. 135; (ii) 'at my proper cost'=at my own expense; 5. 1. 319

PROPERTY (vb.), variously explained: (i) make a tool of, use for one's own ends (cf. *John*, 5. 2. 79 'I am too high-born to be propertied,/To be a... serving-man and instrument'); (ii) take possession of (cf. *Tim.* I. I. 55–8 'His large fortune... Subdues and properties to his love and tendance All sorts of hearts'); (iii) treat like a theatrical 'property' (v. note); 4. 2. 92

PROPRIETY, individuality, personal identity; 5. 1. 146

PURCHASE (after so many years'), the price of land reckoned in terms of its annual rent or return; 4. 1. 22

PURE (adv.), purely, entirely; 5. 1. 82

PUT DOWN, (*a*) make a fool of, (*b*) make incapable with drink; 1. 3. 83, 85

PUT ON, fasten upon; 3. 4. 245

QUESTION, discussion, discourse; 4. 2. 50

QUICK, keen, vigorous (of the appetite), cf. Fuller, *Worthies*, 1661 'they have a quicker palate than I' (*N.E.D.* 20); 1. 1. 9

QUIRK, lit. flourish, hence—caprice (cf. *All's Well*, G.); 3. 4. 246

RECEIVING, understanding, perception; 3. 1. 122

RECOLLECTED, lit. collected, gathered together, hence—studied, far-fetched; 2. 4. 5

RECORD, recollection; 5. 1. 245

RECOVER, get hold of, obtain (*N.E.D.* 6); 2. 3. 190

RELICS, monuments, 'the sights' (cf. *All's Well*, G.); 3. 3. 19

RELISH, trace, tinge, hint; 4. 1. 60

REPORT. A legal term = 'The formal account of a case argued and determined in a court' (*N.E.D.*); 4. 1. 22

RESERVE (vb.), keep for oneself; 1. 5. 189

RESOLUTE, firm, obstinate; 1. 5. 21

RETENTION. A medical term = the body's power to retain its proper contents (v. *N.E.D.* I. a, b), hence metaphorically—stability or consistency of purpose; 2. 4. 96

REVERBERATE (adj.), reverberating. Rare in this active sense, the only known parallel being Jonson, *Masque of Blackness*, 'which skill Pythogoras/First taught to me by a reverberate glass' (*N.E.D.*); 1. 5. 276

REVOLT, a sudden revulsion of mind or feeling, generally in reference to passion (cf. *Two Gent.* 3. 2. 59; *L.L.L.* 5. 2. 74 'gravity's revolt to wantonness'; *M.W.W.* 1. 3. 99 'the revolt of mind is dangerous'; cf. also 'rebellion' *All's Well*, G.); 2. 4. 99

REVOLVE, consider; 2. 5. 147

ROUGH, violent. Probably the regular word for the action of evil spirits upon the 'possessed' (cf. *Luke* ix. 39, 42); 3. 4. 115

ROUND, plain-spoken; 2. 3. 99

RUDESBY, boisterous unmannerly fellow (cf. *Shrew*, 3. 2. 10). The suffix -*by* often used in 16th and 17th cents. in coining descriptive personal appellations, playful or derisive (*N.E.D.* '-by' 2); 4. 1. 51

RULE, conduct, behaviour (*N.E.D.* 13). Luce explains as 'revel' and cites 'night-rule,' *M.N.D.* 3. 2. 5; possibly some connexion with the revels under the Lord of Misrule (v. Chambers, *Med. Stage*); 2. 3. 129

SACK, general name for white Spanish or Canary wines; 'burnt sack' = hot drink made of sack and sugar; 2. 3. 196

SAD, serious; 3. 4. 5

SAUCY, (*a*) insolent, (*b*) seasoned, spiced; 3. 4. 149

SCAB, scurvy fellow; 2. 5. 75

SCATHFUL, harmful; 5. 1. 55

SCHEDULE, 'any tabular or classified statement' (*N.E.D.*); 1. 5. 249

SCOUT (vb.), lie in wait; 3. 4. 180

SCRUPLE, (*a*) lit. an apothecary's weight (20 grains), hence—a minute portion; 2. 5. 4; (*b*) doubt, difficulty, objection; 3. 4. 82

SEASON (vb.), (*a*) salt, preserve by salting, (*b*) embalm; 1. 1. 29

SELF, 'one self,' i.e. one and the same; 1. 1. 38

SEMBLATIVE, resembling. A Shakespearian coinage; 1. 4. 34

SET, deliberate, not spontaneous; 1. 5. 86

SHAPE, figure of the imagination (cf. 2 *Hen. IV*, 4. 3. 108 'full of nimble, fiery and delectable shapes'); 1. 1. 14

SHEEP-BITER, lit. a dog that worries sheep, hence—a sly, sneaking fellow, or (sometimes) a secret woman-hunter, i.e. one who runs after 'mutton' (*N.E.D.*); 2. 5. 7

SHENT, scolded; 4. 2. 105

SHERIFF'S POST. Posts painted in two colours were formerly set up at the side of the door of a mayor, sheriff or other magistrate, as a sign of office (*N.E.D.* 'post'); 1. 5. 148

SHREWISHLY, sharply, ill-temperedly; 1. 5. 160

SHUFFLE OFF, 'get rid of or evade (something irksome) in a perfunctory manner' (*N.E.D.*); 3. 3. 16

SILLY, simple, innocent; 2. 4. 46

SINISTER, discourteous; 1. 5. 177

SINK-A-PACE or cinque-pace (cf. *Ado*, G.), a galliard of five steps. 'The name by which the original galliard was known...it may be that in later times the galliard was so much altered by the addition of new steps, that the original form of the dance came to be distinguished by the name cinque-pace' (*Sh. Eng.* ii. 443–44); 1. 3. 132

SKIPPING, skittish, flighty (cf. *Shrew*, G. 'skipper'); 1. 5. 202

'SLIGHT, an oath meaning 'God's light'; 2. 5. 33

SNECK UP (or snick up), go and be hanged; 2. 3. 98

SOPHY, formerly a title of the Shah of Persia (1500–1736); 2. 5. 184; 3. 4. 280

SOT, (*a*) fool, (*b*) drunkard; 1. 5. 120

SOW, scatter, sprinkle; 5. 1. 164

SPLEEN, sport, merriment. The spleen, regarded as the seat of laughter, is sometimes used for laughter or merriment itself (cf. *L.L.L.* 5. 2. 117 'in this spleen ridiculous'; *Shrew*, Ind. i. 136 'the over-merry spleen'); 3. 2. 66

SQUASH, the unripe pod of a pea; 1. 5. 157

STALLION, (a) ? a dialectal variant of 'staniel' = kestrel-hawk, useless for falconry, (b) male prostitute (v. *N.E.D.* and cf. *Ham.* Q2, 2. 2. 615); 2. 5. 117

STAND BY, (a) stand next door to, (b) depend upon (v. note); 3. 1. 9

STATE, (i) social status; 1. 5. 282; (ii) greatness, high rank; 2. 5. 52; (iii) ceremony, deportment; 2. 3. 155; 2. 5. 154; 3. 4. 74; (iv) chair of state, furnished with a canopy; 2. 5. 45; (v) order, civil discipline; 5. 1. 63

STOCK, stocking; 1. 3. 137

STONE-BOW, 'a cross-bow from which small stones or pellets were shot' in fowling (*Sh. Eng.* ii. 370); 2. 5. 46

STOUP, lit. a measure for liquor (2 quarts), hence—a vessel for wine; 2. 3. 15, 126

STRANGE, distant, reserved; 2. 5. 173

STRIFE, endeavour (cf. *Meas.* 3. 2. 225; *All's Well*, 5. 3. 336); 1. 4. 41

STUCK, thrust, lunge (in fence; cf. *Ham.* 4. 7. 162 'your venomed stuck'); 3. 4. 277

SUPPLY, furnish with an occupant, fill (*N.E.D.* 7. b; cf. *Tim.* 3. 1. 16–8 'an empty box...which...I come to intreat your honour to supply' and *Cor.* 3. 3. 35); 1. 1. 37

SUPPORTANCE, assistance, 'for the supportance of' = for the sake of; 3. 4. 298–99

SWABBER, a sailor who had 'to see the ship kept neat and clean, and that as well in the great cabin as everywhere else betwixt the decks' Nathaniel Boteler, 1634 (*Sh. Eng.* i. 165); 1. 5. 205

SWARTH, a variant of 'swath'; 2. 3. 155

SWAY (vb.), determine opinion, influence judgement; 4. 1. 52

SWEET AND TWENTY, very sweet. The words 'and twenty' are used as an intensive (cf. *M.W.W.* 2. 1. 177 'good even and twenty, Master Page' and *N.E.D.* 'twenty' A. 2). Steevens quotes Tho. Brewer, *Life and Death of the Merry Devil of Edmonton* (1608) 'His little wanton wag-tailes, his sweet and twenties, his pretty pinckineyd pigsnies, etc. as he used to call them'; 2. 3. 53

TABOR, (a) a small drum, used generally with the pipe, and both the traditional instruments of the stage-clown, (b) quibble upon 'tavern' (v. note); 3. 1. 2, 10

TAFFETA, thin silk material of lustrous appearance (cf. *L.L.L.* 5. 2. 159, 406); 2. 4. 74

TAKE UP (a quarrel), make up, settle (cf. *A.Y.L.* 5. 4. 47, 96); 3. 4. 291

TANG, clang, utter like a bell (probably with the bell's reiteration as well as its sound); 2. 5. 154; 3. 4. 73

TARTAR, Tartary, hell; 2. 5. 208

TASTE, make trial of, hence (i) make use of; 3. 1. 78; (ii) test; 3. 4. 246

TAXATION, lit. assessment of dues, hence—imposition; 1. 5. 214

TESTRIL, Aguecheek's diminutive of 'tester' = sixpence (v. note); 2. 3. 35

THROW, 'at this throw' = on this occasion, with a quibble upon a 'throw' at dice; 5. 1. 41

TICKLE, (i) 2. 5. 23, (a) in reference

to 'tickling' trout, (b) flatter, cf. *John*, 2. 1. 573 'That smooth-faced gentleman, tickling Commodity'; (ii) 5. 1. 191 ironically for 'punish, beat'

TILLYVALLY! nonsense! fiddle-sticks! 2. 3. 82

TIME-PLEASER, time-server (cf. *Cor.* 3. 1. 45 'time-pleaser, flatterer'); 2. 3. 154

TOUCH, strain, trait (cf. *Temp.* 5. 1. 21–2 'hast thou...a touch, a feeling/Of their afflictions'; *Two Gent.* 2. 7. 18 'the inly touch of love'); 2. 1. 12

TRADE, business; 3. 1. 75

TREY-TRIP, 'a game at dice, or with dice, in which success probably depended on the casting of a trey or three' (*N.E.D.*); 2. 5. 193

TRIP, a trip in wrestling (*N.E.D.* 5 quotes Palsgrave, 1530, 'I gyue one a tryppe, or caste my foote byfore hym to gyue hym a fall'), with a quibble on 'trip' = trap (*N.E.D.* 7 quotes Robinson trans. More's *Utopia* 'fynde some hole open to set a snare in, wherewith to take the contrarie partie in a trippe'); 5. 1. 166

TRIPLEX, triple time in music; 5. 1. 37

TRUST, conviction, belief; 4. 3. 15

TUCK, rapier; 3. 4. 227

TYRANNOUS, brutal, excessively cruel (as often in Sh.); 3. 1. 121

UNCHARY (adv.), thriftlessly, carelessly; 3. 4. 205

UNCIVIL, (i) disorderly, barbarous, uncivilised; 2. 3. 129; 4. 1. 53; (ii) impolite, discourteous; 3. 4. 254; 5. 1. 111

UNDERTAKER, (a) one who takes up a challenge for another,

(b) ? with a quibble upon 'undertaker' = contractor (v. note); 3. 4. 316

UNFOLD, disclose, reveal; 1. 2. 18

UNHATCHED, without dint or stain, i.e. never used in combat. Probably closely associated with 'hacked' (cf. 1 *Hen. IV*, 2. 4. 288–90 'What a slave art thou, to hack thy sword as thou hast done, and then say it was in fight'); 3. 4. 237

UNKIND, unnatural; 3. 4. 366

UNPRIZABLE, of small account, (of a ship) not worth regarding as a 'prize'; 5. 1. 54

UPSHOT, lit. the final shot in archery, hence—the conclusion of the sport; 4. 2. 72

USURP, (a) supplant, (b) misappropriate (v. note); 1. 5. 188–89

VAINNESS, vanity, boastfulness; 3. 4. 353

VALIDITY, value, strength (cf. *All's Well*, 5. 3. 191; *Ham.* 3. 2. 199); 1. 1. 12

VENERABLE, worthy of veneration or respect; 3. 4. 361

VENT (vb.), lit. discharge, evacuate, hence—utter; 4. 1. 9–12

VICE, the clown in the old interludes (v. note); 4. 2. 123

VIOL-DE-GAMBOYS, violoncello, bass-viol; lit. a viol played between or on the legs; 1. 3. 25–6

VOICE, rumour, report (cf. *Hen. VIII*, 5. 3. 176 'the common voice'); 1. 5. 264

VULGAR, common, well-known; 3. 1. 126

WAINROPE, cart-rope; 3. 2. 58

WANTON, out of hand, equivocal lascivious; 3. 1. 15–20

WARE (bed of). This large bed

measuring 11 feet square, is still to be seen at Rye House, Herts.; 3. 2. 46

WATERS (for all), ready for anything; 4. 2. 64

WEEDS, clothes; 5. 1. 254

WELL-A-DAY! alas; 4. 2. 109

WELL DIVULGED, well-received, of good repute; 1. 5. 264

WESTWARD-HO! The cry of the Thames watermen about to put off from London to Westminster; 3. 1. 136

WHILES, until; 4. 3. 29

WHIRLIGIG, a spinning contrivance of some kind. Probably not a whipping-top (as has generally been supposed), but a mechanical device (a large cage upon a pivot) for the punishment of thieves (cf. *N.E.D.* **2**, quot. 1617); 5. 1. 376

WILL (by my), of my own will, voluntarily; 3. 3. 1

WINDY SIDE, i.e. to the windward (naut.)—so as to be able to escape readily; 3. 4. 168

WOODCOCK, gull, fool (alluding to the ease with which the woodcock could be snared by the fowler); 2. 5. 86; 4. 2. 60

WRACK. Old form of 'wreck,' a wrecked person; 5. 1. 78

YARE, quick, swift; 3. 4. 227

ZANY, a clown's attendant on the stage, who imitates his master in a ludicrously clumsy fashion; 1. 5. 87